A PRINCIPLED APPROACH TO ABUSE OF DOMINANCE IN EUROPEAN COMPETITION LAW

Three questions surround the interpretation and application of Article 82 of the EC Treaty. What is its underlying purpose? Is it necessary to demonstrate actual or likely anticompetitive effects in the marketplace when applying Article 82? And how can dominant undertakings defend themselves against a finding of abuse?

Instead of the usual discussion of objectives, Liza Lovdahl Gormsen questions whether the Commission's chosen objective of consumer welfare is legitimate. While many Community lawyers would readily accept and indeed welcome the objective of consumer welfare, this is not always supported by Article 82 case law. The Community Courts do not always favour consumer welfare at the expense of economic freedom. This is important for dominant undertakings' ability to advance efficiencies and for understanding why the Chicago School arguments cannot be injected into Article 82.

LIZA LOVDAHL GORMSEN teaches competition law at London School of Economics and Political Science and at King's College London.

THE CAMBRIDGE ANTITRUST AND COMPETITION LAW SERIES

Publications within the Series consider various legal, economic and political developments related to competition law and policy. They also consider the application of competition law and policy in sector-specific as well as cross-sector contexts and deal with policy questions ranging from those concerning the formation and adoption of competition law and policy (whether at national, regional or international level) to those dealing with enforcement, and the connection between law and competition in the marketplace. The Series also accommodates different analytical and interdisciplinary viewpoints, such as law and economics; law and political science; and law and economic geography-driven perspectives.

The Series includes publications designed to cater for academic demands as well as practitioner publications catering for the continuously evolving needs of regulators, policy-makers and practitioners, in particular lawyers and economists (who increasingly provide advice on regulatory questions).

The editorial board of the Series welcome proposals by authors and editors who are interested in contributing to the Series through academic monographs; revised PhD theses of high quality; practitioner texts and collections; and edited volumes.

A PRINCIPLED APPROACH TO ABUSE OF DOMINANCE IN EUROPEAN COMPETITION LAW

LIZA LOVDAHL GORMSEN

CAMBRIDGE
UNIVERSITY PRESS

CAMBRIDGE UNIVERSITY PRESS
Cambridge, New York, Melbourne, Madrid, Cape Town, Singapore,
São Paulo, Delhi, Dubai, Tokyo

Cambridge University Press
The Edinburgh Building, Cambridge CB2 8RU, UK

Published in the United States of America by Cambridge University Press, New York

www.cambridge.org
Information on this title: www.cambridge.org/9780521767149

First published 2010

Printed in the United Kingdom at the University Press, Cambridge

A catalogue record for this publication is available from the British Library

Library of Congress Cataloguing in Publication data
Gormsen, Liza Lovdahl.
A principled approach to abuse of dominance in European competition law /
Liza Lovdahl Gormsen.
p. cm. – (The Cambridge antitrust and competition law series)
ISBN 978-0-521-76714-9 (Hardback)
1. Antitrust law–European Economic Community countries.
I. Title. II. Series.
KJE6456.G67 2010
343.24′0721–dc22
2009049663

ISBN 978-0-521-76714-9 Hardback

CONTENTS

PREFACE

According to one study in 2006, the Commission has a 98 per cent success rate in Article 82 cases,[1] and according to another, the Commission has not lost a single Article 82 appeal on substance in twenty years.[2] Yet Article 82, prohibiting abuse of dominance, is in a stage of flux. Perhaps this is because, as eloquently put by Franz Böhm, '[i]t is easier to hold a greased pig by the tail than to control a firm for abuse of a dominant position'.[3]

The Commission's review of Article 82 has created much debate and many excellent participants have tried to find workable solutions to the conundrums raised by Article 82. This author fears the problem of Article 82 is easier to identify than to fix, but hopes it may be possible to design some sensible principles. Unlike most contemporary books on competition law which mainly accept the view that consumer welfare is the main objective of competition law, this book challenges that belief: not because it disregards the importance of consumer welfare, but because it believes the aim of Article 82 is broader than that. The book is not a detailed account of different types of abuse, but draws on case law where relevant for the conceptual discussion.

Some contemporary literature identifies the different goals of Article 82 and expands the analysis to consider the role of economics within the scope of Article 82.[4] This book is not a substitute for any of these other

[1] DG COMP Chief Economist D. J. Neven, 'Competition Economics and Antitrust in Europe' 21(48) *Economic Policy* (2006) 741, 761–2.

[2] C. Ahlborn and D. Evans, 'The *Microsoft* Judgment and its Implications for Competition Policy Towards Dominant Firms in Europe' (2008) 1, 25. Available at: http://papers.ssrn.com/sol3/papers.cfm?abstract_id=1115867.

[3] F. Böhm in F. M. Scherer, *Competition Policies for an Integrated Work Economy* (Washington, DC: Brookings Institution, 1944) 70.

[4] R. O'Donoghue and A. J. Padilla, *The Law and Economics of Article 82 EC* (Oxford: Hart Publishing, 2006); C. D. Ehlermann and I. Atanasiu (eds.), *European Competition Law Annual 2003: What is an Abuse of a Dominant Position?* (Oxford: Hart Publishing, 2006);

works: it merely hopes to complement these by contributing to the scholarly discussion of Article 82. The book includes some discussions of economics, social science and politics. However, the author is a lawyer so the book is written from a legal perspective. Relevant developments are taken into consideration up to 1 March 2009. Since then, the ECJ has given a preliminary ruling in *T-Mobile*[5] and decided the appeal case in *GlaxoSmithKline*.[6] Despite both being cases under Article 81 EC, they are relevant for the point being made about the objectives of Article 82 EC. They both confirm that Article 81, like the other competition rules of the treaty, is designed to protect not only the immediate interests of individual competitors or consumers but also the structure of the market and thus competition as such.[7] This has been the position under Article 82 since *Hoffmann-La Roche*,[8] and was recently reiterated in the *Microsoft* case.[9]

M. Motta, *Competition Policy: Theory and Practice* (Cambridge University Press, 2004); EAGCP Report, *An Economic Approach to Article 82 EC* (July 2005).

[5] Case C-8/08 *T-Mobile Netherlands and others.*

[6] Case C-501/06 etc. *GlaxoSmithKline v. Commission.*

[7] *T-Mobile*, supra note 5, para. 38; *GlaxoSmithKline*, supra note 6, para. 63.

[8] Case 85/76 *Hoffmann-La Roche v. Commission* [1979] ECR 461, para. 125.

[9] Case T-201/04 *Microsoft Corp. v. Commission* [2007] ECR II-3601, para. 664.

ACKNOWLEDGMENTS

Chapter 2 contains some material from Liza Lovdahl Gormsen, 'The Parallels between the Harvard Structural School and Article 82 EC and the Divergences between the Chicago and post-Chicago Schools and Article 82 EC', published in 4(1) *European Competition Journal* (2008) 221–41, and is reproduced by permission of the editors. Chapter 4 includes some parts from a revised version of Liza Lovdahl Gormsen, 'The Conflict between Economic Freedom and Consumer Welfare in the Modernisation of Article 82 EC', published in 3(2) *European Competition Journal* (2007) 329–44, and is reproduced by permission of the editors.

Many of the ideas in this book developed during my time as a doctoral research student at King's College London supervised by Professor Richard Whish and David Bailey. The thesis was examined by Professor Thomas Eilmansberger at the University of Salzburg and Dr Maher Dabbah at Queen Mary, University of London, from both of whom I have received excellent comments.

Other ideas were developed during interesting discussions with my LL B and LL M students while teaching competition law at London School of Economics. I am also grateful for the many and interesting discussions I have had with Margaret Bloom and Alison Jones over the years and all the bright people I have met on my way, in particular at the Office of Fair Trading and the Hellenic Competition Commission.

A number of friends and colleagues, including Philip Marsden, Giorgio Monti, Chris Townley, Anne Aylwin and Bruce Lyons, took their time to review and discuss the whole or parts of this book. I am especially grateful to Anne Aylwin and Chris Townley for endless discussions and to Philip Marsden for his meticulous corrections, which were always given with incredible sensitivity and intelligent understanding, and for reminding me in hard times that the sun is shining somewhere above the cloud. The analysis and conclusions expressed herein are solely those of the author and responsibility for any mistakes remains mine alone.

Wise counselling and encouragement have been given on a daily basis by my dear friends Christina Munck, Yasemin Saltuk and Melanie Smith. I thank you all. Special thanks are owed to my Danish and Greek families for emotional support. Above all, I thank my dear husband Fanis for his endless patience and for always making me laugh.

TABLE OF CASES

European Court of Justice (chronological)

European Court of First Instance (chronological)

Community Commission decisions (chronological)

US cases (alphabetical)

1

Introduction

1. The book's aim

This book identifies some of the uncertainties surrounding the application of Article 82 (formerly Article 86) of the EC Treaty.[1] These are: (i) What is the underlying purpose of Article 82? (ii) Is it necessary to demonstrate actual or likely anticompetitive effects in the marketplace when applying Article 82 and what effects are relevant? (iii) How can dominant undertakings defend themselves against a finding of abuse? These uncertainties led the European Commission (the 'Commission') to initiate a review of Article 82.[2] At the eighth annual conference of the European University Institute in Fiesole in June 2003, former Competition Commissioner Monti announced that the Commission had started an internal review of its policy on abuse of a dominant position. Director General Lowe confirmed the initiation of the review a couple of months later.[3] It became clear early on in the review period that the Commission was keen to emphasise that the aim of Article 82 is consumer welfare.

As will be demonstrated, the Commission and Community Courts, the European Court of Justice (the 'ECJ') and the European Court of First

[1] For simplicity a reference to Article 82 will be made throughout notwithstanding that some of the cases mentioned refer to Article 86, which was the number of the article before the enactment of the Treaty of Amsterdam on 1 May 1999. Quotations will remain in their original form.

[2] The equivalent provision to Article 82 in the US is the Sherman Act Section 2. It falls outside the scope of this study to consider US law in detail; US antitrust will be subject to discussion as such only in relation to consumer welfare in chapter 2. However, it is worth noting that the enforcement of the Sherman Act Section 2 has, like Article 82, been subject to recent review. In June 2006, the Department of Justice ('DOJ') and the Federal Trade Commission embarked on a year-long series of joint hearings. In September 2008, the DOJ issued a report, *Competition and Monopoly: Single-Firm Conduct under Section 2 of the Sherman Act*. The report was withdrawn on 11 May 2009.

[3] That an internal review was initiated was confirmed in October 2003 by DG COMP's Director General Lowe at the annual conference of the Fordham Corporate Law Institute. Available at: http://ec.europa.eu/competition/speeches.

Instance (the 'CFI')[4] have interpreted case law in the light of many objectives. For example, Article 82 has been used as a tool in the Commission's broader effort to liberalise markets in sectors which were previously monopolies, such as the postal sector.[5] Given that objectives other than consumer welfare are relevant within Article 82, the book considers whether the sole focus on consumer welfare is legitimate. From the beginning of the Commission's review, it was assumed that the aim of Article 82 is consumer welfare. At the annual conference at Fordham in 2005, Competition Commissioner Kroes argued that the main and ultimate objective of Article 82 is to protect consumers:[6]

> First, it is competition, and not competitors, that is to be protected. Second, ultimately the aim is to avoid consumers harm … I like aggressive competition – including by dominant companies – and I don't care if it may hurt competitors – as long as it ultimately benefits consumers. That is because the main and ultimate objective of Article 82 is to protect consumers, and this does, of course, require the protection of an undistorted competitive process on the market.

This was echoed in the DG Competition ('DG COMP') *Discussion Paper on the Application of Article 82 of the Treaty to Exclusionary Abuses* (the '*Discussion Paper*') in December 2005.[7] The *Discussion Paper* declared that it wanted to protect competition by enhancing consumer welfare: '[w]ith regard to exclusionary abuses the objective of Article 82 is the protection of competition on the market as a means of enhancing consumer welfare and of ensuring an efficient allocation of resources'.[8] Director General Lowe confirmed this view in his speech at the Federal Trade Commission and Antitrust Division Hearings on Section 2 of the Sherman Act.[9] However, this narrow focus on protecting competition only to promote consumer welfare and allocative efficiency may not be entirely in tune

4 For the sake of clarity, references to the ECJ or CFI will be made individually where appropriate. The term 'Community Courts' will be used when referring to the CFI and the ECJ when they are discussed together.

5 OJ [2001] L331/40 *Deutsche Post AG*.

6 N. Kroes, 'Preliminary Thoughts on Policy Review of Article 82', 23 September 2005, the Fordham Corporate Law Institute New York. Available at: http://ec.europa.eu/competition/speeches.

7 DG COMP's *Discussion Paper on the Application of Article 82 of the Treaty to Exclusionary Abuses* (December, 2005). Available at: http://ec.europa.eu.int/comm/competition/antitrust/others/discpaper2005.pdf. DG COMP has received 107 replies to the public consultation on the Discussion Paper, these are available at: http://eceuropa.eu.int/comm/competition/antitrust/others/article_82_contributions.hml.

8 *Discussion Paper*, supra note 7, paras. 4 and 54.

9 P. Lowe. 'Remarks on Unilateral Conduct', 11 September 2006, Washington, DC, 3 and 6.

with jurisprudence or with the normative structure of the competition rules of the EC Treaty:[10]

> As the law now stands, however, the competition rules contained in the Treaty have a constitutional status and may be interpreted as shaping a *law of economic liberty* from restraints of competition and abuses of private economic power, not only a *law of economic efficiency*. Thus, an efficiency-orientated approach to the Community competition rules may not be in tune with the current normative structure.

Whilst the discussion of objectives is not new, it is necessary. Amato points out that 'it requires a frank discussion [of the goals of competition], because it is doubtful that we all agree on the goals of competition. Generally, however, we refrain from discussing it openly, and ambiguities remain.'[11] This book takes a different turn from the usual discussion of objectives, by questioning whether the Commission's chosen objective of consumer welfare is legitimate. Whilst the review of Article 82 has been going on for many years and has been comprehensive, there has been little focus on the legitimacy of consumer welfare. This objective becomes even more problematic if it conflicts with other objectives. Hawk has highlighted such potential conflict:[12]

> The major policy issue concerns the possible tension between efficiency considerations on the one hand and the Article 86 [now Article 82] market integration and fairness policies on the other hand. To date that tension has largely been resolved in favour of the latter. Whether this will continue may depend on the EEC's willingness to acknowledge the tension and resultant possible trade-offs between allocative efficiency (or consumer welfare according to many economists) and protection of individual firms (or distributive concerns according to many economists).

There is a lack of thorough debate about the potential conflict a focus on consumer welfare may create.[13] Whilst the Commission embraces the objective of consumer welfare, its success in practice depends on whether the Commission can reconcile the objective of consumer welfare with other possible conflicting objectives pursued under Article 82.

[10] J. B. Cruz, *Between Competition and Free Movement: The Economic Constitutional Law of the European Community* (Oxford: Hart Publishing, 2002) 1. Emphasis added.

[11] Panel discussion on competition policy objectives in C. D. Ehlermann and L. L. Laudati (eds.), *European Competition Law Annual 1997: The Objectives of Competition Policy* (Oxford: Hart Publishing, 1998) 3.

[12] B. E. Hawk, 'The American (Anti-trust) Revolution: Lessons for the EEC' 9(1) *European Competition Law Review* (1988) 53, 81.

[13] With the exception of, for example, F. Engelsing, P. Marsden and D. Möller, 'A Bundeskartellamt/Competition Law Forum Debate on Reform of Article 82: a "dialectic" on Competing Approaches' 2 (special supplement) *European Competition Journal* (2006)

The International Competition Network (ICN)'s report on the *Objectives of Unilateral Conduct Laws, Assessment of Dominance/Substantial Market Power, and State-Created Monopolies*, published in May 2007, outlined the following relevant objectives for unilateral conduct on the basis of the responses received: ensuring an effective competitive process; promoting consumer welfare; maximising efficiency; ensuring economic freedom; ensuring a level playing field for small and medium-sized enterprises; promoting fairness and equality; promoting consumer choice; achieving market integration; facilitating privatisation and market liberalisation; and promoting competitiveness in international markets.[14] Set against these, the one-dimensional view focusing on maximising economic efficiency in the form of consumer welfare raises a myriad of problems.

The Commission's one-dimensional view on consumer welfare has been moderated to some extent. In answering the questionnaire to the ICN's working group on unilateral conduct, the Commission said that the objective of unilateral conduct is protecting competition by reducing or eliminating the obstacles to economic change and development, which is fundamental to the broader political aim of the Community, which is the process of integration in economic unions and free-trade areas.[15] This goal is articulated in the EC Treaty[16] as well as being judicially recognised.[17] Moreover, the Commission's *Guidance on the Commission's Enforcement Priorities in Applying Article 82 EC Treaty to Abusive Exclusionary Conduct by Dominant Undertakings* (the '*Guidance Paper*') of 3 December 2008, published in the C-series of the Official Journal,[18] accepts that Article 82 is not only about consumer welfare, but also about other objectives.

211–27; O. Budzinski, 'Monoculture versus Diversity in Competition Economics' 32(2) *Cambridge Journal of Economics* (2008) 295–324; L. L. Gormsen, 'The Conflict between Economic Freedom and Consumer Welfare in the Modernisation of Article 82 EC' 3(2) *European Competition Journal* (2007) 329–44; C. Ahlborn and C. Grave, 'Walter Eucken and Ordoliberalism: An Introduction from a Consumer Welfare Perspective' 2(2) *Competition Policy International* (2006) 196.

14 The report is available at: www.internationalcompetitionnetwork.org/media/library/unilateral_conduct/Objectives%20of%20Unilateral%20Conduct%20May%2007.pdf.

15 The Commission's submission to ICN's questionnaire is available at: www.internationalcompetitionnetwork.org/index.php/en/working-groups/unilateral-conduct/unilateral-conduct-working-group-questionnaire-and-responses.

16 Articles 2 and 3 EC.

17 For example, Case 226/84 *British Leyland plc v. Commission* [1986] ECR 3263; Case 26/75 *General Motors Continental NV v. Commission* [1975] ECR 1367; Case 27/76 *United Brands Company v. Commission* [1978] ECR 207. These are just a few of the cases where market integration considerations had an influence on the outcome.

18 OJ [2009] C45/7 *Guidance on the Commission's Enforcement Priorities in Applying Article 82 EC Treaty to Abusive Exclusionary Conduct by Dominant Undertakings* ('*Guidance*

However, the *Guidance Paper* does not say which objective is the more important one in case of a conflict, so ambiguities remain.

This study will consider whether consumer welfare conflicts with other objectives. A tension between economic freedom[19] and consumer welfare is identified. Consumer welfare takes a neo-classical position whereas economic freedom, as derived from ordoliberalism, values freedom of competition as a fundamental right to ensure individual economic freedom in the market. The study will consider whether economic freedom is considered a fundamental right in the Community legal order. If economic freedom is considered a fundamental right there, then the Commission's priority of a utilitarian goal of consumer welfare is violating a fundamental right.

Instead of a comprehensive review of the underlying purpose of Article 82, the modernisation debate has mainly focused on the Commission's methodology due to the uncertainty about the necessity to examine effects of dominant undertakings' conduct. One of the primary reasons for initiating the review was a greater appreciation of microeconomic theory on the part of the policy-makers and the Commission's perception that the rules under Article 82 must be sufficiently responsive to sound economics. One of the overall conclusions from the 2003 annual conference in Fiesole was that the concept of abuse does not lend itself easily to *per se* rules, and that a rule of reason approach is normally preferable. Another conclusion was that legal formalism should be abandoned in favour of the analysis and evaluation of economic effects.[20] The initiation of the policy review came after growing criticism of the application of Article 82 and, in particular, the insufficient attention to economic principles and apparent lack of rigour of the Commission's policy in this area of law.[21] Some argued that the interpretation of Article 82 was still influenced by old-fashioned formalistic and legalistic principles attributed to

Paper'). This book refers to the paragraphs of the *Guidance Paper* published on DG COMP's webpage on 3 December 2008 in case the numbering is different in the version published in the Official Journal.

19 Freedom of competition and economic freedom are used interchangeably throughout, as they mean the same, which is that the economic system should allow all individuals the freedom to participate in the marketplace unimpaired by the power of other companies.

20 C. D. Ehlermann and I. Atanasiu (eds.), *European Competition Law Annual* 2003: *What is an Abuse of a Dominant Position?* (Oxford: Hart Publishing, 2006).

21 For example, J. Ratliff, 'Abuse of Dominant Position and Pricing Practices: A Practitioner's Viewpoint' and D. Ridyard, 'Article 82 Price Abuses: Towards a More Economic Approach' in Ehlermann and Atanasiu, supra note 20; D. Waelbroeck, '*Michelin II*: A *Per Se* Rule against Rebates by Dominant Companies?' 1(1) *Journal of Competition Law and Economics* (2005) 149, 151.

ordoliberalism.[22] This criticism goes to the heart of the objective of economic freedom (which played a central role in the ordoliberal conception of competition policy).[23]

The study will demonstrate that the Community Courts examine the conduct's harmful effects in some cases, but not in all. Sometimes harmful effects are assumed. The study will highlight the advantages and disadvantages of such assumptions. Relying on assumptions may not be a good idea, unless they are supported by a solid economic theory of how competition is harmed in the market. This is particularly true if the assumptions are conclusive, as it deprives dominant undertakings of the ability to defend themselves. However, the alternative of adopting an effects-based approach in all cases also has some drawbacks. For example, it is likely to create more 'type I errors' and fewer 'type II errors'.[24] A type I error is where a given hypothesis, e.g. that an undertaking has committed an infringement, is rejected although it is true. A type II error is where a hypothesis is accepted, but an alternative hypothesis, e.g. that an undertaking has not committed an infringement, is true.[25] In the first situation (type I) the competition authorities have confidence in the robustness of markets to withstand abuse of a dominant position and do not intervene even though intervention would have been justified. The boundary of public power is set as far ahead as possible to see whether the market can take care of itself – and thereby run the risk of 'private

[22] J. Kallaugher and B. Sher, 'Rebates Revisited: Anticompetitive Effects and Exclusionary Abuse under Article 82' 5 *European Competition Law Review* (2004) 263, 268; see also D. Gerber, *Law and Competition in Twentieth Century Europe: Protecting Prometheus* (Oxford University Press, 1998); W. Möschel, 'Competition Policy from an Ordo Point of View' in A. Peacock and H. Willgerodt (eds.), *German Neo-liberals and the Social Market Economy* (London: Macmillan, 1989) 142.

[23] Not all share the view that case law and practice do not, or even should in all respects, reflect modern economic thinking. Professor Eilmansberger is one of them even though he criticises the lack of a clear, coherent, conceptual basis in decisions concerning exclusionary abuses: see T. Eilmansberger, 'How to Distinguish Good from Bad Competition under Article 82 EC: In Search of Clearer and More Coherent Standards for Anticompetitive Abuses' 42 *Common Market Law Review* (2005) 129, 131.

[24] These are sometimes also known respectively as false negatives and false positives.

[25] Some scholars have identified a 'type III error' which occurs when you get the right answer to the wrong question. In competition law terms, this can be equated with wrong enforcement priority decisions. Type III errors risk over-enthusiastic enforcement activities and can give rise to spurious or speculative complaints from competitors. This in turn gives rise to a form of regulatory drag which is, in principle, just as harmful as unnecessary regulation, wasting resources ultimately to the detriment of consumers. It is also problematic in terms of business planning and strategy, since enforcement which is unpredictable has a cooling effect on commercial behaviour. See Report from IBC conference, *Advanced EC Competition Law* (4–5 May 2006) 64–5.

power' being abused – and thereby accept the risk of private power. In the second situation (type II) the competition authorities have little faith in the robustness of the market and seek to prevent the risk of private power emerging – and thereby run the risk of intrusion by 'public power' – by activating intervention in the markets earlier.[26] In a type II error, competition authorities intervene in circumstances where intervention is not justified. When enforcing Article 82, the Commission has been criticised for being too intrusive when seeking to prevent the risk of private power from emerging.[27]

2. The structure of the book

Given the focus on consumer welfare, chapter 2 considers how economists define the concept of consumer welfare and its relation to allocative, productive and dynamic efficiency. It demonstrates that consumer welfare is concerned with consumer surplus and allocative efficiency. It examines whether Article 82 allows for efficiencies to be advanced despite the lack of an exemption provision like Article 81(3). Despite Article 82's lack of a bifurcate structure between a prohibition and an exemption, dominant undertakings can advance objective justifications. Chapter 3 examines whether case law supports the objective of consumer welfare. It discovers that Article 82 not only aims at promoting consumer welfare, but also seeks to endorse other objectives. The Community Courts rarely articulate their stand on the underlying purpose of Article 82 and, if they do, it is unclear what exactly is meant by these objectives, so ambiguity remains. A consequence of many objectives being considered important is the possibility of a conflict between them. Chapter 4 discusses whether a potential conflict arises between some of the objectives. It finds that there may be a conflict between economic freedom and consumer welfare. Chapter 5 discovers that case law only allows dominant undertakings to advance such justifications based on objective factors going beyond their control and public policy considerations, which do not necessarily

[26] Former Competition Commissioner Monti has said: '[E]nshrined in the Treaty is … an open market economy with free competition … Personally I believe that an open market economy does not imply an attitude of unconditional faith with respect to the operation of market mechanisms': see M. Monti, 'European Competition Policy for the 21st Century', *International Antitrust Law and Policy* (Fordham Corporate Law Institute, 2000) 257.

[27] A criticism acknowledged by P. Lowe, 'New Challenges in Europe', 24 June 2005, King's College London.

include efficiencies. It finds that the Commission and the Community Courts do not always engage in an analysis of effects, but instead make assumptions in some cases that conduct by dominant firms will result in harmful effects. In such cases, efficiencies become illusory. To address the uncertainties surrounding the application of Article 82, the Commission has issued a *Guidance Paper.* Chapter 6 examines whether the *Guidance Paper* clarifies some of the doubts. The *Guidance Paper* emphasises that it is not a statement of law; however, it may still have certain effects for undertakings. The *Guidance Paper* does not address all the uncertainties highlighted in the chapters. Thus, chapter 7 recommends a simple way forward to create more certainty in the application of Article 82.

3. The interpretation of Article 82

Article 82 is the mechanism used in the European Community[28] to control the abuse of a dominant position.[29] The provision is aimed at

[28] In the 1950s, Germany, France, Italy and the Benelux Countries (the Netherlands, Belgium and Luxembourg) decided to establish a system of joint decision-making on economic issues. They formed the European Coal and Steel Community (ECSC), the European Atomic Energy Community (Euratom) and the European Economic Community (EEC). These three communities – collectively known as the European communities – formed the basis of what is today the European Union (EU). The European Community, which is the most important of the three European communities, was originally founded on 25 March 1957 by the signing of the Treaty of Rome under the name of the European Economic Community. The 'Economic' was removed from its name by the Maastricht Treaty in 1992, which also established the EU. The Maastricht Treaty effectively made the European Community the first of three 'pillars' of the EU, the so-called Community (or Communities) pillar. The first pillar corresponds to the European Community, the second comprises the common foreign and security policy (CFSP) and the European security and defence policy (ESDP) and the third consists of police and judicial cooperation in criminal matters. The establishment of the EU in 1992 did not cause the European Community to disappear. It remains part of the EU under the designation 'European Community'. The terminology 'Community' and 'EU' will be used interchangeably. EU law is defined as '[t]he law governing the structure, organs, and functioning of the Council of Europe and other European organizations or institutions; further the law contained in the conventions and agreements of the Council of Europe and the instruments of other European organizations or institutions': see F. W. Hondius, 'The New Architecture of Europe and *Ius Commune Europaeum*' in B. de Witte and C. Forder (eds.), *The Common Law of Europe and the Future of Legal Education* (Deventer: Kluwer Law International, 1992) 215.

[29] If and when the Lisbon Treaty is ratified and comes into force the Treaty of Rome will become the Treaty on the Functioning of the European Union (TFEU). The 'European Community' terminology, which was kept in part after 1992, will be replaced with 'European Union' throughout the TFEU. Article 82 EC will be renumbered Article 102 TFEU. However, it is unknown when – if ever – the Lisbon Treaty will be ratified. Thus, this study will continue to refer to Article 82.

eliminating abusive conduct by prohibiting any abuse by one or more undertakings of a dominant position in a market in so far as it affects trade between Member States. It forms part of the competition provisions established by the Treaty of Rome in 1957,[30] along with Articles 81 and 83–9 EC.[31] Article 82 is the subject of this study, with discussion of the other provisions included only where relevant. The text of Article 82 is as follows:

> Any abuse by one or more undertakings of a dominant position within the common market or in a substantial part of it shall be prohibited as incompatible with the common market in so far as it may affect trade between Member States.
>
> Such abuse may, in particular, consist in:
>
> (a) directly or indirectly imposing unfair purchase or selling prices or other unfair trading conditions;
> (b) limiting production, markets or technical development to the prejudice of consumers;
> (c) applying dissimilar conditions to equivalent transactions with other trading parties, thereby placing them at a competitive disadvantage;
> (d) making the conclusion of contracts subject to acceptance by the other parties of supplementary obligations which, by their nature or according to commercial usage, have no connection with the subject of such contracts.

Article 82(2) has not been interpreted as an exhaustive enumeration, but as a list of examples. This emerges from the wording 'in particular' of Article 82(2) as well as case law.[32] Article 82 does not distinguish between exploitative and exclusionary abuse.[33] Yet, it is a generally accepted distinction, although some abuses can be both.[34]

[30] This study refers to the consolidated version of the EC Treaty.

[31] The provisions in the EC Treaty will be referred to hereinafter by simple number alone rather than by providing the full reference. The complete reference will be included when referring to articles for the first time, or when referring to provisions from other treaties.

[32] Case 6/72 *Europemballage Corporation and Continental Can Co. Inc. v. Commission* [1973] ECR 215, para. 26; Case C-333/94P *Tetra Pak International SA v. Commission* (*Tetra Pak II*) [1996] ECR I-5951, para. 37.

[33] Exploitative abuse is where dominant undertakings take excessive advantages of their market power and obtain a benefit by placing an unfair burden upon their customers or consumers without any effect on the competitive process or the structure of the market in which dominant firms operate: see D. Goyder, *EC Competition Law* (Oxford University Press, 3rd edn, 1998) 369. Exclusionary abuse is where dominant undertakings deny rivals access to the market or expansion in the market.

[34] J. Temple Lang, 'The Requirements for a Commission Notice on the Concept of Abuse under Article 82 EC' CEPS Special Report (2008) 1. Available at: www.ceps.eu.

The meaning of the concepts of dominance and abuse emerge from the case law and practice of the Commission and the Community Courts, as Article 82 is a framework provision and the central terms 'dominance' and 'abuse' are inherently vague. Neither the concept of abuse nor that of dominance is defined in the EC Treaty. The Commission has not sought to publish general secondary legislation or substantive guidance,[35] although it did publish enforcement priorities in December 2008. The *travaux préparatoires* to the Treaty were deliberately never published, although they can be accessed in the Florence archives. In any event, the Community Courts rarely focus on the intent of the drafters of the EC Treaty.

The concept of abuse is not explicitly defined in the EC Treaty. Such a definition could have had a limiting effect on its interpretation, because every decision or judgment would have to fit within the definition. Instead, the interpretation of Article 82 has been developed through case law, which has allowed the concept of abuse to develop to fit the contours of a particular decision and new learning to be integrated into the case law in an ever-changing economy. This allows the analysis of the provision to be updated, as interpretations that seemed adequate years ago may no longer be suitable. However, the lack of substantive guidance as to what does and does not constitute an abuse has led to an *ad hoc* process, swayed by the specific facts that come before the authorities or the courts. It is hard to see a single unifying theory underpinning the interpretation of Article 82.[36] The law of Article 82 is the result of the cases brought before the Community Courts. This has led to some legal uncertainty resulting from the way in which the provision is being applied in practice and the way in which the legal framework is written. This uncertainty, especially with regard to the 'speciality responsibility' of dominant undertakings,[37] may result in dominant firms

[35] However, the Commission has published guidance in specific sectors such as postal services and telecommunications. Some insight into the identification of market power can be gained by analogy from OJ [2002] C165/6 *Commission Guidelines on Market Analysis and Assessment of Significant Market Power under the Community Regulatory Framework for Electronic Communications Networks and Services*, para. 70; EC Directive 2002/21 on a *Common Regulatory Framework for Electronic Communication Service* (the Framework Directive) Article 14(2), where significant market power is equated with dominance under Article 82; 'Commission Issues Market Power Assessment Guidelines for Electronic Communications', press release of 9 July 2002, IP/02/1016.

[36] Dabbah points out that the ECJ has created a jurisprudence under Article 82 which makes it difficult to understand the real aim of Article 82: see M. M. Dabbah, 'Conduct, Dominance and Abuse in "Market Relationship": Analysis of Some Conceptual Issues under Article 82 EC' 21(1) *European Competition Law Review* (2000) 45.

[37] Case 322/81 *Nederlandsche Banden-Industrie Michelin NV v. Commission* (*Michelin I*) [1983] ECR 3461, para. 57.

competing less aggressively. However, formalistic rules, as to what does and does not constitute an abuse in the market, are not helpful or desirable either. It may not be appropriate to rely on case law decided decades ago in today's markets which are often characterised by very rapid technological changes, creation and exploitation of intellectual property rights and a high degree of technical complexity.[38] In general, concepts like dominance and abuse cannot be applied mechanically in today's economic environment and many of the traditional presumptions about what is harmful to competition do not hold in this context.

Article 82 is a legal provision, and one that has been shaped by the interpretation of the Community Courts. The Community is not a static legal environment and the EC Treaty is a 'living instrument', where the interpretation of text is always evolving. While the Community legal system has changed enormously since Article 82 was conceived, the provision itself has remained unchanged since 1957. The question is what tools are available to the Commission in modernising Article 82.

4. Tools available for reforming Article 82

The previous section showed that the concept of abuse has been left to develop through case law, but it is hard to see a single unifying theory underpinning the interpretation of Article 82. The Commission has clarified and reformed its Article 81 and merger control[39] policies in terms of

[38] C. Ahlborn, 'Competition Policy in the New Economy: Is European Competition Law up to the Challenge?' 22(5) *European Competition Law Review* (2001) 156; M. Messina, 'Article 82 and the New Economy: Need for Modernisation?' 2(2) *Competition Law Review* (2005) 73.

[39] OJ [1999] L336/21 Commission Regulation No. 2790/1999, *The Application of Article 81(3) of the Treaty to Categories of Vertical Agreements and Concerted Practices*; OJ [2000] C291/1 Commission Notice, *Guidelines on Vertical Restraints*; OJ [2004] C101/97 Commission Notice, *Guidelines on the Application of Article 81(3) of the EC Treaty*; OJ [2004] L123/11 Commission Regulation No. 772/2004, *The Application of Article 81(3) of the Treaty to Categories of Technology Transfer Agreements*; OJ [2004] C101/2 Commission Notice, *Guidelines on the Application of Article 81 of the EC Treaty to Technology Transfer Agreements*; OJ [2001] C3/2 Commission Notice, *Guidelines on the Applicability of Article 81 of the EC Treaty to Horizontal Cooperation Agreements*; OJ [2004] C101/54 Commission Notice, *Cooperation Between the Commission and the Courts of the EU Member States in the Application of Articles 81 and 82*; OJ [2004] C101/43 Commission Notice, *Cooperation within the Network of Competition Authorities*; OJ [2004] C101/78 Commission Notice, *Informal Guidance Relating to Novel Questions Concerning Articles 81 and 82 of the EC Treaty that Arise in Individual Cases*; OJ [2004] C101/65 Commission Notice, *The Handling of Complaints by the Commission under Articles 81 and 82 of the EC Treaty*; OJ [2004] L24/1 Commission Merger Regulation No. 139/2004; OJ [2004]

economic principles. On the legislative front, the Council of Ministers adopted Council Regulation (EC) No. 1/2003 on the implementation of the rules on competition laid down in Articles 81 and 82 to introduce a more efficient and effective, decentralised system of competition law enforcement.[40] After having thus revised and modernised these areas of competition law, the Commission began the modernisation process of Article 82 in 2003.[41]

Reforming Article 82 is not a simple matter and the tools available are limited. Reform of Article 82 is different from the reform of Article 81, because there is no general secondary legislation on the application of Article 82 which could be revised. Unlike Article 81, Article 82 does not allow the possibility of exemption. The absence of a provision like Article 81(3) means that it is not easy, even though theoretically possible given Article 83 EC, to adopt block exemptions on certain types of conduct, thereby making that type of conduct permissible. The block exemption regulations adopted upon this basis find their limits in the principles enshrined in Articles 81 and 82, excluding any modification of primary law.[42] Article 83 empowers the Council to lay down the 'appropriate regulations or directives to give effect to the principles set out in Articles 81 and 82 EC'. According to subparagraph (b), the Council is empowered to lay down the details of the application of Article 81(3).

Amendments to the text of Article 82 are unlikely. The Lisbon Treaty – if ever ratified – maintains the original text of the provision despite changing the number from Article 82 to Article 102.[43] Unless the Treaty is amended, the reform of Article 82 will depend upon the ECJ reconsidering, or filling the gaps in, its case law and/or the Commission changing its enforcement policy. It is unlikely that earlier case law will be overruled. Those who would like to see a reorientation of the law were disappointed[44] that the Community Courts did not take the opportunity to do so in *British*

C31/5 Commission Notice, *Guidelines on the Assessment of Horizontal Mergers under the Council Regulation on the Control of Concentrations Between Undertakings.*

40 OJ [2003] L/1/1 Council Regulation No. 1/2003, *The Implementation of the Rules on Competition Laid Down in Articles 81 and 82 of the Treaty.* Council Regulation No. 1/2003 applies from 1 May 2004, replacing Council Regulation No. 17/62 OJ [1962] Special edition 204/87 as amended by OJ [1999] L148/5 Council Regulation (EC) No 1216/1999.

41 Lowe, supra note 3.

42 E. J. Mestmäcker and H. Schweitzer, *Europäisches Wettbewerbsrecht* (Munich: Beck, 2nd edn, 2004) 337.

43 Lisbon Treaty: see supra note 29.

44 This is apparent from many of the submissions to the public consultation on the *Discussion Paper*, supra note 7.

Airways[45] and *Michelin II*.[46] Although the ECJ's judgment in *British Airways* contains some promising indications, such as the need for the Commission to establish some form of competitive impact, and an appreciation of economic benefits, these judgments confirm that case law reform of Article 82 is not going to happen immediately. It is a reminder that if the Commission's enforcement policy is to become more economics-based, the impetus cannot be expected to come from the Community Courts alone. It will have to come from the Commission itself and from the national competition authorities, whether through future enforcement decisions or through guidelines. Although substantive guidelines are not legally binding,[47] they would help create a unified body of decisions, rather than a set of individual *ad hoc* and inconsistent measures. As a result, the underlying objectives of Article 82 are more likely to be realised.[48]

The Commission is not precluded from taking a more economics-based approach simply because the ECJ has endorsed its old form-based approach. However, the Commission must use its prosecutorial discretion within the framework of Community case law, as Advocate General Kokott highlighted in her Opinion in *British Airways*: 'even if ... [the Commission's] administrative practice were to change, the Commission would still have to act within the framework prescribed for it by Article 82 EC as interpreted by the Court of Justice'.[49] How far the Commission can go in modernising Article 82, given the case law of the Community Courts, will be discussed in later chapters.

5. Article 82 review

The aim of the Commission's policy review of Article 82 was to bring the law in line with 'mainstream economics'.[50] This may well be the way forward, but modernisation of Article 82 is a sensitive issue surrounded by

45 Case C-95/04P *British Airways plc v. Commission* [2007] ECR I-2331.

46 Case T-203/01 *Manufacture Française des Pneumatiques Michelin v. Commission* [2003] ECR II-4071 ('*Michelin II*').

47 According to Article 249 EC, only regulations, directives and decisions are legally binding measures in the Community.

48 Commission Report, *The Action Plan for Consumer Policy 1999–2001 and on the General Framework for Community Activities in Favour of Consumers 1999–2003* COM(2001) 486, 17–19.

49 Advocate General Kokott in her Opinion in *British Airways*, supra note 45, delivered on 23 February 2006, para. 28.

50 P. Lowe, 'DG Competition's Review of the Policy on Abuse of Dominance' in B. E. Hawk (ed.), *Annual Proceedings of the Fordham Corporate Law Institute: International Antitrust Law and Policy* (New York: Juris, 2004) 165.

many lobbyists from the business community, academia and the legal practice with their own – at times – very different interests.

In the late 1990s, when the Commission was discussing the reform of Article 81, a leading academic in competition policy said 'the reasons why reform or modernization in this area [Article 81] is such a delicate task is the temptation to adjust the rules in light of past disappointments and to open a Pandora's box of new interest and power balancing'.[51] A similar concern can be advanced about the review of Article 82, as it is not unthinkable that some may be tempted to argue that the Commission and the ECJ were pursuing an objective of consumer welfare in the early cases in order to defend the Commission's current commitment to consumer welfare.[52]

Many commentators believe that the underlying principles of Article 82 could be clearer.[53] Some observers point out that the Commission and the Community Courts often place too much emphasis on the 'form' of the conduct, and too little on the economic impact, e.g. the 'effects' of the conduct on the market.[54] This was also the view of the Economic Advisory Group on Competition Policy to the Commission (the 'EAGCP') in its report, *An Economic Approach to Article 82 EC*, published on 21 July

[51] E. J. Mestmäcker, 'The EC Commission's Modernization of Competition Policy: A Challenge to the Community's Constitutional Order' 1 *European Business Organization Law Review* (2000) 401, 413.

[52] See for example N. Kroes, 'European Competition Policy in a Changing World and Globalised Economy: Fundamentals, New Objectives and Challenges Ahead', 5 June 2007, GCLC/College of Europe Conference on '50 years of EC Competition Law', Brussels. Available at: http://ec.europa.eu /competition/speeches. This is however contradicted by Director General Lowe, who argues that case law and decisional practice have been influenced by ordoliberalism: P. Lowe, 'Consumer Welfare and Efficiency: New Guiding Principles of Competition Policy?', 27 March 2007, Thirteenth International Conference on Competition and Fourteenth European Competition Day, 2.

[53] Eilmansberger, supra note 23; J. Vickers, 'Abuse of Market Power' 115 *Economic Journal* (2005) F244; B. Sher, 'The Last of the Steam-Powered Trains: Modernising Article 82' 25(5) *European Competition Law Review* (2004) 243, arguing that there is no internal consistency of application, and that there is no longer any coherent policy basis for applying Article 82; S. Völcker, 'Developments in EC Competition Law in 2003: An Overview' 41 *Common Market Law Review* (2004) 1027, 1048, arguing that Article 82 currently lacks a coherent overall approach and remains largely untouched by the increasing focus on economic analysis that has characterised the development of the law and practice under Article 81.

[54] See for example P. Marsden and S. W. Waller, 'Antitrust Marathon II' 4(1) *European Competition Journal* (2008) 213, 219; L. L. Gormsen, 'Article 82 EC: Where Are We Coming From and Where Are We Going To?' 2(2) *Competition Law Review* (2005) 5, 6; Ratliff and Ridyard respectively in Ehlermann and Atanasiu, supra note 21; Kallaugher and Sher, supra note 22, 268; Waelbroeck, supra note 21, 151.

2005 (the 'EAGCP Report').[55] The report suggests that a 'more economic approach' to Article 82 must be adopted. In this context, a more economic approach is understood to be an approach that 'requires a careful examination of how competition works in each particular market in order to evaluate how specific company strategies affect consumer welfare'.[56] Budzinski does not criticise the more economic approach to competition policy as such, but he warns that it is difficult to achieve because it relies on the following:[57]

(i) the exclusion of actually or allegedly non-economic goals;
(ii) clear, simple and non-ambiguous, preferably quantitative, criteria for the differentiation between pro-competitive and anticompetitive business arrangements and behaviours;
(iii) the facilitation of bringing evidence to the courts;
(iv) the exclusion/reduction of political influences; and
(v) avoiding the difficulties of normative assessments of business arrangements and behaviours by referring to an 'objective and unerring science' instead.

It is probably the most difficult question in competition law to determine what conduct is 'competition on the merits' and therefore legal, and what is 'anticompetitive conduct' and therefore illegal, as the two kinds of conduct often look identical in practice. The great intellectual difficulty over the proper standard of liability governing allegedly exclusionary conduct under Article 82 led DG COMP to publish its *Discussion Paper*. While DG COMP is responsible for competition policy, the Commission will be responsible for applying the principles described in the *Discussion Paper* or any other document if these principles are later adopted in a notice.[58] The *Discussion Paper* was a staff paper, which was meant only for consultation to allow interested parties to express their view on a text that might become substantive guidelines later. Despite not being an authoritative source or even published in the Official Journal, some parts of the

[55] EAGCP Report on *An Economic Approach to Article 82 EC* (July 2005). Available at: http// ec.europa.eu.int/comm/competition/publications/studies/eagcp_july_21_05.pdf.

[56] Ibid., 2.

[57] Budzinski, supra note 13, 295; there are limits of the effects-based analysis: see chapter 5.

[58] DG COMP is the policy branch within the Commission. The main responsibility of DG COMP is making competition policy and the main responsibilities of the Commission are fact-finding, taking action against the infringement of the law and imposing penalties. For a detailed description of the difference between DG COMP and the Commission, see R. Whish, *Competition Law* (Oxford University Press, 6th edn, 2009) 53–4.

Discussion Paper were drafted as substantive guidelines,[59] which raised expectations of the Commission issuing substantive guidance in this area of law.[60] The *Discussion Paper* was never published as substantive guidelines, so it could be considered a document which is no longer relevant. However, in analysing the *Prokent/Tomra* decision,[61] DG COMP officials refer to the *Discussion Paper* to emphasise that the decision took economic analysis into consideration in 'the spirit' of the *Discussion Paper*.[62] This may give the impression that some DG COMP officials actually rely on the principles established in the *Discussion Paper*, in which case it seems to be something more than just a discussion paper. In the light of the above comments by officials regarding the *Prokent/Tomra* decision, the relevance of the *Discussion Paper* cannot be rejected. This is even more so given that there is no secondary legislation or substantive guidelines on the application of Article 82. Despite the publication of the *Guidance Paper*, which is an official notice from the Commission, the *Discussion Paper* is still an important document for understanding what some DG COMP officials are thinking on Article 82. This is in particular because the *Guidance Paper* is a document setting out the Commission's priorities only. For this reason, references to the *Discussion Paper* as well as the *Guidance Paper* will be made throughout.

6. Protecting competition versus protecting competitors

The EAGCP Report[63] specifically emphasised the importance of adopting a more economic approach to Article 82 to avoid confusion between 'protection of competition' and 'protection of competitors'.[64] The distinction between protection of competition and protection of competitors presents an interesting paradox which will remain as long as the meaning of protection of competition is not clear.[65]

Seeking to protect freedom of competition at the same time as promoting consumer welfare may be problematic and create a dilemma: which category of rights to protect at the expense of which other rights. To what

[59] *Discussion Paper*, para. 7.

[60] The issue will be discussed in chapter 6.

[61] COMP/E-1/38.113 *Prokent/Tomra*.

[62] Competition Policy Newsletter, No. 2 (summer 2006) 24.

[63] EAGCP Report, supra note 55.

[64] This was also suggested in the OECD Report on *Competition Law and Policy in the European Union* (October 2005) 30. Available at: www.oecd.org/dataoecd/7/41/35908641.pdf.

[65] Gerber, supra note 22, section 2 of the preface.

extent should the manner in which a large firm exerts its market power to the detriment of competitors, as opposed to the detriment of consumer welfare (or competition) at large, be the concern of competition authorities? Indeed, it is a fine distinction, because by protecting competition and the competitive process, competitors, who make up the fabric of competitive markets, are in fact being protected. If there are no competitors, there is no competitive process to protect.

The uncertainty about how best to protect competition is hardly surprising given that neither the EC Treaty, nor the Community Courts, nor the Commission is very clear. Resolving this uncertainty is nevertheless essential at least for two reasons: first, Article 82 has been and continues to be interpreted in the light of the objective of protection of competition; and second, in order to give the provision an adequate level of predictability and consistency in its application, so that undertakings can understand how Article 82 is applied by national courts and competition authorities.

Whilst it is clearer why competition must be protected, it is less clear how it should be protected. On the one hand, Mestmäcker argues that competition is best protected by ensuring freedom of competition.[66] On the other hand, Competition Commissioner Kroes argues that competition is best protected by protecting consumer welfare.[67] This latter view, in favour of protection of competition to protect the welfare of consumers,[68] is supported in early legal scholarship on Article 82. A study by Joliet in the late 1960s argued that the protection of competition means prohibiting exploitative behaviour[69] which harms consumers.[70] Joliet specifically

[66] E. J. Mestmäcker, *Europäisches Wettbewerbsrecht* (Munich: Beck, 1974).

[67] Kroes, supra note 6.

[68] This view is also supported by Advocate General Jacobs in his Opinion in Case C-7/97 *Oscar Bronner GmbH & Co. KG v. Mediaprint Zeitungs- und Zeitschriftenverlag GmbH & Co. KG* [1998] ECR I-7791, delivered on 28 May 1998, para. 58: '[I]n assessing this issue [access to a competitors' facility] it is important not to lose sight of the fact that the primary purpose of Article 86 [Article 82] is to prevent distortion of competition – and in particular to safeguard the interests of consumers – rather than to protect the position of particular competitors.'

[69] R. Joliet, *Monopolization and Abuse of Dominant Position* (University of Liège, 1970) 250–1.

[70] A consumer may not only mean a member of the public who purchases goods for personal use but also those who purchase goods in the course of their trade: see Whish, supra note 58, 158. Similarly, *Guidance Paper*, supra note 18, footnote 15: 'The concept of "consumers" encompasses all direct or indirect users of the products affected by the conduct, including intermediate producers that use the products as an input, as well as distributors and final consumers both of the immediate product and of products provided

argued that it did not mean preventing competitors' exclusion from the market.[71] His argument has some merits if it is accepted that most exclusionary abuses are also exploitative indirectly. Joliet argued that exclusionary conduct will eventually be caught by prohibiting exploitation because the point of driving competitors out of the market is that the dominant undertaking can acquire the market power necessary to charge monopoly profits. Fox supports this interpretation by arguing that exploitation can sometimes be enabled by market exclusions.[72] Siragusa and others argue that Article 82 applies mainly to exclusionary abuses and its application to exploitative abuses should be limited to the examples listed in Article 82(2).[73] In *Continental Can*, the ECJ also emphasised that consumers must be protected either directly or indirectly.[74] The *Continental Can* case established a connection between consumer harm and significant changes of market structure. The ECJ has confirmed in other cases that Article 82 can be applied to prohibit conduct affecting the structure of the market.[75] However, the connection between consumer harm and changes in the market structure became neglected over time,

by intermediate producers. Where intermediate users are actual or potential competitors of the dominant undertaking, the assessment focuses on the effects of the conduct on users further downstream.' In the context of competition law, the concept of 'consumers' encompasses intermediate and ultimate consumers, OJ [2008]C265/6 *Guidelines on the Assessment of Non-horizontal Mergers under the Council Regulation on the Control of Concentrations Between Undertakings*, para. 16. This is similar in the *Guidelines on the Application of Article 81(3)*, supra note 39, para. 84.

71 Joliet's study was comparative in scope – in particular a comparative analysis of Section 2 of the Sherman Act and Article 82 – and consisted of three parts: American law on single-firm monopolies, a survey of the national laws of the Common Market countries and of Great Britain and, lastly, an analysis of the system of abuse of dominant position under Article 82.

72 E. Fox, 'What is Harm to Competition? Exclusionary Practices and Anticompetitive Effect' 70 *Antitrust Law Journal* (2002) 371, 382; this is also supported by Advocate General Kokott, supra note 49, para. 68, where she says that 'where competition as such is damaged, disadvantages for consumers are also to be feared'.

73 M. Siragusa, *The Application of Art. 86: Tying Agreements, Refusal to Deal, Discrimination and Other Cases of Abuse* (Bruges, 1974); E. J. Mestmäcker, 'Die Beurteilung von Unternehmenszusammenschlüssen nach Artikel 86 des EWG-Vertrags' in *Festschrift für Walter Hallstein zu seinem 60: Probleme des Europäischen Rechts* (Frankfurt am Main: Klostermann, 1966); V. Van Themaat, 'Zusammenschlüsse über die Grenze im Rahmen des EWG-Bereichs', Conference Paper of the Fourth International Conference on European Law, Rome, 1968.

74 *Continental Can*, supra note 32, para. 26.

75 Case 85/76 *Hoffmann-La Roche AG v. Commission* [1979] ECR 461, para. 91; *Michelin I*, supra note 37, para. 70.

so even insignificant change in the market structure became associated with harm to consumers.[76]

Having introduced some of the problems and uncertainties surrounding Article 82 in this chapter the concept of consumer welfare will be defined in the next chapter.

[76] See E. Rousseva, 'Modernizing by Eradicating: How the Commission's New Approach to Article 81 EC Dispenses with the Need to Apply Article 82 EC to Vertical Restraints' 42 *Common Market Law Review* (2005) 587, 592; L. Lovdahl Gormsen, 'The Parallels between the Harvard Structural School and Article 82 EC and the Divergences between the Chicago and Post-Chicago Schools and Article 82 EC' 4(1) *European Competition Journal* (2008) 221, 242.

2

Consumer welfare theory, different schools of thought and efficiencies

1. Introduction

Many jurisdictions embracing competition law state that the objective is to improve consumer welfare.[1] Some argue that consumer welfare is also an objective in European competition law.[2] To be able to examine whether consumer welfare conflicts with any other objectives pursued in Article 82, it is necessary to clarify the concept. There is no precise definition of the term 'consumer welfare'. The EC Treaty has not assigned a specific meaning to the concept of consumer welfare, or other variants of welfare, and its meaning is not entirely clear. The expression 'consumer welfare' has several interpretations and it has sometimes been misunderstood in competition law analysis.[3] Consequently, the term 'consumer welfare' requires clarification. This chapter is written from a legal perspective, so it does not attempt to suggest a new definition of consumer welfare, but will describe the current understanding of the term and its contours for the purpose of examining a potential conflict. Subsequent chapters will also refer to consumer welfare, so this chapter provides a point of reference which will continuously be referred to and used in later chapters.

1 UNCTAD, 'Objectives of Competition Law and Policy: Towards a Coherent Strategy for Promoting Competition and Development' 4, submitted for the OECD in 2003. Doc. CCNM/GF/COMP/WD (2003) 31.

2 N. Kroes, 'Preliminary Thoughts on Policy Review of Article 82', speech given on 23 September 2005 at the Fordham Corporate Law Institute, New York, available at: www.europa.eu.int/comm/competition/speeches; M. E. Janow, 'International Perspectives on Abuse of Dominance' in OECD paper GD(96)131 on *Abuse of Dominance and Monopolisation* (1996) 34; OJ [2004] C101/97 Commission Notice, *Guidelines on the Application of Article 81(3) of the EC Treaty*, para. 33; OJ [2000] C291/1 Commission Notice, *Guidelines on Vertical Restraints*, para. 7; M. Monti, 'Comments to the Speech given by Hew Pate, Assistant Attorney General, US Department of Justice, at the Conference "Antitrust in a Transatlantic Context"', 7 June 2004, Brussels. Available at: http://ec.europa.eu/competition/speeches.

3 J. F. Brodley, 'The Economic Goals of Antitrust: Efficiency, Consumer Welfare and Technological Progress' 62 *New York University Law Review* (1987) 1020, 1032.

Consumer welfare is an economic term, but is increasingly used in the legal sphere, including the sphere of European competition law, where the Commission has devoted itself to a more 'economic approach' in respect of competition law.[4] The marrying of economics and law is not new, but can be found in the works of, for example, Posner and Bork.[5] These scholars, among others, are concerned with welfare economics[6] (or normative economics)[7] and aim to identify situations where efficiencies are not achieved and to prescribe corrective solutions.

The chapter introduces the different types of efficiency and their correlation with the various welfare standards. This is necessary to understand what kinds of efficiencies are accepted when adopting a consumer welfare standard, which becomes relevant for examining whether advancing efficiencies in Article 82 is a possibility. Whether efficiencies can be advanced and how they are evaluated depends on which welfare standard is adopted. For example, if the aim is to improve total welfare then it is irrelevant whether either producers or consumers gain from efficiencies. If the aim is to improve consumer welfare, then consumers must benefit from efficiencies. This requires redistribution in the form of wealth transfer from producers to consumers. Thus, what welfare standard is adopted is important for deciding who is the more deserving of welfare.

The chapter also discusses how different schools of thought have treated market power. This is to examine whether ordoliberalism, which has influenced the application of Article 82, is in effect the Harvard 'structural' School's European sister. This is important for analysing whether the beliefs of the Chicago School can be injected into Article 82. In the US, the Harvard School believed that competition policy is aimed at multiple goals. It was sceptical about efficiency and did not necessarily believe that an accumulation of power was due to efficiency. The Chicago School

4 OJ [1999] C132/1 Commission White Paper, *Modernisation of the Rules Implementing Articles 85 and 86 of the EC Treaty*, point 78. Available at: http://ec.europa.eu/comm/competition/antitrust/wp_modern_En.pdf. The EAGCP Report on *An Economic Approach to Article 82 EC* (July 2005) has suggested an economics-based approach to Article 82.

5 R. Posner, *Antitrust Law* (University of Chicago Press, 2nd edn, 2001); R. Bork, *The Antitrust Paradox: A Policy at War with Itself* (New York: Free Press, 1993).

6 Welfare economists view the social desirability of alternative arrangements of economic activities and allocation of resources. It is, in effect, the analysis of the optimal behaviour of individual consumers rather than of society as a whole. See C. M. Price, *Welfare Economics in Theory and Practice* (London: Macmillan, 1977) 3. For an in-depth definition see G. Bannock *et al.*, *Dictionary of Economics* (New York: Bloomberg Press, 4th edn, 2003) 302.

7 As opposed to positive economics, which views economics exclusively as an empirical science, i.e. without reference to value judgements.

adopted a competition policy aimed at economic efficiency only. It adopted a positive view on efficiency. For example, it believed that higher profits are due to the lower costs of larger firms, because they have economies of scale. In Europe, the ordoliberal school of thought viewed the protection of individual economic freedom of action as a value in itself. Efficiency was seen as a possible by-product rather than an aim in itself.

Finally, the chapter examines whether efficiencies are relevant in Article 82 and, if so, whether they are considered as a part of the overall analysis of abuse or as a defence. This is connected to the discussion of consumer welfare as a goal of Article 82 as well as the discussion of presumptions in chapter 5.

2. Efficiency and welfare standards

This section describes three different types of efficiency underpinning competition law: allocative, productive and dynamic efficiency. In a similar vein, it describes the different welfare standards – consumer surplus, producer surplus or total surplus[8] – and their correlation to efficiency. There is a great deal of debate about which welfare standard is the best.[9] The answer depends on an assessment of whether it is more important to protect the interests of consumers, or producers, or both. This in turn depends on which efficiencies are considered most beneficial in a given system. Given the close relationship between efficiency and welfare standards, they are discussed together in this section. Depending on which welfare standard a system is seeking to pursue, the different types of efficiency can explain whether welfare is increased or not. It is believed that an economy is operating at maximum efficiency when society is obtaining the greatest value – the highest level of welfare – from its scarce resources.[10] This section illustrates, with Williamson's trade-off

[8] Consumer surplus on each unit consumed is the difference between the market price and the maximum price the consumer would pay to obtain the unit. Producer surplus is the sum of all profits made by producers in an industry. Total surplus is the sum of consumer and producer surplus: see for example R. Lipsey, *An Introduction to Positive Economics* (London: Weidenfeld and Nicolson, 7th edn, 1989) 90; M. Motta, *Competition Policy: Theory and Practice* (Cambridge University Press, 2004) 18.

[9] For example, S. Bishop and M. Walker, *The Economics of EC Competition Law: Concepts, Application and Measurement* (London: Sweet & Maxwell, 2nd edn, 2002) 25–7; Motta, supra note 8, 18–22.

[10] P. Lowe, 'Consumer Welfare and Efficiency: New Guiding Principles of Competition Policy?', 27 March 2007, the Thirteenth International Conference on Competition and Fourteenth European Competition Day, 2. Available at: http://ec.europa.eu/competition/speeches.

model,[11] how economic resources are most inefficiently and efficiently allocated in order to minimise or maximise consumer surplus.[12]

The DG COMP's *Discussion Paper* suggests that consumer welfare to enhance allocative efficiency is the welfare standard preferred within the sphere of Article 82: '[w]ith regard to exclusionary abuses the objective of Article 82 is the protection of competition on the market as a means of enhancing consumer welfare and of ensuring an efficient allocation of resources'.[13] This was also the welfare standard preferred within Article 81 until *GlaxoSmithKline v. Commission*.[14] Article 81 is not the subject for discussion here and will be discussed only where relevant, as Articles 81 and 82 are pursuing the same aim although at a different level.[15]

2.1 Allocative, productive and dynamic efficiency

Allocative efficiency[16] refers to the way in which competition serves to allocate resources to their highest and best use by creating incentives for producers to compete to expand output in a market until the cost of the last unit of output (marginal cost)[17] equals the price consumers are willing to pay for the product (marginal revenue).[18] At that point, the market is allocating the optimal amount of society's total resources to production of that market's good or service.[19] Allocative efficiency is harmed

[11] O. E. Williamson, 'Economies as an Antitrust Defense: The Welfare Tradeoffs' 58(1) *American Economic Review* (1968) 18.

[12] Williamson's trade-off model shows how an increase in market power and an increase in prices causing a loss in allocative efficiency can, despite this, lead to an increase in welfare due to cost savings.

[13] DG COMP's *Discussion Paper on the Application of Article 82 of the Treaty to Exclusionary Abuses* (December 2005) ('*Discussion Paper*'), paras. 4 and 54.

[14] See Case T-168/01 *GlaxoSmithKline Services Unlimited v. Commission* [2006] ECR II-2969, paras. 118 and 273. On appeal, the ECJ overturned the CFI's view that Article 81(1) is only about consumer welfare: see Joined Cases C-501/06 etc. *GlaxoSmithKline Services v. Commission*, para. 63.

[15] Case 6/72 *Europemballage Corporation and Continental Can Co. Inc. v. Commission* [1973] ECR 215, para. 25.

[16] In the broad sense allocative efficiency encompasses efficient pricing on both the input and the output side of the market; in the narrow sense it focuses solely on the seller's behaviour in output markets.

[17] The increase in the total costs of a firm caused by increasing its output by one extra unit. If all costs are fixed, the marginal cost of the first unit of output will be very high, but all subsequent units can be made for nothing.

[18] Bork, supra note 5, 91.

[19] According to Bork, supra note 5, allocative efficiency is not well suited as a policy guideline, since it is difficult to achieve in practice.

when producers agree directly or indirectly to increase price and reduce output. Producers engaging in such conduct expect to obtain more surplus from consumers than would be possible if competition prevailed, as they shift surplus from consumers to themselves. This will lead to allocative inefficiency as shown in Williamson's trade-off model illustrated in figure 2.1. This model provides an illustration of the effects on resource allocation when output is restricted from quantity Qc to quantity Qm and price is increased from the competitive price to monopoly price, compared to that under perfect competition, leading to deadweight loss.[20] The deadweight loss is the cost to society of a market which does not operate efficiently.[21] The consumers who were willing to pay only the competitive price will no longer buy the product. Consumer surplus is no longer maximised for those consumers and not all consumer surplus is turned into producer surplus and there will be deadweight loss where neither consumers nor producers benefit.

Productive efficiency refers to the effective use of resources by a particular firm, meaning that a given set of products is produced at the lowest possible cost, given the current technology.[22] Productive efficiency is generated when production is improved to produce the same level of output using fewer resources or to produce more valuable output of better quality using the same resources. Unlike allocative efficiency, which is maximised when the price consumers are willing to pay equals marginal cost, and which cannot be improved beyond that point,[23] productive efficiency can always be improved and never maximised. If technical progress is improved, productive efficiency will improve by freeing up resources to expand the economy's output and providing the means for deriving more value from the existing use of resources.[24]

Allocative and productive efficiency are predicated on the static economic model of perfect competition,[25] developed in the nineteenth century by neo-classical economists like Cournot and Marshall.[26] In a market characterised by perfect competition, production methods and prices are

[20] This illustration is taken from Williamson, supra note 11, 21. This book's author is graphically challenged so many thanks to P. Akman for allowing me to use her drawing.

[21] D. W. Carlton and J. M. Perloff, *Modern Industrial Organization* (Boston: Addison Wesley, 4th edn, 2005) 71–2; Bishop and Walker, supra note 9, 22.

[22] Bishop and Walker, supra note 9, 20.

[23] What a consumer is willing to pay depends on an initial allocation of resources. Rich people are more willing/able to pay a higher price than poor people.

[24] Bork, supra note 5, 91. [25] Bishop and Walker, supra note 9, 20.

[26] See L. Pepall, D. Richards and G. Norman, *Industrial Organization: Contemporary Theory and Practice* (Cincinnati, OH: South Western, 1999) 236 ff.

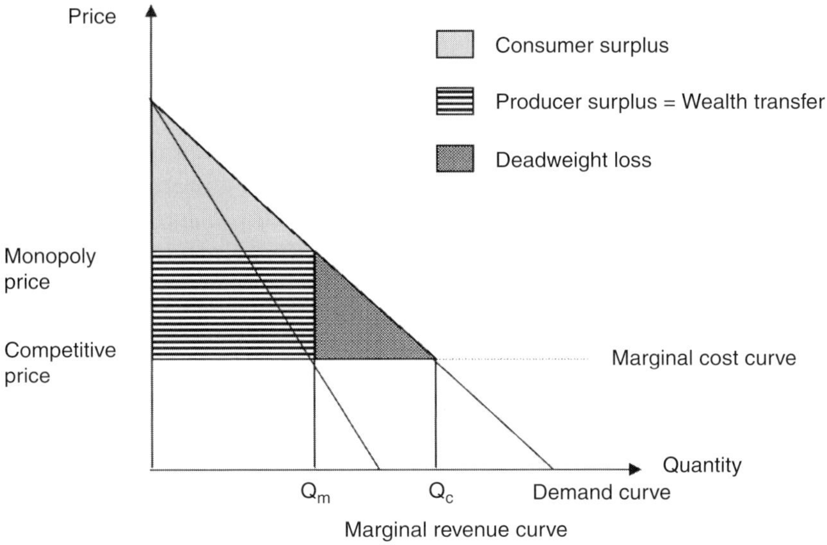

Figure 2.1 Illustration of allocative inefficiency and deadweight loss

transparent. This means that although the firm may lower its average cost of production and earn 'supernormal profit'[27] in the short term, in the long term the firm will earn 'normal profit', because other firms will copy the new production method. The price of the goods will decrease to the new lowest point on the average cost curve – the curve that shows total production costs per unit of output. There will be no divergence between average cost and marginal revenue, because no firm can restrict output and set output short of the lowest point. Moreover, there are many players acting in the market to buy and sell homogeneous products. In the theory of perfect competition there are no barriers to entry or exit and, because of the free entry of other firms, competition will push prices down to the lowest point in each firm's average cost curve. Thus, in a market with perfect competition the price of a product would be equal to the marginal cost of producing the product. Perfect competition delivers both productive and allocative efficiency.[28]

Dynamic efficiency refers to the extent to which a company introduces new products or new processes of production.[29] An undertaking has the possibility to adopt a process of innovation if it can produce at a lower marginal

[27] Any profit over and above normal profit.

[28] Bishop and Walker, supra note 9, 20.

[29] Ibid., 36–9; Motta, supra note 8, 55–64.

cost compared to the current cost.[30] If the undertaking does not innovate, because it has no incentive, either because it has a monopoly or because competition is too strong, it will lead to dynamic inefficiency and result in a welfare loss. It may sound surprising that a highly competitive market could lead to a disincentive to innovate, but in a system pursuing a consumer welfare standard, prices are constantly forced down to marginal cost to improve allocative efficiency, which may reduce the possibility of appropriating the results of the investment. For example, once produced, an idea can be used by an infinite number of people indefinitely with little or no additional cost. As the cost of producing the idea remains fixed, regardless of how many people consume it, there is a zero marginal cost in allowing additional consumption. Hence, if marginal cost pricing were enforced in relation to ideas, the cost of producing the idea could never be recovered and there would be no incentive to come up with it. To avoid dynamic efficiency being undermined over time, it is important that a system favouring a consumer welfare standard is balanced between the long-term need for innovation and the risk of short-term loss in allocative efficiency when innovation occurs. In the short term, there may be loss in allocative efficiency if prices rise above marginal cost in order to pay for the investment, but in the long term, allocative benefits may increase due to the innovation.

The examination of the different types of efficiency is useful in order to consider the relationship between these efficiencies and the different welfare standards. Knowing the different benefits of the various types of efficiency, the question is which welfare standard to pursue. The answer depends on an assessment of whether it is more important to protect the interests of consumers, or producers, or both. This will be explored in the following subsection.

2.2 *The different welfare standards and their correlation with efficiency*

Economic efficiency is defined in terms of consumer surplus, producer surplus and total welfare.[31] Competition law systems favouring the total welfare standard, which is defined by most economists as the sum of producer surplus and consumer surplus,[32] will choose to protect productive

[30] Motta, supra note 8, 56.

[31] K. J. Cseres, *Competition Law and Consumer Protection* (The Hague: Kluwer Law International, 2005) 17–18.

[32] W. K. Viscusi, J. M. Vernon and J. E. Harrington, *Economics of Regulation and Antitrust* (Cambridge, MA: MIT Press, 2nd edn, 1995) 63; Bishop and Walker, supra note 9, 23–7; Posner, supra note 5, 23; and Motta, supra note 8, 20.

and dynamic efficiency more than allocative efficiency. This is because these systems believe that improvements in productive and dynamic efficiency, either by an increase in output in the market where the asset is deployed, or by freeing up resources in order to increase output in other markets, will lead to an increase in total welfare. Even if an improvement in efficiency leaves price unchanged and end consumers (i.e. consumers in that particular market) do not benefit directly, end consumers may benefit indirectly in a partial equilibrium framework. This is because those consumers are able to consume incremental goods and services produced in other markets from the freed-up resources. A system which believes in total welfare opposes exclusionary conduct[33] because it reduces production and innovative efficiency by raising the costs or lowering the return of rival firms with no offsetting benefits to society.

In a competition law system favouring the consumer welfare standard in the form of consumer surplus, productive efficiencies are relevant only where they translate into lower prices and are converted into consumer surplus. Gain in producer welfare would only be acceptable under the consumer welfare standard if there was sufficient competition to force the producers to pass such benefits on to consumers. For systems pursuing a consumer welfare standard, reductions in allocative efficiency are unacceptable, because consumers suffer. Thus, unless producer welfare is translated into lower prices or gains which are passed on to consumers, the beneficial effect on producer welfare is irrelevant. However, as argued above, focusing on allocative efficiency gains in the short term can risk reducing the scope for investment in research and development in the long term as prices fall to marginal cost. Thus, it is important to balance long-term gain in dynamic and productive efficiency with short-term loss in allocative efficiency, as consumers may favour a reduction in allocative efficiency in the short term in order to achieve dynamic efficiencies in the long term.

The consequence of consumer welfare is that the gain in consumer surplus is not a gain to society as a whole, because it comes at the expense of a corresponding loss in producers' profits. Proponents of the producer welfare standard and the total welfare standard argue that there is no economic reason for favouring a dollar in the hands of consumers over a

[33] Exclusionary conduct is defined in the *Discussion Paper*, supra note 13, para. 1, as action to deny rivals access to the market or expansion in the market without offsetting benefits to consumers: '[b]y exclusionary abuses are meant behaviours by dominant firms which are likely to have a foreclosure effect on the market, i.e. which are likely to completely or partially deny profitable expansion in or access to a market to actual or potential competitors and which ultimately harm consumers'.

dollar in the hands of the producers or their shareholders, who can also be consumers.[34] Moreover, they argue that the consumer welfare standard does not discriminate among consumers, i.e. between relatively poor and relatively well-off consumers, therefore profit may end up in the pockets of consumers who are already wealthy. However, critics of the total welfare standard argue that it treats consumers and shareholders alike even when they are different.

In summary, this section has argued that efficiencies are related to a discussion of welfare standards. Which efficiencies are relevant depends on which welfare standard is chosen for a given system. This is relevant for the discussion of efficiencies in Article 82 later in this chapter. Having introduced the basic theory of the different welfare standards and their correlation with the various forms of efficiency, the following section describes the different schools of thought on market power and its correlation with efficiency. This is important to examine whether the Chicago School's arguments, which were accepted in US antitrust in the 1970s, can be injected into Article 82. This depends on whether ordoliberalism can be seen as the equivalent Harvard structural School in Europe.[35]

3. Different schools of thought in law and economics

While consumer welfare has been on the Commission's political agenda explicitly since at least when Sir Leon Brittan became Competition Commissioner in 1989, there is relatively little analytical work to guide policy-makers. Some insights may be found in the US where the Harvard School and the Chicago School have influenced the US Supreme Court.[36] These schools of thought have had an impact on US antitrust and spill-over effects on European competition law.[37] Considering these formative influences in the evolution of US antitrust can help in the analysis of the

[34] C. F. (Rick) Rule, 'Consumer Welfare, Efficiencies, and Mergers', 17 November 2005, hearing of the Antitrust Modernization Commission, 6.

[35] 'Competition law' is the usual term used in Europe whereas 'antitrust law' is the term used in the US.

[36] United States' submission to OECD, 'The Objectives of Competition Law and Policy', CCNM/GF/COMP (2003); Hovenkamp in C. D. Ehlermann and L. L. Laudati (eds.), *European Competition Law Annual 1997: The Objectives of Competition Policy* (Oxford: Hart Publishing, 1998) 328. The Chicago School started in the 1960s and culminated in the 1970s and 1980s. Besides Bork, some of its originators are Stigler, Demsetz and Brozen.

[37] Cseres, supra note 31, 41.

development of law and policy towards dominant undertakings. However, it must be stressed that these are insights rather than solutions as there are political, economic and cultural differences between the US and the EU.[38]

Section 3.1 will introduce the Harvard 'structural' School. This is necessary to show that the Harvard structural School is different from the Chicago School, which will be discussed in section 3.2, and the Post-Chicago School, which will be considered in section 3.3. Sections 3.2 and 3.3 show how the Harvard structural School's line of thinking was 'replaced' by the Chicago and Post-Chicago Schools' line of thinking. This becomes important for the question whether the Chicago School's foundation can be injected into Article 82 to change the way in which this provision is applied, like it changed the way in which the Sherman Act was applied. Article 82 has been influenced by ordoliberalism, which will be subject to analysis in section 3.4.[39] If ordoliberalism can be seen as the Harvard structural School's European sister, there is no reason why the Chicago School's ideology cannot be injected into Article 82. Whether ordoliberalism is functionally the Harvard structural School's sister or is so fundamentally different that it could never be influenced by the Chicago School or the later Harvard School's arguments will be discussed in section 3.5.

Some may argue that what happened many years ago can hardly be relevant for today's review of Article 82. This author believes that historical context is a useful source for the review of Article 82 and thus discusses the foundations of different schools of thought below. As Ludwig von Mises said: 'if we wish to understand contemporary events, we would do well to read the books written 20 or 30 years ago'.[40]

3.1 The Harvard School

Early jurisprudence on the Sherman Act Section 2 centres on the different meaning and influence given to both the structural and the conduct

[38] B. McDonnell and D. A. Farber, 'Are Efficient Antitrust Rules Always Optimal?' 48(3) *Antitrust Bulletin* (2003) 807, 808–9, 814–15.

[39] B. E. Hawk, 'Article 82 and Section 2' in OECD, *Report on Competition on the Merits* (March 2006) 253, available at: www.oecd.org/dataoecd/7/13/35911017.pdf; D. Gerber, 'Constitutionalizing the Economy: German Neo-liberalism, Competition Law and the "New" Europe' 42 *American Journal of Comparative Law* (1994) 25, 73; D. Evans, 'Roundtable Discussion about the US Supreme Court's Decision in *Verizon v. Trinko*' *Global Competition Review* (2004) 26.

[40] F. Böhm, 'Democracy and Economic Power' in *Cartel and Monopoly in Modern Law* (Karlsruhe: C. F. Müller, 1961) 36.

elements.[41] For example, *Standard Oil* shows that the accumulation of wealth in the hands of a few was perceived as a threat to both the economic order and democracy.[42] The need to consider both the economic implications and the political dimension made it difficult for the courts to interpret Section 2. To make the application of Section 2 more orientated towards industry and markets in general, a line of Industrial Organisation thinking – the so-called Harvard 'structural' School[43] – developed the S-C-P paradigm as a measurement of harm to competition.[44] The S-C-P paradigm is based on the assumption that there is a causal relationship between structure, conduct and performance, such that market structure influences a firm's conduct, which in turn influences its performance. This is an approach focusing on process, in contrast to the output approach using productive and allocative efficiency to measure harm to competition advocated by the Chicago School (elaborated below). The S-C-P paradigm became dominant in the 1930s, 1940s and 1950s and was associated with Harvard economists such as Bain,[45] Mason[46] and Kaysen.

The Harvard structural School is to be distinguished from the modern Harvard School, taking shape in the early 1970s and linked to scholars such as Areeda and Turner.[47] Unlike the Harvard structural School, the modern Harvard School shares many similarities with the Chicago School.[48] For example, both schools embrace economic

[41] This section of the chapter is expanded in L. Lovdahl Gormsen, 'The Parallels between the Harvard Structural School and Article 82 EC and the Divergences between the Chicago and Post-Chicago Schools and Article 82 EC' 4(1) *European Competition Journal* (2008) 221.

[42] *Standard Oil of New Jersey v. United States*, 221 US 1, 50 (1911).

[43] H. Hovenkamp, 'The Harvard and Chicago Schools and the Dominant Firm' University of Iowa Legal Studies Research Article No. 07-19 (September 2007) 1.

[44] 'The Economics of Antitrust Laws', in B. Bouckaert and G. De Geest, *Encyclopedia of Law and Economics* (Cheltenham: Elgar, 2000) vol. III, 473; J. Faull and A. Nikpay, *The EC Law of Competition* (Oxford University Press, 2nd edn, 2007) 6.

[45] For example, J. Bain, *Barriers to New Competition: Their Character and Consequences in Manufacturing Industries* (Harvard University Press, 1956); J. Bain, 'Relation of Profit Rate to Industry Concentration: American Manufacturing, 1936–40' 65 *Quarterly Journal of Economics* (1951) 293.

[46] For example, E. Mason, *Economic Concentration and the Monopoly Problem* (Harvard University Press, 1957).

[47] See P. Areeda and D. Turner, 'Predatory Pricing and Practices under Section 2 of the Sherman Act' 88 *Harvard Law Review* (1975) 697.

[48] Kovacic refers to the 'Chicago/Harvard Double Helix', W. Kovacic, 'The Intellectual DNA of Modern US Competition Law for Dominant Firm Conduct: The Chicago/Harvard Double Helix' *Columbia Business Law Review* (2007) 1.

efficiency in their assessment of single-firm conduct under Section 2 of the Sherman Act.[49]

The Harvard structural School did not believe in one single goal of economic efficiency for antitrust. Instead, multiple goals were seen as important: distribution of equity, economic stability, decentralisation of economic power, optimal factor allocation and consumer sovereignty.[50] It did not aim to protect economic efficiency, but rather to restrict the growth of large firms. It was believed that markets are fragile and prone to failure. The Harvard structural School argued that high concentration enables a firm to exercise market power and earn high profits, due to market power rather than efficiency. A leading firm's market shares provide a meaningful indication of the likelihood of market power – not necessarily superior efficiency.

The role of market entry was important to the Harvard structural School. Barriers to entry were used as an alternative explanation for highly concentrated markets. Bain defined the conditions for entry as 'the extent to which, in the long run, established firms can elevate their selling prices above the minimal average costs of production and distribution … without inducing potential entrants to enter the industry'.[51] Bain showed that high barriers to entry can lead to foreclosure and concentrated markets where collusion is expected.[52] Moreover, there is a relationship between profit and structural characteristics of the industry (profitability–concentration relationship).[53] To prove its different points, the Harvard School relied on empirical data from specific industries and case studies.

Antitrust authorities had large discretionary powers to control conduct by large firms and impose regulation on a given market. This led to a broad interpretation of illegal conduct and an interventionist approach. During the peak of the Harvard structural School, its structural approach was to a certain extent reflected in the case law.[54] This approach captured a wide range of conduct which sufficed to create liability for dominant

[49] M. Jacobs, 'An Essay on the Normative Foundations of Antitrust Economics' 74 *North Carolina Law Review* (1995) 219, 228–32.

[50] Cseres, supra note 31, 56.

[51] J. Bain, *Industrial Organization* (New York: Wiley, 2nd edn, 1968) 252.

[52] Bain (1956), supra note 45. [53] Bain (1951), supra note 45.

[54] For example *US v. Aluminium Co. of America,* 148 F.2d 416 (2d Cir. 1945); *American Tobacco Co. v. United States,* 328 US 781 (1946); *US v. United Shoe Machinery Corp,* 110 F. Supp. 295 (1953), 347 US 521 (1954). This is also supported by L. White, 'The Growing Influence of Economics and Economists on Antitrust: An Extended Discussion' Working Article 08–05 (February 2008) 6. Available at: www.reg-markets.org/author/page.php?id=38.

firms[55] and expanded the rights of the perceived victims of economic exploitation.[56]

The Harvard structural School adopted a generally negative view of vertical mergers.[57] Concentrations were believed to facilitate collusion, and so the School advocated a prohibition of any vertical merger in which the acquiring firm had 20 per cent or more of its market. The Harvard structural School also disliked vertical restraints, which it argued should be illegal. The courts adopted a similarly negative view towards vertical restraints such as tying, bundling, exclusive dealing,[58] requirements contracts,[59] territorial restraints[60] and resale price maintenance.[61]

3.2 The Chicago School

While the Harvard structural School was dominant in the decades following the Second World War, there was another line of Industrial Organisation thinking developing in the 1950s, under the intellectual leadership of Aaron Director: the so-called Chicago School.[62] Associated with Director were economists such as Friedman, Stigler,[63] Telser,[64]

[55] Kovacic, supra note 48, 6.

[56] E. Fox and L. Sullivan, 'Antitrust – Retrospective and Prospective: Where Are We Coming From? and Where Are We Going?' 62 *New York University Law Review* (1987) 936, 954.

[57] The Court condemned vertical mergers in *US v. EI du Pont de Nemours & Co.*, 353 US 586 (1957); *Brown Shoe Co. v. US*, 370 US 294 (1962); *Ford Motor Co. v. US*, 405 US 562 (1972).

[58] Exclusive dealing was condemned by the courts in *Standard Fashion Co. v. Magrane-Houston Co.*, 258 US 346, 42 S.Ct. 360, 66 L.Ed. 653 (1922); *Standard Oil Co. of California et al. v. US*, 337 US 293 (1949); *FTC v. Motion Picture Advertising Service Co.*, 344 US 392 (1953).

[59] The Court condemned requirements contracts in *Standard Oil*, supra note 58; *Richfield Oil Corp. v. US*, 343 US 922 (1952). However, in *Tampa Electric Co. v. Nashville Coal Co.*, 365 US 320 (1961), the Court said that a requirements contract and exclusive dealing should be judged by a rule of reason.

[60] The Court prohibited territorial restraints as a *per se* violation in *US v. Arnold Schwinn & Co. et al.*, 388 US 365 (1967).

[61] The Court condemned retail price maintenance as a *per se* violation in *Dr Miles Medical Co. v. John D. Park and Sons Co.*, 220 US 373 (1911). This was reaffirmed in *US v. Bausch & Lomb Optical Co.*, 321 US 707 (1944); *US v. Parke, Davis & Co.*, 362 US 29 (1960); *Simpson v. Union Oil Co.*, 377 US 13 (1960); *Albrecht v. Herald Co.*, 390 US 145 (1968).

[62] For a good article on the distinction between the Harvard School and Chicago School, see R. Posner, 'The Chicago School of Antitrust Analysis' 127 *University of Pennsylvania Law Review* (1979) 925; see also Cseres, supra note 31, chapter 2.

[63] G. Stigler, 'The Dominant Firm and the Inverted Price Umbrella' 8 *Journal of Law and Economics* (1965) 167.

[64] L. Telser, 'Why Should Manufacturers Want Fair Trade?' 3 *Journal of Law and Economics* (1960) 86.

Demsetz,[65] McGee, Bowman[66] and Burstein.[67] They were all sceptical of the S-C-P paradigm and more sympathetic to vertical restraints and generally supportive of market outcomes.[68] Unlike the Harvard structural School, which believed in multiple goals, the Chicago School believed in one single goal of economic efficiency.[69]

According to one commentator, '[i]n antitrust, the beginning of all wisdom is understanding the true nature of consumer welfare'[70] and by 'true' he meant the way in which the Chicago School has articulated consumer welfare. Others point out that consumer welfare in the Chicagoan sense is not consumer welfare at all.[71] The latter view is understandable given that Bork – one of the protagonists of the Chicago School – identified consumer welfare as improving allocative efficiency without impairing productive efficiency in *The Antitrust Paradox*:[72]

> [T]he whole task of antitrust can be summed up as the effort to improve allocative efficiency without impairing productive efficiency so greatly as to produce either no gain or a net loss in consumer welfare.[73]
>
> The argument of this book [*The Antitrust Paradox*], of course, is that competition must be understood as the maximization of consumer welfare, or, if you prefer, economic efficiency.

Bork discussed maximisation of consumer welfare, which he equated with economic efficiency. Improving allocative efficiency without impairing productive efficiency can be equated with economic efficiency, which

[65] H. Demsetz, 'Two Systems of Belief about Monopoly' in H. Goldschmid, H. Mann and J. Weston (eds.), *Industrial Concentration: The New Learning* (New York: Columbia University Press, 1974) 164–84.

[66] W. Bowman, 'Tying Arrangements and the Leverage Problem' 67 *Yale Law Journal* (1957) 19.

[67] M. Burstein, 'The Economics of Tie-in Sales' 42 *Review of Economics and Statistics* (1960) 68; M. Burstein, 'A Theory of Full-line Forcing' 55 *Northwestern University Law Review* (1960) 62.

[68] S. Peltzman, 'Aaron Director's Influence on Antitrust Policy' 43 *Journal of Law and Economics* (2005) 313.

[69] That antitrust should be concerned with one goal only is supported by W. Baxter (former Assistant Attorney General in Antitrust Division, DOJ), who said that 'the sole goal of anti trust is economic efficiency' in the *Wall Street Journal* on 4 March 1982, 28, but opposed by H. B. Thorelli, who concluded that, in the absence of a single-minded legislative intent to pursue efficiency goals, antitrust should manifest concern for other social values: see H. B. Thorelli, *The Federal Antitrust Policy* (Baltimore: Johns Hopkins Press, 1955).

[70] Rule, supra note 34, 14.

[71] Fox and Sullivan, supra note 56, 946.

[72] Bork, supra note 5, 91 and 427 respectively.

[73] Bork reiterated this in R. H. Bork, 'Legislative Intent and the Policy of the Sherman Act' 9 *Journal of Law and Economics* (1966) 7.

is based on the total welfare standard that seeks to maximise total surplus. Consumer welfare in the form of consumer surplus is explicitly concerned with consumer gain.[74] Thus, to avoid any conceptual confusion, it must be stressed that when Bork speaks about improving allocative efficiency without impairing productive efficiency, he is concerned about total welfare and not consumer welfare in the form of consumer surplus only.[75] As argued above, systems which favour consumer surplus are concerned with productive efficiencies only where they translate into lower prices and are converted into consumer surplus. Systems which favour productive efficiency are concerned with producer surplus (the aggregated measure of the surplus made by all producers), not the issue of wealth distribution between consumers and producers.[76] Bork is concerned with total welfare, implicitly taking the view that the identity of the winners and losers is unimportant, as long as it is ensured that there are more gains than losses.[77]

It is important to distinguish between total welfare and consumer welfare, because the implication of the choice of welfare standard can be significant. For example, an exclusive buying arrangement that lowers the price of a good or service to the end consumer by £10, but raises a rival's cost by £30, could be lawful under a consumer surplus standard but not necessarily under a total welfare standard. That said, some argue that consumer welfare and total welfare coincide in the very long run if cases are analysed in a dynamic perspective.[78] Others reject this by arguing that the analysis of individual cases should not be conducted in a long-term perspective.[79] One commentator has said 'it is difficult to say whether

[74] R. Whish, *Competition Law* (Oxford University Press, 6th edn, 2009) 4; Brodley, supra note 3, 1020–1.

[75] See discussion and critique of Bork's definition of consumer welfare in R. H. Lande, 'The Rise and (Coming) Fall of Efficiency as the Rule of Antitrust' 33 *Antitrust Bulletin* (1988) 429, 433–5.

[76] Motta, supra note 8, 18; Bork, supra note 5, 111; F. M. Scherer, 'Antitrust, Efficiency, and Progress' 63 *New York University Law Review* (1987) 998, 998–9; O. E. Williamson, 'Economies as an Antitrust Defense Revisited' 125 *University of Pennsylvania Law Review* (1977) 699, 710.

[77] One criticism of Bork's ideas is that the total welfare standard ignores marginal utility. Marginal utility describes the additional benefit derived from an additional unit of wealth, which after a point diminishes with each additional unit.

[78] For example, S. C. Salop, 'Efficiencies in Dynamic Merger Analysis', Statement before the US Federal Trade Commission (FTC) Hearings on Global and Innovation-Based Competition (2 November 1995), available at: www.ftc.gov/opp/global/saloptst.htm; Motta, supra note 8.

[79] J. Farrell and M. L. Katz, 'The Economics of Welfare Standards in Antitrust' 2(2) *Competition Policy International* (2006) 1, 6.

competition authorities and courts favour in practice a consumer welfare or total welfare objective'.[80] According to the Chicago School, this is because a policy of maximising total welfare will most effectively accomplish the goal of protecting consumers' interests. Whilst this may be true where monopolies are easily broken up or unstable, in the view of this author, this is not the case for markets characterised by stable monopolies. In a society with stable monopolies, a competition policy pursuing a total welfare standard[81] would mean that it would be legitimate for a monopoly to keep the gain of any cost savings even though consumers would have to pay higher prices.

The Chicago School reviewed business practices in terms of their effects on efficiency and prices. To show harm to competition, it relied on the neo-classical price theory and general economic theories.[82] Bork argued that it was only workable to view markets from an economic efficiency point of view, since the social-political framework was so amorphous.[83] Indeed, Bork even pronounced all contrary views as being so incapable of use as to be 'unconstitutional'.[84]

The Chicago School believed that the basic tenets of firms were rationality and profit maximisation.[85] For example, firms would engage in vertical price fixing to avoid free-riding. Therefore, vertical price fixing should not be prohibited, as it guarantees better services to consumers. In relation to predation, the Chicago School believed that aggressive prices are generally pro-competitive and enhance economic efficiency, except in rare situations where the predator has sufficient market power to recoup its losses through long-term, supra-competitive prices achieved

[80] Motta, supra note 8, 19.

[81] Recalling that, when pursuing an objective of total welfare, it does not make a difference whether producers or consumers gain from wealth maximisation, as long as society as a whole is better off.

[82] Jacobs, supra note 49, 228–9.

[83] The proponents of one single objective (that of economic efficiency) do not all necessarily mean to imply any disagreement with other objectives, such as more equitable distribution of income or the diffusion of economic power. They simply believe that a competition policy concentrated on the efficiency objective is likely to be applied more consistently and effectively. Furthermore, they believe that if the distribution of income is unfair, then it can be redistributed later using other means.

[84] R. H. Bork, 'The Role of the Courts in Applying Economics' 54 *Antitrust Law Journal* (1985) 21, 24.

[85] The Chicago School relied on neo-classical economics which makes a number of assumptions: people have rational preferences among outcomes that can be identified and associated with a value; individuals maximise utility and firms maximise profits; and people act independently on the basis of full and relevant information.

after its rivals have been eliminated.[86] Thus, in this view rational firms will not engage in predatory pricing since they cannot be successful. Therefore the Chicago School considered that predatory pricing should be of no concern for antitrust policy. The Chicago School believed that collusion is difficult to enforce for market players and thus unlikely, except in regulated industries. From a competition policy point of view, the Chicago School believed that markets would be self-correcting and intervention should be in exceptional circumstances only. As for barriers to entry, the Chicago School viewed legal barriers to entry as the only ones of importance.[87] Stigler argued that only a cost of production which is borne by the entrant, seeking to enter the market, but not by the incumbent, must be considered a barrier to entry.[88] In other words, barriers to entry exist only where the cost of entering the market is higher for the potential entrant than it is for the incumbent. According to this view, there are no or few artificial barriers to entry, thus a private monopoly can only be temporary.[89]

From the 1970s onwards, the US Supreme Court implemented some of the Chicago School philosophy.[90] For example, the rule of reason found its way into *Continental TV*.[91] The court declared that territorial restraints should be examined under a rule of reason, rather than being condemned as *per se* illegal as in *Schwinn*.[92] As regards tying arrangements, the court did not suspend the *per se* rule adopted in *Northern Pacific Railway*.[93] However, in *United States Steel Corporation*,[94] the court upheld that, in the absence of market power in the tying market, a tying arrangement was acceptable. This was reinforced in *Jefferson Parish Hospital*.[95] In the area of maximum retail price maintenance, the court's previously strict

[86] The Chicago School's economic analysis of predation was accepted by the US Supreme Court in 1992 in *Brooke Group Ltd v. Brown & Williamson Tobacco Corporation*, 509 US 209 (1993).

[87] Cseres, supra note 31, 50.

[88] G. Stigler, *The Organization of Industry* (Homewood, IL: R. D. Irwin, 1968) 67.

[89] Jacobs, supra note 49, 228–32.

[90] For example, *Illinois Brick Co v. Illinois*, 431 US 720 (1977) 731–44; *Brooke Group*, supra note 86. In *Reiter v. Sono-tone Corporation*, 442 US 330 (1979) 343 the court said 'Congress designed the Sherman Act as a "consumer welfare prescription"' and then cited Bork's *The Antitrust Paradox*, supra note 5.

[91] *Continental TV Inc. v. GTE Sylvania Inc.*, 433 US 36 (1977), in particular 50–9 and footnote 21.

[92] *US v. Arnold Schwinn*, supra note 60.

[93] *Northern Pacific Railway Co. v. US*, 356 US 1, 5; 78 S.Ct. 514, 2 L.Ed.2d 545 (1958).

[94] *United States Steel Corp. v. Fortner Enterprises Inc.*, 429 US 610 (1977).

[95] *Jefferson Parish Hospital District No. 2 v. Edwin G. Hyde*, 466 US 2 (1984).

view in *Albrecht* condemning conduct *per se* was loosened to a rule of reason in *State Oil v. Khan*.[96]

Economics has moved on from the Chicago School because it is now known that information can be asymmetric, transaction costs exist, consumers may behave differently over time and counterfactuals may be incomplete. This has led to some criticism of the Chicago School's theory,[97] which will be discussed in the following subsection.

3.3 Main critique of the Chicago School: the Post-Chicago School

The Chicago School reliance on neo-classical economics has been criticised for making questionable assumptions[98] which fail to explain strategic behaviours taking advantage of market imperfections, where firms can make profits without being efficient.[99] This, together with the Chicago School's philosophy that antitrust should only protect economic efficiency, has led to some criticism.[100] The main criticism came from the so-called Post-Chicago School, of which Hovenkamp was one of the main proponents. The Post-Chicago School was in essence unconvinced about the Chicago School's ability to prove its assumptions.

In addition, three other main points of critique were as follows. First, applying economic theory only and excluding political values when assessing possible competition law problems is neither desirable nor possible.[101] Economics itself is arguably not value-neutral, as it reflects political preference. Hovenkamp, for example, argued that 'wealth maximization must include everything to which people assign a value',[102] whereas the Chicago School excludes the phases of production of goods and services by considering exclusively the exchange between suppliers

[96] *State Oil v. Khan*, 522 US 3 (1997).

[97] The so-called Chicago School critique: see for example the EAGCP Report, supra note 4.

[98] See the Chicago School's assumptions, supra note 85.

[99] H. Hovenkamp, 'Antitrust Policy after Chicago' 84 *Michigan Law Review* (1985) 213, 261.

[100] For example, R. H. Lande, 'Wealth Transfers as the Original and Primary Concern of Antitrust: The Efficiency Interpretation Challenged' 34 *Hastings Law Journal* (1982) 65; J. May, 'Antitrust in the Formative Era: Political and Economic Theory in Constitutional and Antitrust Analysis, 1880–1918' 50 *Ohio State Law Journal* (1989) 257, 260; R. J. Peritz, 'A Counter-History of Antitrust Law' 40(2) *Duke Law Journal* (1990) 263, 272–4.

[101] R. Pitofsky, 'The Political Content of Antitrust' 127 *University of Pennsylvania Law Review* (1979) 1051.

[102] Hovenkamp, supra note 99, 242.

and consumers.[103] Second, the Chicago School reduces the importance of enforcement to measure welfare in terms of economics only, and excludes the specific interests of the firm, which would normally be considered a part of the legal analysis. Hovenkamp argued that it is illogical to have economic efficiency as the only goal, as economic efficiency is not verifiable.[104] Third, the Chicago School adopted the concept of economic efficiency without defining it in such a way that it could be quantified. Indeed, Bork had acknowledged that economic performance is difficult, if not impossible, to measure scientifically: 'the real objection to performance tests and efficiency defenses in antitrust law is that they are spurious. They cannot measure the factors relevant to consumer welfare, so that after the economic extravaganza was completed we should know no more than before we began.'[105]

Thus, Bork applied Stigler's definition of 'competitive effectiveness' to assess whether total welfare was increased. By applying competitive effectiveness, it would be possible to find the most efficient firm in the market by examining which firm had the most success in the marketplace without collusion or predation.[106]

Critique aside, the Chicago and Post-Chicago Schools agree that the essence of antitrust is economics.[107] Both schools rejected the relevance of subjective inquiries which they attributed to the political approaches of the past. However, they disagreed on market failures. The Chicago School believed that markets tend towards efficiency, that market imperfections are normally temporary, and that intervention should proceed cautiously.[108] On the other hand, the Post-Chicago School believed that market failures are not necessarily self-correcting, and that firms can therefore take advantage of imperfections to produce inefficient results even in competitive markets. Moreover, it also considered that the distortions to competition made possible by market imperfections should prompt intervention to scrutinise a wider variety of conduct.[109]

Having described how the different US schools of thought considered market power and efficiency, the following subsection introduces the European school of thought, ordoliberalism. This is appropriate as the

[103] P. McNulty, 'Economic Theory and the Meaning of Competition' 82(4) *Quarterly Journal of Economics* (1968) 639, 646.

[104] Hovenkamp, supra note 99, 234.

[105] Bork, supra note 5, 124.

[106] Ibid., 192.

[107] J. Baker, 'Recent Developments in Economics that Challenge the Chicago School Views' 58(3) *Antitrust Law Journal* (1989) 645, 646.

[108] F. H. Easterbrook, 'The Limits of Antitrust' 63 *Texas Law Review* (1984) 1, 2.

[109] Jacobs, supra note 49, 223.

concept of economic power is one of the features of German and European competition law thinking that most clearly distinguishes it from US antitrust law analogies.[110] Again this is necessary for the question of whether the Chicago School's line of thinking can be introduced into Article 82.

3.4 Ordoliberalism

Director General Lowe has also confirmed that case law and decisional practice have been influenced by ordoliberalism.[111] Ordoliberal influence on the application of Article 82 can be seen from the Commission and the Community Courts' adoption of economic freedom, amongst other objectives.[112] Economic freedom can be traced back to ordoliberalism where the aim of competition policy is 'the protection of individual economic freedom of action as a value in itself, or vice versa, the restraint of undue economic power'.[113] Thus, it is necessary to understand ordoliberalism.

Ordoliberalism is an ideology developed in the 1930s and 1940s by a group of neo-liberals at Freiburg University in Germany.[114] Their ideologies were grouped together under the term ordoliberalism, which became shorthand for the underlying set of ideas behind the social market economy.[115] The ideas of ordoliberalism took shape in response to the economic, political and social crises starting with the fall of the Weimar Republic in 1933 and the rise of Nazi Germany.[116] One of the greatest European calamities resulted from the totalitarian Nazi regime misusing the powerful iron and steel industry (the German *Schwerindustrie*)[117] by turning private economic power into political power. Well-run cartels[118] and monopolies resulted in

[110] Gerber, supra note 39, 51. [111] Lowe, supra note 10, 2.

[112] This will be discussed in chapter 3.

[113] W. Möschel, 'The Proper Scope of Government Viewed from an Ordoliberal Perspective: The Example of Competition Policy' 157 *Journal of Institutional and Theoretical Economics* (2001) 3; W. Möschel, 'Competition Policy from an Ordo Point of View' in H. Willgerodt and A. Peacock (eds.), *German Neo-liberals and the Social Market Economy* (London: Macmillan, 1989) 146.

[114] The founders of the Freiburg School were economist Walter Eucken and lawyers Franz Böhm and Hans Grossmann-Doerth. Some protagonists of ordoliberalism were Wilhelm Röpke, Alexander Rüstow, Alfred Müller-Armack and Leonhard Miksch.

[115] H. Giersch, K. H. Paque and H. Schmieding, *The Fading Miracle: Four Decades of Market Economy in Germany* (Cambridge University Press, 1992) 31.

[116] Nazi economic policy was not concerned with protecting the process of competition but with the elimination, or at least marginalisation, of it.

[117] W. Röpke, *German Commercial Policy* (London: Longmans, 1934) 24–7.

[118] Especially the chemical cartel Interssen Gemeinschaft Farben (IG Farben), from which the major source of Hitler's power derived. Germany processed large quantities of coal and a German scientist discovered the process of converting coal into gasoline in 1909,

powerful economic concentration in conjunction with great accumulation of political power, which led to the abandonment of democratic principles.[119] Ordoliberals believed that the accumulation of power resulted from the inability of the legal system to prevent the creation and misuse of private economic power.[120] They alleged that both the lack of adequate safeguards against the rise of private economic power and the weakness of the state ultimately replaced economic and political freedom with an unrestrained dictatorship, which became unstoppable and led to the Second World War.[121]

Ordoliberals disliked both totalitarianism and socialism, because they considered that these ideologies were contrary to the principles of private property and the free-market economy, and paid little attention to the rule of law.[122] The ordoliberals therefore rejected notions of both totalitarianism and socialism, and developed the idea of the 'social market economy' (*Soziale Marktwirtschaft*).

3.4.1 Ordoliberal ideology

In developing the social market economy, one of the founders of ordoliberalism, Eucken, advanced the idea of order-based policy (*Ordnungspolitik*) which consisted of two fundamental 'orders'. These were the transaction economy (*Verkehrswirtschaft*) and the administered economy (*Zentralverwaltungswirtschaft*). According to the first order (the transaction economy), economic conduct was organised through private transactional decision-making. Private companies could act on the basis of incentives and disincentives created by economic competition. According to the second order (the administered economy), economic activity was organised according to criteria external to the economic system.[123] These two fundamental orders were incompatible, as the transaction economy would be harmed by governmental intervention and the administered economy would be harmed without governmental intervention. According to Eucken, the failure to recognise the incompatibility of the two orders was a major problem of the twentieth century.[124] In order to avoid the repetition of history and to prevent private economic

but the technology was not completely developed during the First World War. In August 1927, the US company Standard Oil agreed to embark on a cooperative programme of research and development of the hydrogenation process to refine the oil and on 9 November 1929, Standard Oil and IG Farben signed a cartel agreement.

[119] Röpke, supra note 117, 24–7. [120] Gerber, supra note 39, 29.

[121] Giersch, Paque and Schmieding, supra note 115, 27–8.

[122] S. Pejovich, 'From Socialism to the Market Economy: Postwar West Germany versus Post-1989 East Bloc' 1 *Independent Review* (2001) 27, 27.

[123] Gerber, supra note 39, 42. [124] Ibid., 43.

power turning into political power, it was imperative for the ordoliberals to establish the appropriate economic order, protected by the appropriate legal framework.

The government's policies should be designed to create and maintain the chosen economic order through *Ordnungspolitik*.[125] If the economic constitution calls for a transaction economy, then the *Ordnungspolitik* must ensure the creation of conditions within an industrialised economy which allow the development of a functioning and an economic order.[126] The task of the *Ordnungspolitik* is to search for a normative order.[127] The ordoliberal approach is a 'programme of freedom' embedded in and subordinated to a constitutionally theoretical set of conditions where order becomes a prerequisite for freedom.

Ordoliberalism was dedicated to achieving an economic order – a competitive order – which was able to control private economic and political power in order to ensure a prosperous and humane society which guaranteed individual economic freedom and price stability. Price stability was seen as essential for a society where long-term contracts would act as the cement for civil society, whilst the competitive order was seen as necessary both to prevent the accumulation of private economic power in too few hands and to sustain economic development.[128] The higher the level of competition in the economy, the more effectively the system functioned.

The social market economy became the name for the economic order, the competitive order, underlying the transaction economy. The individual characteristics of the transaction economy were private property, the protection of economic freedom and low barriers to entry into markets. These characteristics tended to reinforce each other and thereby increase the effectiveness of the system as a whole.[129] The social market economy advocated by ordoliberals became the actual economic system created in (the then) West Germany by Ludwig Erhard.[130] It represented

[125] D. Gerber, *Law and Competition in Twentieth Century Europe: Protecting Prometheus* (Oxford University Press, 1998) 246–7.

[126] W. Eucken, 'Die Wettbewerbsordnung und ihre Verwirklichung' 2 ORDO (1949) 1, 21. (An English translation of this article can be found in 2(2) *Competition Policy International* (2006) 219.)

[127] W. Eucken, *Grundsätze der Wirtschaftspolitik* (Berne, 1952) 14.

[128] R. Barrell and K. Dury, 'Choosing the Regime: Macroeconomic Effects of UK Entry into EMU' NIESR Discussion Paper No. 168 (2000) 5.

[129] Gerber, supra note 39, 42.

[130] N. Goldsmith and A. Berndt, 'Leonhard Miksch (1901–1950): A Forgotten Member of the Freiburg School', Walter-Eucken-Institute, Freiburg Discussion Papers on Constitutional Economics No. 3 (2002).

the ordoliberal vision of society, where individual economic freedom and competition were sources of political freedom, and the 'economic constitution' of society. Competition law was the main pillar of the social market economy and was represented as constitutional in scope.[131] Ordoliberals intertwined legal and economic perspectives and discourses by arguing that the characteristics and effectiveness of the economy depended on its relationship with the political and legal systems. This view is based on a belief that the economic order was formed through political and legal decision-making. Ordoliberals believed that the institutional framework that constituted a well-functioning market could not be expected to arise naturally. The economic constitution emphasised the need for competition laws to control the economic power of private firms and prohibit conduct by firms with market power which would otherwise interfere with the process of competition.

The economic constitution was by definition not political as it was not subject to political intervention. It was committed to economic rationality and a system of undistorted competition implemented and protected by a legal framework. The legal framework would regulate and limit the emergence of private economic power by prohibiting cartels, the growth of single-firm market power and contracts that created unjustified limits on the competitive autonomy of firms. From the ordoliberal perspective, private economic power threatened the competitive process, so the primary function of competition law was to eliminate private economic power in order to protect the process of competition. When a system had chosen a transaction economy in its economic constitution, then that choice required the government to make the system function effectively.

3.4.2 Ordoliberal competition policy

The origin of ordoliberalism was in humanist values rather than economic efficiency.[132] In the ordoliberal view the aim of competition policy was limitation and control of private power, or at least of its harmful effects,[133] in order to protect individual economic freedom in the interest of a free and fair political and social order.[134] Ordoliberals also believed that competition provided the best way to organise social change.[135] They encouraged open access to the market, as they believed that this would be the best control of private and political power. Competition needed

[131] Gerber, supra note 125, 277 and 282. [132] Gerber, supra note 39, 36.
[133] Gerber, supra note 125, 251. [134] Möschel (1989), supra note 113, 146.
[135] Ibid.

to be protected by law as it was viewed as the most 'ingenious instrument of deprivation of power in history'.[136] Ordoliberals saw competition as a process whereby market actors participate in the economy without being disproportionately constrained by either private or public power. Under the ordoliberal model, the aim of competition policy is 'the protection of individual economic freedom of action as a value in itself, or vice versa, the restraint of undue economic power'.[137] Ordoliberals would prefer a state of inefficiency coupled with freedom rather than a totalitarian, but efficient, state.[138] Effectively every power – whether political or economic – must be associated with checks, constraints and countervailing forces. When it came to political and economic power, ordoliberals argued strongly for representative democracy and against the economic power of dominant undertakings. Their dislike of power was due to their belief that individual freedom was eroded from within by the rise of private economic power. The deprivation of power was one of the core ideas of ordoliberalism.[139]

The theory of ordoliberalism breaks competition policy down to four concepts. First, the primary goal of competition policy is individual economic freedom. Second, the state retains a strong role in protecting the basic parameters of the system of competition, but with strict limits on more direct intervention. Third, competition policy is shaped by the rule of law rather than by *ad hoc* political decision-making. Fourth, competition policy is embedded in the economic order of a free and open society.[140]

Ordoliberal theory has two basic starting points: first, that individual economic freedom is an essential accompaniment to political freedom, and second, that competition is necessary for the economic liberty of the individual.[141] In the so-called ordoliberal view of society, individual economic freedom and competition are the source not only of prosperity, but also of political freedom. Thus, the legal framework, the economic constitution, should include basic principles to counteract any tendencies that neutralise competition. It should regulate and limit the emergence of private economic power by prohibiting cartels, the growth of single-firm

136 Eucken, supra note 126, 23. 137 Möschel (1989), supra note 113.

138 C. Watrin, 'Germany's Social Market Economy' in A. Kilmarnock (ed.), *The Social Market and the State* (London: Social Market Foundation, 1999) 91–5.

139 E. J. Mestmäcker, 'Competition Policy and Antitrust: Some Comparative Observations' 136 *Zeitschrift für die Gesamte Staatswissenschaft* (1980) 387.

140 Möschel (1989), supra note 113, 142.

141 F. A. Hayek, *New Studies in Philosophy, Politics, Economics and the History of Ideas* (University of Chicago Press, 1978) 179–90.

market power and contracts that create unjustified limits on the competitive autonomy of firms.

The legal framework should protect the competitive order by allowing 'liberal state intervention' (but without intervening to achieve particular results). Intervention should control the accumulation of economic power, preventing individual economic freedom from being endangered. Ordoliberalism did not regard capitalism (pure economic liberalism) as a self-generating, self-equilibrating and self-correcting system, but rather believed that the state should intervene to cure market failures. Eucken declared that 'the economic system cannot be left to organize itself',[142] and Röpke regarded 'undiluted capitalism' as intolerable.[143] They argued that a free economic market is good but may have undesirable outcomes. Röpke was concerned with the undesirable social consequences of the pure market mechanism, despite the fact that he was being 'pro-market'.[144] He argued in favour of state intervention to correct the outcome of the market process through, for example, direct transfers and subsidies.[145] However, he argued against interference with the market mechanism itself: for example, he was not in favour of fixing prices and quantities.[146] Eucken was concerned with securing and maintaining the competitive order and argued in favour of state intervention 'directed at securing the order of the economy, not at the steering of the economic process'.[147] Along the same lines, Miksch argued that a 'free economy can only be an economy which is organized by the state according to liberal principles'. Thus, competition is a 'game that is regulated by the state'.[148]

Ordoliberal theorists acknowledged that both individuals and society need to be protected from power. Thus, the framework assigned a positive role to the state in the form of power to intervene in the market to protect the autonomy of the individual, and to guarantee private contractual autonomy, freedom of occupation and trade, individual property rights and free movement of persons. State intervention could achieve this by imposing restrictions on cartels and abusive behaviour by dominant companies.[149] Besides imposing restrictions on the players in the

142 W. Eucken, *The Unsuccessful Age* (Edinburgh: William Hodge, 1951) 93.

143 W. Röpke, *Social Crisis of Our Time* (London: Thames and Hudson, 1958) 119.

144 W. Röpke, *Civitas Humana. Grundfragen der Gesellschafts- und Wirtschaftsreform* (Erlenbach-Zurich, 1944).

145 W. Röpke, *Die Gesellschaftskrisis der Gegenwart* (Erlenbach-Zurich, 1942) 252–8.

146 Giersch, Paque and Schmieding, supra note 115, 31.

147 Eucken, supra note 127, 336.

148 L. Miksch, *Wettbewerb als Aufgabe Grundsätze einer Wettbewerbsordnung* (Stuttgart: Godesberg, 2nd edn, 1947) 9.

149 P. Manow, 'Ordoliberalismus als Ökomische Ordnungstheologie' 21 *Leviathan* (2001) 179.

market, the legal framework should impose restrictions on the political system in order to protect the free market against political intrusion.[150] The legal framework should be respected both by the political system, to avoid opportunism under the pressure of socio-economic forces exerted by political parties, and by private cartels and dominant undertakings.

Whilst traditional liberalism maintained that the rule of law was mainly to protect the individual against government coercion (political power),[151] ordoliberalism attached equal importance to safeguarding individual economic freedom from intrusion by private undertakings. Ordoliberalism thereby differentiates itself from traditional classical liberalism in two respects: first, in that an unregulated free market is not the most efficient means of allocating resources, and second, in that individual economic freedom needs to be protected from both political and private economic power. Ordoliberalism considers free enterprise and free competition as being inseparable from the concepts of liberty and prosperity. The idea of liberal state intervention makes ordoliberalism decidedly different from other liberal strands.[152]

3.4.3 Complete competition

The competitive order underlying the transaction economy was the only economic order ordoliberals considered capable of achieving the beneficial result of a democratic and humane society. In order for the transaction economy to function effectively the government should adopt an *Ordnungspolitik* with a legal system constructed in such a way that it could maintain conditions of complete competition.[153] Ordoliberals considered that only complete competition could produce this beneficial outcome. It exists in a market where no firm has the power to coerce conduct of other firms.[154] Where complete competition exists, therefore, certain kinds of behaviour which could potentially amount to an abuse, such as predatory pricing or loyalty rebates, would not constitute an abuse. Instead, such behaviour would constitute performance competition, as the firm engaging in pricing below cost or offering the rebate would not have market power.[155]

150 F. Böhm, *Wirtschaftsordnung und Staatsverfassung* (Tübingen: Mohr, 1950).

151 B. Leoni, *Freedom and the Law* (Indianapolis: Liberty Fund, 3rd edn, 1991).

152 Goldsmith and Berndt, supra note 130, 12.

153 Gerber, supra note 125, 246. 154 Eucken, supra note 126, 23.

155 The term 'competition on the basis of performance' or 'performance competition' is interrelated with the term 'competition on the merits'. Some scholars think that it is no more than a semantic difference, but the ECJ seems to mean that it is the same in substance, e.g. in Case 85/76 *Hoffmann-La Roche AG v. Commission* [1979] ECR 461, para. 91

Complete competition could be achieved through competition on both the supply and demand sides of the market.[156] To have competition on both sides of the market would require that no market player on either the supply or the demand side of the market was restricted in their freedom to compete. It was therefore imperative to protect individuals' freedom to compete. The complete competition model has similarities with the model of perfect competition. The term 'complete competition' in German is '*vollständiger Wettbewerb*'. It is generally translated as 'perfect competition'. However, as noted by Möschel:[157]

> [T]he scholars of ordoliberalism have also used economic models for the description of their ideas, for instance, the model of perfect competition as it was developed in the traditional theory of competition. Such models, however, served only for the description of general effects of a market system, illustrating them in what might be called a chemically pure form. That did not imply, however, that those partly unreal premises were to be integrated as goals into practical competition policy.

Market power was inconsistent with complete competition. A firm with market power could hinder the performance of its rivals and that was structurally inconsistent with complete competition. Therefore the conduct of a firm with market power was to be limited so that it was not capable of harming its competitors or society in general.[158] There is fear of what power can lead to. Thus, market power is sufficient to impose an obligation upon firms with such power. Where an individual firm has economic power it must be controlled, as it is otherwise capable of obstructing social justice. An independent competition authority should impose a positive obligation on such a dominant undertaking in order for it to conduct itself 'as if' it were faced with complete competition.[159] The theory of complete competition would require market players to act 'as if' they

where the text discusses competition 'on the basis of commercial operators'. This is a poor translation of the authentic German version in which the court used the term 'leistungswettbewerbs auf der grundlage der leistungen der marktbürger abweichen' where 'leistungswettbewerb' is the legal concept of 'competition on the basis of performance'. A better translation would therefore have been 'competition on the basis of performance'. In Case 62/86 *AKZO Chemie BV v. Commission* [1991] ECR I-3359, para. 70 the text mentions 'competition on the basis of quality' whereas in the original French version the court uses the term 'concurrence par les mérites'. A better translation therefore would have been 'competition on the merits'.

[156] Eucken, supra note 126, 26. [157] Möschel (1989), supra note 113, 146.

[158] Gerber, supra note 39, 52.

[159] D. Schmidtchen, 'German Ordnungspolitik as Institutional Choice' 140 *Zeitschrift für die Gesamte Staatswissenschaft* (1984) 60.

were faced with complete competition.[160] It was believed that the dominant undertaking would thereby be forced to compete on performance in order to be profitable, rather than use its power to gain an unfair advantage over rivals. The dominant undertaking would therefore have an obligation not to impair its rivals' freedom and right to compete. Ordoliberals assumed that the 'as if' standard would provide clear guidelines for applying the abuse concept by basing it on the proposition that economic science could effectively use perfect competition as a model against which to measure actual economic behaviour.[161]

3.5 Is ordoliberalism in effect the Harvard School?

Having briefly discussed the Harvard structural School, the Chicago and Post-Chicago Schools and ordoliberalism, it is apparent that the latter is fundamentally different. Ordoliberalism sounds like the Harvard structural School in that both schools of thought focus on the process more than the outcome. Like ordoliberalism, the Harvard structural School was not aimed at protecting economic efficiency, but rather at restricting growth of large firms. Both believed that markets are fragile and prone to failure. Moreover, the role of market entry was important to both the Harvard structural School and ordoliberalism. However, ordoliberalism is not the Harvard School's European sister, as it is fundamentally different. Despite the *Guidance Paper*[162] adopting the Harvard structural School's definition on barriers to entry, where it sees economies of scale as a barrier to entry instead of efficiency like the Chicago School, it does not implement the Harvard structural School.

Ordoliberalism was not only about controlling private economic power, but also about preventing political power in order to ensure a prosperous and humane society. The origin of ordoliberalism was in humanist values rather than economic efficiency. Ordoliberals would prefer a state of inefficiency coupled with freedom rather than a totalitarian, but efficient, state. Thus, the aim of competition policy was limitation and control of private

[160] The use of the 'as if' standard requires a comparison between markets with and without market power. According to Miksch, such a comparison could be made by using the equilibrium-theoretical analyses of A. Marshall and L. Walras: see Goldsmith and Berndt, supra note 130, 4.

[161] Gerber, supra note 125, 308.

[162] OJ [2009] C45/7 *Guidance on the Commission's Enforcement Priorities in Applying Article 82 EC Treaty to Abusive Exclusionary Conduct by Dominant Undertakings* ('*Guidance Paper*').

power to protect individual economic freedom in the interest of a free and fair political and social order and competition provided the best way to organise social change. Effectively every power – whether political or economic – must be associated with checks, constraints and countervailing forces. Both individuals and society need to be protected from power. Thus, the legal framework assigned a positive role to the state in the form of power to intervene in the market to protect the autonomy of the individual, and to guarantee private contractual autonomy, freedom of occupation and trade, individual property rights and free movement of persons.

Given the fundamental difference between the Harvard structural School and ordoliberalism, this section concludes that the Chicago School's line of thinking cannot be injected into Article 82 as it was into the application of the Sherman Act Section 2 by 'replacing' the Harvard structural School. This is not to say that consumer welfare and efficiency are irrelevant to Article 82, but to say that these concepts may not be introduced into Article 82 in a similar fashion to how they were introduced into US antitrust. This becomes important as to whether efficiencies are a possible defence to certain kinds of conduct. There is a difference between accepting market power where it leads to a better outcome for consumers in the form of efficiency and not accepting market power – not because it does not lead to a better outcome in the form of efficiency, but because it impairs other market participants' economic freedom. In the latter scenario, it becomes hard to imagine how efficiencies can counterbalance a powerful firm's attempts to grow in the market even where the growth benefits consumers. Thus, the final section of this chapter examines how efficiencies are dealt with in Article 82. This is also relevant for chapter 5, which will discuss the Commission's various assumptions in this area of law.

4. Efficiency considerations under Article 82

The wording of Article 82 is silent on efficiencies and there is no secondary legislation or other legislative document embracing efficiencies under Article 82. The *Guidance Paper* does accept that efficiencies play a role in Article 82,[163] but, as will be shown in section 4.2, this is illusory unless the aim of Article 82 is consumer welfare.[164] The first question to be answered in section 4.1 is whether Article 82, despite not containing an exemption provision like Article 81(3), allows efficiencies to be advanced. This is important for the overall argument of the legitimacy of consumer welfare

[163] Ibid. paras. 45, 61, 73 and 89.

[164] This will be discussed in more detail in chapter 6.

as the main goal of Article 82. If the aim is consumer welfare then it is relevant to examine the benefits of efficiencies to consumers. If recognisable efficiency gains are so large that the conduct can no longer be said to harm consumers, then the Commission must be prepared to accept the conduct. In this way, the analysis of efficiencies is directly tied to the analysis of the conduct's competitive effects on consumers. Thus, pursuing a consumer welfare objective cannot ignore the question of efficiencies. Section 4.2 examines whether efficiencies are relevant and if so, how they should be treated in Article 82. Again, this is linked to the objective of consumer welfare, as efficiencies are mainly relevant if the aim of Article 82 is consumer welfare. Section 2 showed the correlation between the consumer welfare standard and efficiencies and section 3.4 showed that economic freedom, for example, is about achieving economic freedom in the market for all market participants, not about promoting efficiencies for consumers.

4.1 The structure of Article 82

Article 82 does not contain a framework for the assessment of possible efficiency benefits explicitly. Article 82 is not bifurcated like Article 81,[165] as explained by the ECJ in *Continental Can*: 'Article 86 [Article 82] does not contain the same explicit provisions, but this can be explained by the fact that the system fixed there for dominant positions, unlike Article 81(3), does not recognise any exemption from the prohibition.'[166] This was further elaborated by the CFI in *Atlantic Container Line AB and others (TACA)*:[167]

> [I]t must be noted at the outset that there is no exception to the principle in Community competition law prohibiting abuse of a dominant position.

[165] If an agreement restricts competition and therefore violates Article 81(1), the undertaking must, in order to assess whether the agreement creates any efficiencies, examine whether the agreement has economic benefits. The undertaking must prove that the agreement restricting competition improves production, distribution or technical and economic progress and does not impose unnecessary conditions, that consumers get a fair share of the benefits, and that the agreement does not eliminate competition. The notification for agreements for individual exemption was abandoned after 1 May 2004 so there is no longer any such thing as an individual exemption. The undertakings and their advisers must conduct their own self-assessment of the application of Article 81(3): see Whish, supra note 74, 149.

[166] *Continental Can*, supra note 15, para. 25.

[167] Joined Cases T-191/98 and T-212 to 214/98 *Atlantic Container Line AB and others v. Commission* (*TACA*) [2003] ECR II-3275, para. 1109.

> Unlike Article 85 of the Treaty [now Article 81], Article 86 of the Treaty [now Article 82] does not allow undertakings in a dominant position to seek to obtain exemption for their abusive practices ... Furthermore, according to the case-law, dominant undertakings have a special responsibility not to allow their conduct to impair genuine undistorted competition on the common market ... Consequently, there can be no exceptions to the prohibition of abuse by dominant undertakings.

It is clear that Article 82 does not contain a statutory or a case law developed exemption provision like that of Article 81. The question is whether efficiency considerations are excluded from Article 82 because the provision does not contain a specific exemption provision.

According to Competition Commissioner Kroes' 2005 Fordham speech, the answer is probably no. She said: 'Article 82 does not expressly foresee the possibility of "exempting" abusive behaviour under Article 82 because of efficiencies. However, we must find a way to include efficiencies in our analysis. We must take into account that the same type of conduct can have efficiency-enhancing as well as foreclosure effects. This should be reflected in our analytical framework.'[168]

In Commissioner Kroes' 2008 Fordham speech she continued to suggest that, for reasons of consistency, 'the analytical framework for reviewing efficiencies under Article 82 should not differ much from those used under Article 81 and the Merger Regulation'.[169] She highlighted the process for assessing efficiencies in Article 82:[170]

- the efficiencies have been or are likely to be realised and are a result of the conduct;
- the conduct is indispensable to the realisation of the efficiencies in the sense that there must be no realistic and less anticompetitive alternatives to the conduct that are capable of generating the same efficiencies;
- the firm's conduct benefits consumers by producing efficiencies that outweigh any anticompetitive effects on consumers; and
- the conduct does not eliminate effective competition, by removing all or most existing sources of actual or potential competition.

Unlike Article 81(3), there is no requirement that consumers must get a 'fair share', just that the efficiencies must benefit consumers. This makes it hard to know how much it takes to benefit consumers. Getting a fair share

[168] Kroes, supra note 2, 5. [169] Ibid.

[170] N. Kroes, 'Exclusionary Abuses of Dominance: The European Commission's Enforcement Priorities', speech given on 25 September 2008 at the Fordham Corporate Law Institute New York (speech/08/457), available at: www.ec.europa.eu/comm/competition/speeches.

implies that the passing on of benefits must at least compensate consumers for any actual or likely negative impact on them from the restriction of competition found under Article 81(1).[171] Although, there is no 'fair share' requirement, it must be assumed that consumers' benefits cannot be negative.[172] This is of course not much comfort to dominant undertakings given that the Commission has a great deal of discretion.

According to these policy statements, efficiencies do have a place in Article 82 even though Article 82 does not contain an exemption provision. While this may be a reasonable position to take, it is ultimately for the Community Courts to decide whether or not there is scope for efficiencies within Article 82. While the case law referred to above makes clear that Article 82 does not contain a case law developed exemption provision, it does not appear, in theory, to exclude the possibility of assessing efficiencies as one of the factors to be considered in the main assessment of abuse. This appears to be the CFI's position in *Laurent Piau*, where it indicated that it would be prepared to accept an efficiency defence under Article 82.[173] DG COMP also relied upon this case in its *Discussion Paper*,[174] taking the position that an efficiency defence is possible in Article 82. In some cases, the Community Courts have considered quantity rebates reflecting a genuine cost saving for the dominant supplier,[175] and therefore considered them to be lawful.[176] In *Irish Sugar*,[177] the CFI held that a dominant undertaking is allowed to protect its commercial position[178] where it is based on economic efficiency and in the interest of consumers:[179]

> [E]ven if the existence of a dominant position does not deprive an undertaking placed in that position of the right to protect its own commercial

[171] *Guidelines on the Application of Article 81(3)*, supra note 2, para. 85.

[172] See an analogy to mergers in OJ [2004] C31/5 *Guidelines on the Assessment of Horizontal Mergers under the Council Regulation on the Control of Concentrations between Undertakings*, para. 79.

[173] Case T-193/02 *Laurent Piau v. Commission* [2005] ECR II-209, para. 119.

[174] *Discussion Paper*, supra note 13, para. 8 footnote 6.

[175] Case T-203/01 *Manufacture Française des Pneumatiques Michelin v. Commission* [2003] ECR II-4071, para. 58; Case C-163/99 *Portuguese Republic v. Commission* [2001] ECR I-2613, paras. 50–2.

[176] L. Gyselen, 'Rebates: Competition on the Merits or Exclusionary Practice?' in C. D. Ehlermann and I. Atanasiu (eds.), *European Competition Law Annual 2003: What is an Abuse of a Dominant Position?* (Oxford: Hart Publishing, 2006) 287.

[177] Case T-228/97 *Irish Sugar plc v. Commission* [1999] ECR II-2969.

[178] If it does not interfere with the independence of a small customer: see Case 27/76 *United Brands Co. v. Commission* [1978] ECR 207, paras. 189–94.

[179] *Irish Sugar*, supra note 177, para. 189.

> interests when they are threatened …, the protection of the commercial position of an undertaking in a dominant position with the characteristics of that of the applicant at the time in question must, at the very least, in order to be lawful, be based on criteria of economic efficiency and consistent with the interests of consumers.

In *British Airways*,[180] the CFI reiterated that economic efficiency can be taken into consideration.[181] On appeal, the ECJ tied the analysis of efficiencies directly to the analysis of the conduct's competitive effects on consumers:[182]

> It has to be determined whether the exclusionary effect arising from such a system [discount system], which is disadvantageous for competition, may be counterbalanced, or outweighed, by advantages in terms of efficiency which also benefit the consumer. If the exclusionary effect of that system bears no relation to advantages for the market and consumers, or if it goes beyond what is necessary in order to attain those advantages, that system must be regarded as an abuse.

The ECJ acknowledged that the discount that may foreclose may bring efficiencies, which is a step towards a more economics-based approach. However, even though an economics-based approach naturally lends itself to a rule of reason approach to competition policy by balancing efficiencies against the conduct,[183] the court does not employ the language of a rule of reason.

Accordingly, if the recognisable efficiency gains are so large that the conduct can no longer be said to harm consumers, then the Commission must be prepared to accept this conduct. In this sense, efficiency gains must 'cleanse' the conduct in order for the conduct not to be deemed anti-competitive in the first place. In this fashion, the analysis of efficiencies is directly tied to the analysis of the conduct's competitive effects on consumers. Only when the Commission is convinced that the negative effects have been eliminated will it allow the conduct. Measuring efficiency gains can be a difficult task, as Posner acknowledges: 'it is very difficult to measure the efficiency consequences of a challenged practice. And so throughout this book [*Antitrust Law*, 2001] we shall continually be searching for ways of avoiding prohibiting efficient, albeit noncompetitive, practices without having to compare directly the gains and losses from a challenged practice.'[184]

[180] Case T-219/99 *British Airways plc v. Commission* [2003] ECR II-5917.
[181] Ibid., para. 280.
[182] Case C-95/04P *British Airways plc v. Commission* [2007] ECR I-2331, para. 86.
[183] EAGCP Report, supra note 4, 3. [184] Posner, supra note 5, 29.

The difficulty arises because balancing anticompetitive effects and efficiencies clearly involves a trade-off between gains in efficiency and the effects of the anticompetitive conduct. The Economic Advisory Group on Competition Policy, the EAGCP, admits that trade-offs involve an element of redistribution between groups of consumers, who can be both final and intermediate consumers as seen above. It suggests that when faced with such trade-offs, which require making a choice, the competition authority must exercise its judgement, which necessarily involves a certain element of subjectivity. The latter should however 'not absolve the competition authority from the requirement to be clear about the trade-offs themselves and to indicate precisely what consumer welfare effects are relevant to its decision'.[185]

That said, the Community Courts have interpreted efficiencies very narrowly.[186] Moreover, efficiency concerns have not been considered an aim in themselves.[187] This is probably because of the historical concern with preventing increases in industrial concentration and the possible political ramifications of conjoining economic and political power.

The Community Courts have been reluctant to interpret objective justifications as efficiency justifications.[188] The way in which Commissioner Kroes suggests adopting efficiencies is as a 'defence'. The terminology gives rise to a procedural issue regarding the burden of proof.[189] In addition to examining

[185] EAGCP Report, supra note 4, 10.

[186] Case 311/84 *Centre Belge d'Études de Marche Telemarketing v. CLT and IPB* [1985] ECR 3261, paras. 25–7; Case C-418/01 *IMS Health GmbH & Co. OHG v. NDC Health GmbH & Co. KG* [2002] ECR I-3401, para. 38; Case T-30/89 *Hilti AG v. Commission* [1991] ECR I-1439, paras. 105–7; Case C-333/94P *Tetra Pak International SA v. Commission* (*Tetra Pak II*) [1996] ECR I-5951, para. 79. However, the Commission has justified exclusionary behaviour based on economic grounds in its decision of 26 April 1989 in *Filtrona/Tabacalera*, where it rejected a complaint under Article 82 *based on economic grounds* from a Spanish cigarette filter producer against the Spanish tobacco monopoly holder. The latter had increased its own production of cigarette filters from 44 to 100 per cent, but justified its behaviour in vertical integration on the economic grounds that producing all its filter requirements would allow it to achieve economies of scale and generally reduce its production costs.

[187] E. Fox, 'Monopolization and Dominance in the United States and the European Community: Efficiency, Opportunity, and Fairness' 61 *Notre Dame Law Review* (1986) 981, 985; T. Eilmansberger, 'How to Distinguish Good from Bad Competition under Article 82 EC: In Search of Clearer and More Coherent Standards for Anticompetitive Abuses' 42 *Common Market Law Review* (2005) 129, 136.

[188] E. Rousseva, 'The Concept of "Objective Justification" of an Abuse of a Dominant Position: Can it Help to Modernise the Analysis under Article 82 EC?' 2(2) *Competition Law Review* (2006) 27, 58. For a distinction between objective justifications and efficiency justifications see L. Lovdahl Gormsen, 'The European Commission's Priority Guidelines on Article 82 EC' 14(3) *Communications Law* (2009) 83, 86.

[189] For a general discussion of the burden of proof within the scope of Article 82 see R. Nazzini, 'The Wood Began to Move: An Essay on Consumer Welfare, Evidence and Burden of Proof in Article 82 Cases' 31(4) *European Law Review* (2006) 518, 523 ff.

whether efficiencies are considered a 'factor' in the overall assessment of abuse or a 'defence' to an abuse, the following section analyses whether and how efficiencies are linked to the goal of consumer welfare in Article 82.

4.2 *Efficiencies as a 'defence' or a 'factor' and the link to consumer welfare*

The *Discussion Paper* suggested including efficiencies in Article 82 as a defence.[190] Although the terminology of 'defence' is removed from the *Guidance Paper*, the evidential burden of proving efficiencies still lies on the dominant undertaking, which must demonstrate 'that its conduct produces efficiencies which outweigh any anticompetitive effects on consumers'.[191] Despite the removal of the word 'defence', it is clear from Commissioner Kroes' 2008 Fordham speech, referred to above, that the Commission sees efficiencies in Article 82 as a defence.

While it makes perfect sense to require the dominant undertaking to prove that its conduct will create efficiencies to the benefit of consumers – if the aim is to promote consumer welfare – as it is in the best place to know this, it shifts the evidential burden of proof. Article 2 of Regulation 1/2003 establishes that it should be for the authority or the party alleging an infringement of Articles 81(1) and 82 to prove the infringement and there is no legal basis for reversing the legal burden of proof. It is important to distinguish between the legal and the evidential burden of proof, as only the latter can switch between the parties whereas the legal burden of proof will always be on the party alleging an infringement. This raises the question whether 'defence' refers to a rebuttal presumption of a first order inference, based on evidence, that the conduct is anticompetitive, or whether it is a defence to a final conclusion. In the light of Regulation 1/2003, it is not enough that the Commission establishes a series of presumptions, and thereafter requires the dominant undertaking to disprove these presumptions, but rather the Commission must prove the alleged infringement. In order to clarify the issue, former Deputy Director for DG COMP Emil Paulis has said:[192]

> A defence to a violation of a statute is not only an express defence stated in the law or in the text book. Any countervailing factor such as objective

[190] The conditions proposed in the *Discussion Paper*, supra note 13, para. 84 are clearly modelled upon Article 81(3) – although not in the same order.

[191] *Guidance Paper*, supra note 162, para. 27.

[192] E. Paulis, 'The Burden of Proof in Article 82 Cases', speech given on 13 September 2006 at the Fordham Corporate Law Institute, New York, 5, available at: www.ec.europa.eu/comm/competition/speeches.

> justifications or efficiencies which render Article 82 inapplicable can qualify as a defence, for which the burden of proof normally has to be on the person invoking such defence. The fact that the countervailing factor has to be brought forward by the defending party does not preclude a global integrated assessment and balancing of all effects under Article 82. It does not either change the fact that the authority has the burden of proving the ultimate violation of Article 82. This means that if the defendant comes forward with sufficient evidence of facts which contradict the facts alleged by the authority or which outweigh or neutralise the negative effects identified by the authority, the authority/plaintiff either accepts this outcome or has to prove with further evidence that the evidence put up by the dominant firm is not sufficient to outweigh the negative effects shown by the authority.

Paulis acknowledges that the authority has the legal burden of proof, but also that it is for the party advancing efficiencies to neutralise the negative effects identified by the authority. It is assumed that the word 'identified' means 'proved' otherwise it is nothing more than a presumption that reverses the burden of proof. Paulis does not talk about creating a framework where efficiencies are considered a defence and thereby creating a two-stage analysis, but does refer to a global integrated assessment. This is similar to the framework for analysing objective justifications suggested by the CFI in *Microsoft*[193] and by Advocate General Jacobs in his Opinion in *Syfait*:[194]

> I would add that the two-stage analysis suggested by the distinction between an abuse and its objective justification is to my mind somewhat artificial. Article 82, by contrast with Article 81 EC, does not contain any explicit provision for the exemption of conduct otherwise falling within it. Indeed, the very fact that conduct is characterised as an 'abuse' suggests that a negative conclusion has already been reached, by contrast with the more neutral terminology of 'prevention, restriction, or distortion of competition' under Article 81 EC. In my view, it is therefore more accurate to say that certain types of conduct on the part of a dominant undertaking do not fall within the category of abuse at all.[195]

Case law on Article 82 has dealt with objective justifications by making them a part of the overall assessment of conduct.[196] There is no reason

[193] Case T-201/04 *Microsoft Corporation v. Commission* [2007] ECR II-3601, para. 688.

[194] Advocate General Jacobs' Opinion in Case C-53/03 *Synetairismos Farmakopoion Aitolias & Akarnanias (Syfait) and others v. GlaxoSmithKline AEVE* [2005] ECR I-4609, delivered on 28 October 2004, para. 72.

[195] This was also the view of Advocate General Kokott in her Opinion in *British Airways*, supra note 182, delivered on 23 February 2006, paras. 42–3, which considered an objective justification as part of a demonstration of unlawful conduct, not as a defence.

[196] For example, COMP/C-3/37.792 *Microsoft*; Case T-83/91 *Tetra Pak International SA v. Commission* [1994] ECR II-755; Case T-65/98 *Van den Bergh Foods Ltd v. Commission* [2003] ECR II-4653; *Tetra Pak II*, supra note 186; *Irish Sugar*, supra note 177; *Portuguese*

why efficiencies should be treated any differently, *if* the aim is to promote consumer welfare. Thus, where the efficiencies outweigh the conduct in question, an abuse ought not to be found in the first place.[197] Therefore, it is not as a defence to a final conclusion that conduct is anticompetitive. Rather, the 'defence' terminology refers to the rebuttal of a first-order inference from a portion of the evidence that proves the conduct is anticompetitive and violates Article 82. It is a defence to a *prima facie* case, not a defence to a final conclusion. However, whether efficiencies are a 'factor' or a 'defence' does not really matter. What matters for dominant undertakings' ability to advance efficiencies is whether Article 82 aims at promoting consumer welfare. Efficiencies are only important for achieving that aim. On the contrary, if the objective of Article 82 is to achieve economic freedom for all market participants, the aim is not to promote efficiencies for consumers, the efficiencies are not relevant. If by protecting economic freedom, consumers gain in terms of greater efficiencies, then this is an additional benefit, but not the aim. In this way, dominant undertakings' possibility of advancing efficiencies either as a 'factor' or as a 'defence' depends on what Article 82 is trying to achieve.

The *Guidance Paper*'s section on efficiencies reveals that the test for dominant undertakings is not whether the conduct in question is efficient, but rather whether it eliminates effective competition.[198] If the aim is consumer welfare, then the dominant undertaking should be allowed to prove that its conduct was efficient despite an elimination of effective competition. However, it is clear from the efficiency section that *even if* the dominant undertaking proves its conduct is efficient and it benefits consumers, it may not escape the prohibition in Article 82. The test of eliminating effective competition means that dominant undertakings are only allowed to compete aggressively if they do not impair effective competition at the same time. Whether or not effective competition is eliminated ought not to matter if it benefits consumers.

The test of elimination of effective competition makes it more likely that Article 82 is about economic freedom, in which case efficiency is not the aim. According to the ECJ in *Continental Can*,[199] dominant undertakings can neither *strengthen* nor *use* their dominant position where

Republic, supra note 175; *Michelin*, supra note 175; *Hilti*, supra note 186. Objective justifications were not discussed on appeal to the ECJ in *Hilti*.

197 See for example Commission decision of 26 April 1989 in *Filtrona/Tabacalera*, supra note 186.

198 *Guidance Paper*, supra note 162, para. 29, fourth bullet point.

199 *Continental Can*, supra note 15.

this eliminates effective competition. Thus, allowing a dominant undertaking to advance efficiencies is all very well in theory, but impossible in practice if the aim is not consumer welfare. If however the aim is consumer welfare, then it should not matter whether the dominant undertaking *strengthens* its dominance (unlike if the objective is economic freedom), but only whether the dominant undertaking *uses* its dominant position.

This section concludes that Article 82 does not contain an exemption provision. Despite that, the *Guidance Paper* acknowledges that efficiencies play a role in Article 82, but the test applied makes it impossible for dominant undertakings to advance efficiencies, as efficiencies will only be accepted where they do not eliminate effective competition. However, whether effective competition is eliminated or impaired ought to matter if the aim is consumer welfare. What matters in the application of a consumer welfare standard is whether consumers ultimately benefit and not whether effective competition is eliminated. Efficiencies can only fully be advanced as a defence against an abuse if Article 82 is about consumer welfare, but consumer welfare is not the only goal in Article 82, as will be shown in chapter 3.

5. Conclusion

The aim of this chapter was to examine the concept of consumer welfare. This was necessary for later chapters, which consider whether consumer welfare conflicts with any other objectives pursued in Article 82. The chapter was divided into three main sections. Section 2 introduced the basic theory of consumer welfare, the different forms of efficiency and the correlation between them, which is essential to understanding what kinds of efficiencies are accepted when adopting a consumer welfare standard. It found that what kind of efficiency is relevant depends on which welfare standard is chosen for a given system. This was significant for the discussion of efficiencies in Article 82.

Section 3 discussed how different schools of thought have treated market power and those schools' views on efficiency. This was to examine whether ordoliberalism, which has influenced the application of Article 82, is in effect the equivalent of the Harvard 'structural' School in Europe. If it is, it may be possible to inject Chicago School arguments into Article 82 like they were injected into US antitrust in the 1970s. However, the main difference between the two schools was their view of efficiency. Whilst the Harvard 'structural' School did not believe efficiency was always an explanation for market power, it still believed efficiency was an important goal – although not the only one – of antitrust. On the contrary, ordoliberalism viewed the protection of individual economic freedom of action as a value in itself. Efficiency was seen as a possible by-product rather than an aim in itself. Thus, section 3 concluded that ordoliberalism is something fundamentally different from the Harvard 'structural' School and therefore not susceptible to Chicago School arguments.

Section 4 questioned whether Article 82, despite not containing an exemption provision like Article 81(3), allows efficiencies to be advanced. This is important for the overall argument of the legitimacy of consumer welfare as the main goal in Article 82. If the aim is consumer welfare, then it is relevant to examine the efficiencies' benefits to consumers. The section concluded that in theory dominant undertakings can advance efficiency as an objective justification. However, upon analysing how efficiencies should be treated in Article 82, it transpired that the test for efficiencies is not whether or not the conduct in question is efficient or inefficient to the advantage or disadvantage of consumers, but rather whether effective competition is eliminated. This ought not to matter if the conduct in question benefits consumers. Section 4 concluded that efficiencies can only fully be advanced by dominant undertakings if Article 82 is about consumer welfare. Chapter 3 will discuss the objectives of Article 82.

3

Objectives

1. Introduction

This chapter discusses what the goals of Article 82 are and why they are pursued. Understanding why an objective is pursued helps identify whether it conflicts with any other objective. Conflicts must be identified to see how the Commission balances the various interests and which of the conflicting objectives is given precedence.

The lack of clarity regarding the objectives of Article 82 has intensified the long-standing controversy regarding the proper legal standards to govern abusive conduct. Many decisions and judgments are not clear in their analysis of exclusion or in their implications. The Commission acknowledges that it needs to be better at explaining its decisions:[1]

> [T]he Commission must always work to improve its decisions and its policies. The review [of Article 82] is about a better focus and a better argumentation in future cases. Furthermore, the fact that if the discussion paper leads to a more refined economic analysis, the Commission would in future argue a case in a different way than in the past, does not mean that the decision taken in a past case was wrong, only that the argumentation would today have been different.

In the light of the Commission's policy review and its commitment to consumer welfare, some may be tempted to argue that the Commission and the Community Courts have aimed at promoting consumer welfare in previous cases decided under Article 82. However, the unrealistic counterfactuals and lack of efficiency analysis in much of the Article 82 case law make it difficult to believe that the main aim has been consumer welfare.

As this chapter will show, Article 82 does not pursue one objective only, which gives rise to the question whether it is fair that the Commission puts so much emphasis on consumer welfare. The competition provisions are not only concerned with competition in the narrow sense of the term, but also with broader issues such as industrial, social and political

[1] Commission Discussion Paper on Abuse of Dominance – Frequently Asked Questions, Memo of 19 December 2005, MEMO/05/486.

policies.[2] Community competition law has attempted to protect competition against distortion in many different ways, such as safeguarding freedom of competition (economic freedom),[3] promoting economic efficiency, and the reduction or elimination of obstacles to economic change and development in the name of market integration.[4] These are not easily categorised, but, broadly speaking, they could be thought of as pursuing:

(i) political goals;
(ii) economic goals; and
(iii) socio-economic goals.

For example, Article 82 has been used as a tool to liberalise markets in sectors which were previously monopolies. Liberalisation is not easily categorised because it is a process for achieving an open market. Access to markets protects undertakings' freedom of competition (their economic freedom) and enhances the process of competition. This may (or may not) turn into consumer welfare. Interpreted in this way, liberalisation is a wider objective, which is used as a means to an end of a variety of other objectives. This is similar to market integration, which serves as a political as well as an economic objective of EU competition policy.[5]

This chapter consists of six sections. In section 2 the role of undistorted competition is considered. Section 3 examines market integration as an objective of Article 82 and why it is pursued. Section 4 analyses whether jurisprudence supports an objective of consumer welfare. Section 5 considers the objective of economic freedom. Section 6 concludes.

2. Undistorted competition

One of the Treaty's goals is 'a system ensuring that competition in the internal market is not distorted'.[6] Article 82 has been interpreted by

[2] P. Jebsen and R. Stevens, 'Assumptions, Goals and Dominant Undertakings: The Regulation of Competition under Article 86 of the European Union' 64 *Antitrust Law Journal* (1996) 443, 446.

[3] Freedom of competition and economic freedom are used interchangeably in this chapter, as they mean the same, which is that the economic system should allow all individuals the freedom to participate in the marketplace unimpaired by the power of other companies.

[4] G. Monti, 'Article 81 EC and Public Policy' 39(5) *Common Market Law Review* (2002) 1057, 1069–70.

[5] A. Schaub, Working Paper in C. D. Ehlermann and L. L. Laudati (eds.), *European Competition Law Annual 1997: The Objectives of Competition Policy* (Oxford: Hart Publishing, 1998) 126.

[6] Article 3(1)(g) of the EC Treaty: Consolidated version [1997] OJ 340/173. Article 3(1)(g) will be moved to a protocol when the Lisbon Treaty is ratified.

reference to this object and purpose from the very first case, *Continental Can*,[7] where the ECJ said:[8]

> Article 86 [Article 82] is part of the chapter devoted to the common rules on the community's policy in the field of competition. This policy is based on Article 3(f) of the Treaty [Article 3(1)(g)] according to which the community's activity shall include the institution of a system ensuring that competition in the common market is not distorted. The applicants' [Continental Can] argument that this provision merely contains a general programme devoid of legal effect, ignores the fact that Article 3 considers the pursuit of the objectives which it lays down to be indispensable for the achievement of the community's tasks. As regards in particular the aim mentioned in (f), the Treaty in several provisions contains more detailed regulations for the interpretation of which this aim is decisive.
>
> But if Article 3(f) provides for the institution of a system ensuring that competition in the common market is not distorted, then it requires a fortiori that competition must not be eliminated. This requirement is so essential that without it numerous provisions of the Treaty would be pointless. Moreover, it corresponds to the precept of Article 2 of the Treaty according to which one of the tasks of the community is 'to promote throughout the community a harmonious development of economic activities'. Thus the restraints on competition which the Treaty allows under certain conditions because of the need to harmonize the various objectives of the Treaty are limited by the requirements of Articles 2 and 3. Going beyond this limit involves the risk that the weakening of competition would conflict with the aims of the common market.

The CFI reiterated in *Tetra Pak* that: 'Article 86 [Article 82] must accordingly be interpreted by reference to its object and purpose as they have been described by the Court of Justice, … in accordance with the general objective set out in Article 3(f) [Article 3(1)(g)] of the Treaty as it was then.'[9] Other cases have confirmed this view.[10]

It is clear that Article 82 must be read in its Community context. It is not a stand-alone provision, but part of the EC Treaty, and a teleological[11] analysis of Article 82 means that it must be interpreted in light of the Treaty's

[7] Case 6/72 *Europemballage Corporation and Continental Can Co. Inc. v. Commission* [1973] ECR 215.
[8] Ibid., paras. 23–4.
[9] Case T-83/91 *Tetra Pak International SA v. Commission* [1994] ECR II-755, para. 114.
[10] For example, COMP/C-3/37.792 *Microsoft*, para. 836; Case C-361/98 *Malpensa* [2001] ECR I-385, para 31.
[11] For a general explanation of the different methods of interpretation, see S. Weatherill and P. Beaumont, *EU Law* (London: Penguin Books, 3rd edn, 1999) 184 ff.

aims. To achieve the aims set out in Article 2 EC,[12] the Community shall conduct certain activities listed in Articles 3 and 4 EC. One of the activities listed in Article 3 is to ensure that competition in the internal market is not distorted.[13] Some see 'undistorted competition' as an objective,[14] whereas others see it as an activity.[15] In any event, Article 82 is an implementation provision, meaning that it assists Article 2 in establishing a common market and implementing common policies.[16]

Traditionally, the Community Courts have interpreted the basic objective of protection of competition by adopting a teleological interpretation, as opposed to a literal, historical or contextual interpretation.[17] For Article 82, this method of interpretation has been used since *Continental Can*. The teleological interpretation has given the Community Courts an opportunity to develop the law and implement suitable objectives. According to the ECJ, interpreting Article 82 in the light of the overall objectives of the Treaty is necessary because the activities of Article 3 are 'indispensable for the achievement of the Community's tasks'.[18]

Regulation 1/2003 recital 9 recognises that both Articles 81 and 82 have as their objective the protection of competition on the market. This

[12] Under Article 2 EC, the Community has as its task to promote a 'harmonious, balanced and sustainable development of economic activities, a high level of employment and of social protection, equality between men and women, sustainable and non-inflationary growth, a high degree of competitiveness and convergence of economic performance, a high level of protection and improvement of the quality of the environment, the raising of the standard of living and quality of life, and economic and social cohesion and solidarity among Member States'. One of the means of obtaining these goals is by ensuring that competition in the common market is not distorted.

[13] Article 3(1)(g): 'A system ensuring that competition in the internal market is not distorted'.

[14] T. Eilmansberger, 'How to Distinguish Good from Bad Competition under Article 82 EC: In Search of Clearer and More Coherent Standards for Anticompetitive Abuses' 42 *Common Market Law Review* (2005) 129, 132–3.

[15] Letter from M. Petite from the Commission's legal service to the editor of the *Financial Times*, 27 June 2007.

[16] See C. Townley, 'Is Anything More Important than Consumer Welfare (in Article 81 EC)? Reflections of a Community Lawyer' *Cambridge Yearbook* (Cambridge University Press, 2007) 9.

[17] The ECJ has been accused of being rather political in its purposive interpretation and has been criticised by P. J. G. Kapteyn and P. Verloren Van Thematt in L. W. Gormley (ed.), *Introduction to the Law of the European Communities after the Coming into Force of the Single European Act* (Deventer: Kluwer, 2nd edn, 1989) 169–73; H. Rasmussen, 'Between Self-Restraint and Activism: A Judicial Policy for the European Court' 13 *European Law Review* (1988) 28, 28–9 and 37.

[18] *Continental Can*, supra note 7, para. 23.

however raises the fundamental question of what is harm to, or distortion of, competition.[19]

The ECJ explained in *Continental Can*[20] that restraints on competition are acceptable to the extent that they are needed to harmonise the various goals of the Treaty, but may not go beyond what is necessary to achieve these goals, as that would conflict with the overall aims of the Treaty. The aim is not to protect competition against *any* distortion, but to avoid competition being distorted in such a way that it prevents the achievement of the broader objectives of the Treaty. In this way, competition is not promoted or protected as an end in itself but as a means to achieve the broader objectives.[21] This requires a fine balance between conduct which distorts competition in such a way that the wider objectives are jeopardised, and conduct which distorts competition only insignificantly and therefore does not prevent the broader objectives from being achieved. However, the Treaty does not define which conduct distorts competition and which does not. Case law is helpful in showing which conduct distorts competition. For example, the acquisition of a competitor which would leave no competition in the market distorts the market structure and therefore is abusive.[22] A refusal to supply a competitor might be treated as adversely affecting the structure of the market by destroying the competitor's capacity to compete effectively.[23] Fidelity rebates that pressurise firms into dealing with a dominant firm may distort competition in the market, unless there is 'economic equivalency' in the transactions.[24] Dominant undertakings' strategies to limit the independence of a smaller business imply coercion, which is abusive and distorts competition.[25]

However, case law is not very helpful in defining what kinds of conduct do *not* distort competition. Only by knowing what Article 82 is trying to achieve is it possible to benchmark the conduct in question against those objectives, and in that context determine whether the specific conduct

[19] J. Vickers, 'Abuse of Market Power', 115 *Economic Journal* (2005) F244, F254.

[20] *Continental Can*, supra note 7, para. 24.

[21] K. Van Miert, 'Competition Policy in the 1990s', 11 May 1993, Royal Institute of International Affairs. Available at: http://ec.europa.eu.int/comm/competition/speeches; Commissioner Monti's foreword to the Commission's thirty-third *Annual Report on Competition Policy* (2003).

[22] *Continental Can*, supra note 7.

[23] Case 6–7/73 *Istituto Chemioterapico Italiano SpA and Commercial Solvents Corporation v. Commission* [1974] ECR 223.

[24] Case 85/76 *Hoffmann-La Roche AG v. Commission* [1979] ECR 461; Case 322/81 *Nederlandsche Banden-Industrie Michelin NV v. Commission* (*Michelin I*) [1983] ECR 3461.

[25] Case 27/76 *United Brands Co. v. Commission* [1978] ECR 207.

distorts or promotes competition. For example, if the objective is market integration, conduct creating any barriers to trade that the rules on free movement[26] are trying to dismantle cannot be allowed. If however the objective is consumer welfare, only conduct which harms consumers must be prevented. On the other hand, if the objective is protecting freedom, conduct restricting the freedom to participate in the market must be prohibited. Whilst it is necessary to know which objectives are important in the application of Article 82, it is equally significant to comprehend why these objectives are pursued. They may not all pursue that same overall aim, and so a conflict between the objectives may arise. To avoid a conflict, it is necessary to balance them. The rest of this chapter will attempt to identify which objectives Article 82 is trying to achieve and why those objectives are pursued. By answering the latter, it will be possible to identify whether there is a conflict between any of the goals. How to balance conflicting goals against one overarching objective will be discussed in chapter 7.

The remaining part of the chapter accepts that the aim of Article 82 is to avoid competition being distorted significantly so as to jeopardise the wider objectives of the Treaty. However, neither the Treaty nor jurisprudence has defined exactly what is meant by undistorted competition, presumably because it changes over time. Thus, it is necessary to discuss why the various objectives are pursued besides avoiding competition being distorted.

3. Market integration

Competition is fundamental to the broader political aims of the Community, one of which is the process of integration in economic unions and free trade areas. This section examines why market integration is pursued. Is it an intermediate objective of consumer welfare or is it an intermediate objective of economic freedom?

The Commission has called market integration a wider objective of Community competition policy.[27] As chapter 5 will demonstrate, sometimes market integration is distorted and the conduct in question is prohibited because such distortion restricts the economic freedom of some market participants, whereas at other times, market integration needs to be protected to achieve consumer welfare. The Community Courts

[26] Articles 28, 39, 43 and 49.

[27] OJ [2009] C-45/7 *Guidance on the Commission's Enforcement Priorities in Applying Article 82 EC Treaty to Abusive Exclusionary Conduct by Dominant Undertakings* (*Guidance Paper*) para. 1.

have recognised that market integration is an important objective.[28] It is clear that market integration is an objective pursued in Article 82, but the question is what the underlying rationale for pursuing it is. Some consider market integration as a means to an end of other objectives.[29] Different reasons are given for pursuit of the single market. For example, some believe market integration promotes economic freedom;[30] others argue that economic efficiency justifies this goal;[31] or market integration may be considered a rationale for economic integration. Whilst the latter seems obvious, some argue that the market integration objective does not necessarily promote economic integration.[32] For Mestmäcker, market integration is a means to an end of undistorted competition, which can be achieved by ensuring economic freedom. This economic freedom – in essence the freedom to participate in the market – is ensured by Treaty articles governing the freedom of services, free movement of goods and freedom of establishment.[33] By linking market integration with the competition rules, Articles 81 and 82 also become a tool to protect the result of eradicating barriers to free movement. Market integration is not achieved if economically powerful firms are allowed to manipulate the market or hinder the flow of trade between Member States.[34] It works both ways: market integration is a means to an end of undistorted competition, which can be achieved by ensuring economic freedom, but economic freedom can also be ensured by integrating the market. Waelbroeck believes that the original focus on the free movement of goods in the Spaak

[28] For example, Case 226/84 *British Leyland plc v. Commission* [1986] ECR 3263; Case 26/75 *General Motors Continental NV v. Commission* [1975] ECR 1367; *United Brands*, supra note 25; Joined Cases C-468/06 to C-478/06 *Sot. Lelos kai Sia EE and others v. GlaxoSmithKline AEVE* [2008] ECR I-7139.

[29] G. Glöckler, L. Junius, G. Scappucci, S. Usherwood, and J. Vassallo, *Guide to EU Policies* (London: Blackstone Press, 1998) 91.

[30] Monti, supra note 4, 1063; E. Mestmäcker, 'Die Beurteilung von Unternehmenszusammenschlüssen nach Artikel 86 des EWG-Vertrags', reprinted in Mestmäcker, *Wirtschaft und Verfassung in der Europäischen Union* (Baden-Baden: Nomos Verlagsgesellschaft, 2nd edn, 2006) 597.

[31] For example, M. Waelbroeck, 'Competition, Integration and Economic Efficiency in the EEC from the Point of View of the Private Firm' in *Festschrift zu Ehren von Eric Stein* (Baden-Baden: Nomos Verlagsgesellschaft, 1987); R. Van Den Bergh, 'Modern Industrial Organisation versus Old-fashioned European Competition Law' 17(2) *European Competition Law Review* (1996) 75, 76–80.

[32] D. J. Neven, Working Paper in Ehlermann and Laudati, supra note 5, 117.

[33] Mestmäcker, supra note 30, 606.

[34] G. Marenco, 'Competition between National Economies and Competition between Businesses: A Response to Judge Pescatore' 10 *Fordham International Law Journal* (1987) 420, 429–30.

Report[35] was 'a means of increasing competition, which itself was seen as a means of enhancing economic efficiency'.[36]

In the *United Brands* case,[37] United Brands Company (UBC) delivered its Chiquita bananas to various ports within the Community. From these ports distributors would transport the bananas to their ripening facilities throughout the common market. The prices charged to each distributor depended upon the country in which the distributor operated: for example, the price charged in Ireland was the lowest and the prices charged in Belgium and Denmark were the highest. Data showed that there were substantial differences of 30–50 per cent between the highest and lowest prices charged to customers in the various Member States during some weeks. UBC controlled the arbitrage between the high-priced and low-priced Member States by having a clause in its distribution contracts prohibiting the resale of green bananas.[38] The ECJ held that geographic price discrimination created a partitioning of national markets and therefore was prohibited by Article 82:[39]

> Although the responsibility for establishing the single banana market does not lie with the applicant [UBC], it can only endeavour to take 'what the market can bear' provided that it complies with the rules for the regulation and coordination of the market laid down by the Treaty.
>
> These discriminatory prices, which varied according to the circumstances of the member states, were just so many obstacles to the free movement of goods and their effect was intensified by the clause forbidding the resale of bananas while still green and by reducing the deliveries of the quantities ordered.
>
> A rigid partitioning of national markets was thus created at price levels which were *artificially* different, placing certain distributor/ripeners at a competitive disadvantage, since compared with what it should have been competition had thereby been distorted.

Following the Commission's decision United Brands had to bring the infringement to an end.[40] In respect of its sales of Chiquita bananas, it

[35] The *Rapport des Chefs de Délégation aux Ministres des Affaires Étrangères* (in English: *Report of the Heads of Delegation of the Governmental Committee*) set up by the Messina Conference, named after Paul-Henri Spaak, then the Belgian prime minister, was presented on 21 April 1956 and led to the Treaty of Rome of 1957. Available at: www.aei.pitt.edu/995/01/Spaak_report.pdf.

[36] Waelbroeck, supra note 31, 302. [37] *United Brands*, supra note 25.

[38] This was in effect an export ban, because once bananas are yellow they are perishable and soft, which means that it is impossible to transport them without damaging them. It is slightly surprising that the Commission did not consider this under Article 81.

[39] *United Brands*, supra note 25, paras. 227 and 232–3. Emphasis added.

[40] OJ [1976] L95/1 *Chiquita*, Article 3(a).

had to stop charging other trading parties, namely distributor/ripeners, dissimilar prices for equivalent transactions. This part of the decision was not set aside on appeal. The consequence of this was that United Brands could not price discriminate between high-income and low-income countries. This would benefit wealthier consumers but not poorer consumers. Before the judgment, United Brands could charge high prices in high-income countries, for example Denmark and Germany, and lower prices in low-income countries such as Ireland. Because United Brands would have to charge a non-discriminatory price, the price would probably be an average price between the lowest and the highest of the discriminatory prices to avoid losing its profit margin. If this assumption is correct, the price in the higher-income countries would be lower than when United Brands could discriminate. Welfare (in the form of a lower price) for consumers in high-income countries would increase. Consumers who did not buy bananas before due to the high price might start buying bananas at the lower price. Consumers who did buy bananas before would be able to buy them at a lower price. These consumers would be better off than before. However, the price in the lower-income countries, such as Ireland, would probably be higher than when United Brands could discriminate if the assumption of the average price holds. Some Irish consumers might no longer want to buy bananas because of the price increase, and the ones still buying bananas would have to pay a higher price for the same quality as before. These consumers would be worse off than before the judgment. The distributional effect is that income is distributed away from a poorer part of Europe to a wealthier part of Europe. This led one commentator to argue that a ban on geographic price discrimination can lead to undesirable distributive consequences.[41] Another commentator argued that the court appears more inclined to protect existing competitors rather than competition and that the court did not make consumers better off, nor did it pursue efficiency.[42]

Despite the arguments of some,[43] the single-market objective remains relevant, as the ECJ confirmed recently in *Sot. Lelos kai Sia EE*.[44] In this case, GlaxoSmithKline asked the court to abandon its normal (strict)

[41] W. Bishop, 'Price Discrimination under Article 86: Political Economy in the European Court' 44 *Modern Law Review* (1981) 282, 287–8.

[42] L. Zanon, 'Price Discrimination under Article 86 of the EEC Treaty: The *United Brands* Case' 31 *International and Comparative Law Quarterly* (1982) 36, 50–1.

[43] P. Marsden and S. Bishop, 'Intellectual Leaders Still Need Ground to Stand On' editorial 3(2) *European Competition Journal* (2007) 315, 315.

[44] *Sot. Lelos kai Sia EE*, supra note 28. See analysis of this case in chapter 5.

position on parallel trade, because the parallel trade in the pharmaceutical market does not give the final consumers a lower price.[45] In other words, despite its intention to restrict competition, there is no effect on final consumers, so the conduct should not be prohibited under Article 82.[46] The court explained that practices of an undertaking in a dominant position which are aimed at avoiding all parallel exports from one Member State to another cannot escape the scope of Article 82.[47] Unlike in the Spanish *GlaxoSmithKline* case, where the CFI saw market integration as an intermediate to achieving the objective of consumer welfare,[48] the ECJ opined that where there is harm to free trade due to restriction of parallel exports, it does not matter that consumers in the importing Member State are actually not harmed.

The Community Courts seemed to seek to achieve market integration and economic freedom at the expense of consumer welfare in *United Brands* and *Sot. Lelos kai Sia EE*. In the former case, United Brands had discontinued supplies of Chiquita bananas to the Danish ripener/distributor Olesen, because it had taken part in a campaign mounted by Castle and Cooke to promote Dole bananas. Olesen tried to obtain Chiquita bananas from some of United Brands' other ripener/distributors in Denmark and from a German company, Scipio, but without success. United Brands' refusal to supply Olesen would discourage other ripener/distributors from actively promoting competing brands. Its justification for refusing to supply Olesen was that the refusal did not affect actual competition on the Danish market.[49] The ECJ rejected this. The court held that although UBC was allowed to protect its own commercial interests by taking reasonable steps, such steps could not interfere with the independence of 'small and medium-sized firms in their commercial relations with the undertaking in a dominant position'.[50] In the *Sot. Lelos kai Sia EE* case, the aim of GlaxoSmithKline's refusal to supply its wholesalers was to prevent parallel exports. The court said that without any objective justification, refusal to supply existing customers constitutes an abuse.[51] GlaxoSmithKline

[45] Ibid., para. 31.

[46] According to Cases C-199/92P etc. *Huls AG v. Commission* [1999] ECR I- 4287, para. 163, and C-51/92P etc. *Hercules Chemicals NV v. Commission* [1999] ECR I-4235, concerted practice is caught by Article 81(1) even in the absence of anticompetitive effects on the market, but in Case T-25/95 etc. *Cimenteries CBR SA v. Commission* [2000] ECR II-491, para. 1865, the CFI said that there would be no infringement of Article 81 if the parties could prove that the conduct had no anticompetitive effect.

[47] *Sot. Lelos kai Sia EE*, supra note 28, para 66.

[48] Case T-168/01 *GlaxoSmithKline v. Commission* [2006] ECR II-2969, para. 118.

[49] *United Brands*, supra note 25, para. 178.

[50] Ibid., para. 193.

[51] *Sot. Lelos kai Sia EE*, supra note 28, para. 34.

argued that it would not earn its monopoly rent, which it was entitled to because of research and development, and furthermore that parallel trade in pharmaceuticals was not going to have an impact on final consumers. The ECJ rejected these arguments.[52]

Some have commented that the goal of market integration takes priority over other efficiency goals, including that of consumer welfare.[53] These cases appear to support this. However, consumer welfare may sometimes be desired at the expense of market integration and freedom, as seen in the Spanish *GlaxoSmithKline* case, although that was rejected on appeal before the ECJ.[54] As explained by some, market integration is only set aside in circumstances where efficiency resulting from the conduct in question is greater than the restriction of competition.[55] This section concludes that consumer welfare is not always desired at the expense of market integration and freedom.

4. Consumer welfare

Some believe that competition must be protected against distortion because competition fosters economic growth. They believe economic efficiency is the main goal of competition. To examine whether competition is distorted they would, as described in chapter 2, balance the disadvantages of anticompetitive conduct (allocative inefficiency – the deadweight loss) against the advantages of productive efficiency using Williamson's trade-off model.[56] Williamson's trade-off model shows how an increase in market power and an increase in prices causing a loss in allocative efficiency can nevertheless lead to an increase in welfare due to cost savings. Allocative efficiency is the welfare standard preferred within the sphere of Article 82, as articulated in the *Discussion Paper*: '[w]ith regard to exclusionary abuses the objective of Article 82 is the protection of competition on the market as a means of enhancing consumer welfare and of ensuring an efficient allocation of resources'.[57] Whilst this book challenges the view that consumer welfare is the main objective of Article 82, it accepts that in so far as consumer welfare is relevant it is in the form of consumer surplus

[52] Ibid., para. 57.

[53] K. J. Cseres, *Competition Law and Consumer Protection* (The Hague: Kluwer Law International, 2005) 276.

[54] *GlaxoSmithKline*, supra note 48; Case C-501/06 etc. *GlaxoSmithKline v. Commission*, para 63.

[55] Monti, supra note 4, 1094.

[56] O. E. Williamson, 'Economies as an Antitrust Defense: The Welfare Tradeoffs' 58 (1) *American Economic Review* (1968) 18.

[57] DG Competition *Discussion Paper on the Application of Article 82 of the Treaty to Exclusionary Abuses* (December 2005) ('*Discussion Paper*') paras. 4 and 54.

as defined in chapter 2. The legitimacy of consumer welfare is discussed in the next chapter.

The EC Treaty does not mention consumer welfare directly, and some argue that, unlike in US antitrust, it is not the overriding interest in European competition analysis.[58] Despite this, some believe that it is one of the core objectives of EC competition law.[59] The following section will examine whether consumer welfare is an objective pursued in Article 82, and if so, why it is pursued and whether it conflicts with any other objectives.

Consumer welfare has been on the agenda for some time. The Commission emphasised the importance of consumers in its first *Annual Report on Competition Policy* in 1971:[60]

> Through the interplay of decentralised decision-making machinery, competition enables enterprises continuously to improve their efficiency, which is the *sine qua non* for a steady improvement in living standards and employment prospects within the countries of the Community. From this point of view, competition policy is an essential means for satisfying to a great extent the individual and collective needs of our society … Competition policy … encourages the best possible use of productive resources for the greatest possible benefit of the economy as a whole and the benefit, in particular, of the consumer.

Consumer welfare became more apparent when Sir Leon Brittan became Competition Commissioner in 1989. The introduction to the Commission's *Annual Report on Competition Policy* in 1990 specifically highlights the importance of an efficient allocation of resources and of economic growth, in order to maximise consumer welfare.[61] It states that Member States must develop along the lines dictated by economic efficiency.[62] According to the *Discussion Paper* of 2005, consumer welfare is the main objective of Article 82.[63] The focus on consumers was maintained in the Commission's *Guidance Paper* of 2008, which says that in applying Article 82 to exclusionary conduct by dominant undertakings, the Commission will focus on those types of conduct that are

[58] I. Haracoglou, 'Competition Policy Law, Consumer Policy and the Retail Sector: The Systems' Relation and the Effects of a Strengthened Consumer Protection Policy on Competition Law' 3(2) *Competition Law Review* (2007) 175, 180; Cseres, supra note 53, 20.

[59] Cseres, supra note 53, 255; M. Motta, *Competition Policy: Theory and Practice* (Cambridge University Press, 2004) 23; Monti, supra note 4, 1064; Neven, supra note 32, 118.

[60] First *Annual Report on Competition Policy* (1971) 11–12.

[61] Twentieth *Annual Report on Competition Policy* (1990) 11.

[62] Ibid., 12.

[63] *Discussion Paper*, supra note 57, paras. 4, 54, 55 and 88.

most harmful to consumers.[64] Some policy statements have confirmed this view.[65]

4.1 *Signs of consumer welfare in early jurisprudence*

In the first Article 82 case to come before the ECJ, the *Continental Can* case, the court specifically emphasised that Article 82 prohibits exclusionary conduct only where it harms consumers directly or indirectly.[66] The court analysed how consumers are likely to be harmed where there is harm to the structure of competition.

Continental Can, the world's largest producer of metal containers, acquired a 91 per cent interest in a Dutch metal can manufacturer, Carnaud of France and Thomassen & Drijver-verblifa NV (TDV), through its holding company Europemballage Corporation. Continental Can had transferred its 85 per cent share of a German company, Schmalbach-Lubeca-Werke AG (SLW), to Europemballage to buy the shares of TDV. In December 1971, the Commission concluded that the merger with TDV constituted an abuse of a dominant position and thus violated Article 82. Europemballage had rendered any future competition between TDV and SLW impossible and thereby distorted competition in West Germany and the Benelux countries, which represented a substantial part of the common market.[67] On appeal, the Commission put forward the following arguments:[68]

(1) The basic aims of the Treaty are to ensure competition;
(2) Article 82(2)(b) together with Article 3(1)(g) constitutes a broad mandate to prohibit the effect of prejudice to consumers;
(3) A change in the structure of competition which reduces the consumer's market alternatives is an effect which is prohibited as prejudicial; and
(4) Because it is the effect of reducing competition that is abusive, neither the type of conduct nor the existence of a causal relationship between the dominance and that conduct is relevant to proving an abuse.

[64] *Guidance Paper*, supra note 27, para. 5

[65] N. Kroes, 'Preliminary Thoughts on Policy Review of Article 82', 23 September 2005, Fordham Corporate Law Institute New York; Philip Lowe, 'Consumer Welfare and Efficiency: New Guiding Principles of Competition Policy?', 27 March 2007, the thirteenth International Conference on Competition and fourteenth European Competition Day, 9.

[66] *Continental Can*, supra note 7, para. 26.

[67] OJ [1972] L7/25 *Continental Can*; 2 CCH Comm. Mkt Rep. 8171 (1973).

[68] W. M. H. Haubert II, '*Continental Can*: New Strength for Common Market Anti-trust' 11 *San Diego Law Review* (1973–4) 227, 233.

Continental Can argued that Article 82 does not prohibit the existence of a dominant position, but only the abusive exploitation thereof, so even a monopoly is permitted. A mere increase in market share is permissible.

Advocate General Roemer emphasised in his Opinion that '[t]he only question of interest in the present case ... is purely whether Article 86 [Article 82] also applies if an undertaking in a dominant position on the market, by means of the acquisition of another undertaking, reinforces its position on the market, to such an extent that "in practice" nothing remains in the way of competition of economic significance'.[69] By using the word 'also', Roemer considered whether Article 82, in addition to exploitative practices where the undertaking *uses* its power to harm consumers directly, also prohibits practices where the undertaking *strengthens* its market power in such a way that no competition of significance is left in the market. He concluded that there is no legal basis in Article 82 for finding that dominant undertakings are not allowed to increase their market power by acquiring another undertaking. Roemer based his conclusion on several observations, three of which were: (i) Article 82 does not distinguish between different degrees of dominance, (ii) Article 82 does not contain a provision such as the merger provision in Article 66 of the ECSC Treaty[70] and (iii) Article 82 does not prohibit the mere 'hindrance' of competition. The latter point is in tune with the intentions of some of the drafters of the Treaty. For example, Hans Von der Groeben held that: 'what should be prohibited in the case of monopolies is not the hindrance of competition but only abuse of a dominant position in the market'.[71]

However, the ECJ interpreted 'abuse' to cover changes in the structure of an undertaking which lead to a disturbance of competition in the common market.[72] The court relied on a teleological interpretation by examining Article 82 in the light of Article 3(1)(g), according to which competition must not be distorted.[73] This shows that abuse of a dominant position cannot be examined in isolation, and that the focus should not only be on the conduct itself, but also on its impacts. Interpreting Article 82 in the light of Article 3(1)(g) means that conduct of a dominant

[69] Opinion of Advocate General Roemer in *Continental Can*, supra note 7, delivered on 21 November 1972, 254.

[70] The ECSC Treaty was in force at the time.

[71] This quote is taken from I. Forrester, 'The Modernisation of EC Antitrust Policy: Compatibility, Efficiency, Legal Security' in C. D. Ehlermann and I. Atanasiu (eds.), *The Modernisation of EC Antitrust Policy* (Oxford: Hart Publishing, 2001) 75, 84.

[72] *Continental Can*, supra note 7, para. 20.

[73] Ibid., paras. 23 and 26.

undertaking is abusive if it runs counter to the purpose of protecting competition in the common market from distortions.

The court concluded that an abuse may occur 'if an undertaking in a dominant position strengthens such position in such a way that the degree of dominance reached substantially fetters competition, i.e. that only undertakings remain in the market whose behaviour depends on the dominant one'.[74] Article 82 'is not only aimed at practices which may cause damage to consumers directly, but also at those which are detrimental to them through their impact on an effective competition structure'.[75] The court explained that Article 82 is also designed to protect the structure of the market, which is an important step towards protecting competition. By protecting the structure of competition, consumers are protected indirectly, presumably because where competition is impaired disadvantages for consumers are also feared, at least in the long term. Thus, the objective is to guarantee effective competition for the benefits it delivers to consumers.[76] An alteration to the competitive structure in itself is not objectionable, and may even follow from a natural selection of the best competitors. However, it becomes unacceptable where the alteration of the market structure is so significant that it harms the process of competition and thereby harms consumers. Thus, the court explained that an alteration to the structure of the market can harm consumers by endangering their freedom of action in the market:[77]

> If it can, irrespective of any fault, be regarded as an abuse if an undertaking holds a position so dominant that the objectives of the treaty are circumvented by an alteration to the supply structure which seriously endangers the consumer's freedom of action in the market, such a case necessarily exists, if practically all competition is eliminated. Such a narrow precondition as the elimination of all competition need not exist in all cases. But the Commission, basing its decision on such elimination of competition, had to state legally sufficient reasons or, at least, had to prove that competition was so essentially affected that the remaining competitors could no longer provide a sufficient counterweight.

Not only did the court establish a connection between significant changes of market structure and harm to consumers, it also sent a clear message to the Commission. Where the Commission reaches a decision based on elimination of competition (exclusion), it will have to explain or prove how

[74] Ibid., para. 26. [75] Ibid., para. 26.

[76] S. Bishop and M. Walker, *The Economics of EC Competition Law: Concepts, Application and Measurement* (London: Sweet & Maxwell, 2nd edn, 2002) 244.

[77] *Continental Can*, supra note 7, para. 29.

consumers are affected. Despite the *Continental Can* case not using the terminology of consumer welfare in the form of efficiency as defined in chapter 2, the ECJ was concerned with the prejudice to consumers. Some argue that the connection between significant changes of market structure and harm to consumers has been neglected over time, such that even insignificant changes in the market structure have become associated with harmful effects on consumers, and therefore have been caught by Article 82.[78]

4.2 *Signs of consumer welfare in recent jurisprudence*

Harm to end consumers is directly apparent in some cases,[79] but in other cases it is difficult to detect direct harm to consumers.[80] In *Österreichische Postsparkasse AG*, the CFI referred directly to the welfare of end consumers.[81] Although the case concerned the interpretation of 'legitimate interest within the meaning of Article 3(2) of Regulation No. 17', the court held that 'the ultimate purpose of the rules [competition rules] that seek to ensure that competition is not distorted in the internal market is to increase the well-being of consumers'.[82] Similarly in the Spanish *GlaxoSmithKline* case, the CFI said: 'the objective assigned to Article 81(1) EC ... is to prevent undertakings, by restricting competition between themselves or with third parties, from reducing the welfare of the final consumer of the products in question'.[83] The case specifically concerned Article 81, but as the ECJ emphasised in *Continental Can*, Articles 81 and 82 'seek to achieve the same aim on different levels'.[84]

In *Oscar Bronner*,[85] Mediaprint had refused to give a rival newspaper access to its nationwide home-delivery scheme. The ECJ had to consider whether this refusal to give access was an abuse of Article 82. Advocate

[78] E. Rousseva, 'Modernizing by Eradicating: How the Commission's New Approach to Article 81 EC Dispenses with the Need to Apply Article 82 EC to Vertical Restraints' 42 *Common Market Law Review* (2005) 587, 592.

[79] For example, COMP 37.685 *GVG/FS*, para. 145; OJ [2000] L5/55 *1998 Football World Cup*, para. 100; *General Motors*, supra note 28, paras. 11–12; Case C-241/91P *RTE and ITP v. Commission (Magill)* [1995] ECR I-743, para. 54.

[80] See discussion in chapter 5.

[81] Joined Cases T-213/01 and T-214/01 *Österreichische Postsparkasse AG and Bank für Arbeit und Wirtschaft AG v. EC Commission* [2006] ECR II-1601, para. 103.

[82] Ibid., para. 115.

[83] *GlaxoSmithKline*, supra note 48, para. 118. This was overturned on appeal, supra note 54, para. 63.

[84] *Continental Can*, supra note 7, para. 25.

[85] Case C-7/97 *Oscar Bronner GmbH & Co. KG v. Mediaprint Zeitungs- und Zeitschriftenverlag GmbH & Co. KG* [1998] ECR I-7791, [1999] 4 CMLR 112.

General Jacobs emphasised in his Opinion[86] that the primary purpose of Article 82 is to prevent distortion of competition to safeguard the interests of consumers, rather than to protect competitors. He particularly considered consumers' long-term interest:[87]

> In the long term it is generally pro-competitive and in the interest of consumers to allow a company to retain for its own use facilities which it has developed for the purpose of its business. For example, if access to a production, purchasing or distribution facility were allowed too easily there would be no incentive for a competitor to develop competing facilities. Thus while competition was increased in the short term it would be reduced in the long term. Moreover, the incentive for a dominant undertaking to invest in efficient facilities would be reduced if its competitors were, upon request, able to share the benefits. Thus the mere fact that by retaining a facility for its own use a dominant undertaking retains an advantage over a competitor cannot justify requiring access to it.

The ECJ considered whether Mediaprint's refusal would eliminate all competition in the daily newspaper market. It found that was not the case, as there were other methods of distributing daily newspapers, such as by post and through sale in shops and at kiosks.[88] Moreover, that it would not be impossible, or even unreasonably difficult, for any other publisher of daily newspapers to establish, alone or in cooperation with other publishers, its own nationwide home-delivery scheme.[89] This resulted in the court concluding that there were no technical, legal or even economic obstacles to establishing such a delivery. It is difficult to say whether the court considered the refusal to give access acceptable because either (i) it did not make it impossible, or even unreasonably difficult, for any other publisher of daily newspapers to participate in the market, and therefore the refusal did not restrict their freedom, or (ii) because not all competition was eliminated, so consumers would not be harmed.

The conclusion of this section is that the Commission appeared to view consumer welfare as an important objective of Article 82, but the Community Courts have been reluctant to use the terminology of consumer welfare in Article 82 cases. Despite this, some cases appear to be concerned with the welfare of consumers. However, the lack of an explanation of the counterfactuals makes it difficult to say whether the courts were really concerned with consumer welfare. Despite the Commission focus on consumer welfare, Article 82 cannot be reduced to consumer

[86] Opinion of Advocate General Jacobs in *Oscar Bronner*, ibid., delivered on 28 May 1998.

[87] Ibid., para. 57. [88] *Oscar Bronner*, supra note 85, para. 43.

[89] Ibid., para. 44.

welfare only, as Article 82 has pursued a variety of other objectives.[90] Moreover, the objective of consumer welfare potentially conflicts with that of freedom of competition. The latter will be discussed before considering the potential conflict in section 2.1 of chapter 4.

5. Freedom of competition

Competition is seen as 'the best stimulant of economic activity since it guarantees the widest possible freedom of action to all'.[91] Some argue that the objective of economic freedom (freedom of competition), defined as the freedom to participate in the marketplace unimpaired by the power of other companies,[92] associated with ordoliberalism, has had an impact on Article 82.[93] As chapter 2 explained, for ordoliberalism the main objective of competition policy was the protection of economic freedom of action of all market players.[94] The Commission emphasised the importance of economic freedom, 'the freedom and right of initiative of the individual economic operators', in its foreword to the *Annual Report on Competition Policy* in 1985.[95] This section now discusses whether economic freedom is considered an objective in some Article 82 jurisprudence, and why it is pursued.

5.1 Traces of economic freedom in jurisprudence

The previous sections showed that the free movement rules give economic actors several economic rights, while the competition rules impose some

[90] V. Mertikopoulou, 'DG Competition's Discussion Paper on the Application of Article 82 of the EC Treaty to Exclusionary Abuses: The Proposed Economic Reform from a Legal Point of View' 28(4) *European Competition Law Review* (2007) 241, 251.

[91] First *Annual Report*, supra note 60, 11.

[92] Supra note 3.

[93] C. Ahlborn and C. Grave, 'Walter Eucken and Ordoliberalism: An Introduction from a Consumer Welfare Perspective' 2(2) *Competition Policy International* (2006) 196; Monti, supra note 4; L. Lovdahl Gormsen, 'Article 82 EC: Where Are We Coming From and Where Are We Going To?' 2(2) *Competition Law Review* (2005), 5; D. Gerber, *Law and Competition in Twentieth Century Europe: Protecting Prometheus* (Oxford University Press, 1998); Rousseva, supra note 78; D. Evans, 'Roundtable Discussion about the US Supreme Court's Decision in *Verizon v. Trinko*' 7(2) *Global Competition Review* (2004) 26; B. Hawk, 'Article 82 and Section 2' in OECD, *Paper on Competition on the Merits*, DAF/COMP(2005)27; L. Lovdahl Gormsen, 'The Conflict between Economic Freedom and Consumer Welfare in the Modernisation of Article 82 EC' 3(2) *European Competition Journal* (2007) 329.

[94] W. Möschel, 'Competition Policy from an Ordo Point of View' in H. Willgerodt and A. Peacock (eds.), *German Neo-liberals and the Social Market Economy* (London: Macmillan, 1989) 146.

[95] Commission's fifteenth *Annual Report on Competition Policy* (1985).

limits upon economic actors' economic power so as to avoid distortion of competition. Thus, all market participants have the freedom to participate in the marketplace as long as they do not exceed the limits placed upon them by the competition rules.

In the *Commercial Solvents* case, the ECJ confirmed, as will be discussed below, that a refusal to supply a downstream customer was an abuse of Article 82.[96] Judge Pescatore, then President of the ECJ, confirmed in a speech that the court had intended 'to protect a small firm, rather than free competition for the benefit of consumers'.[97] This is an interesting insight and it could indicate that the ECJ reached its conclusion by protecting the economic freedom of Zoja. Some commentators have supported Judge Pescatore's viewpoint.[98] Moreover, the Commission's *Annual Report on Competition Policy* in 1978 also appeared to support the view.[99] In order to guarantee equality of opportunity, freedom of access to business and freedom of choice within the common market, dominant companies cannot refuse to supply long-standing customers.[100]

Commercial Solvent Corporation (CSC), an American corporation, produced 1-nitropropane (nitropropane) and a derivative thereof, 2 amino-1-butanol (aminobutanol), an intermediate product for the production of ethambutol. The latter was a compound used in the treatment of pulmonary tuberculosis. CSC supplied aminobutanol to customers in the common market through its Italian subsidiary, Istituto Chemioterapico Italiano SpA (ICI), in which it owned 51 per cent of the shares.[101] At the time of the judgment, the three main producers of ethambutol in the common market were the American company Cyanamid Company (acting through its Italian subsidiary Cyanamid Italia), CSC/ICI (ICI acted as a re-seller for CSC in the common market) and an Italian company Laboratorio Chimico Farmaceutico Giorgio Zoja (Zoja). Aminobutanol was an essential material in the production of ethambutol. CSC used to have a patent in the method of production of nitropropane for producing aminobutanol. The patent had expired, but CSC held a *de facto* monopoly due to its know-how, and the high barriers to entry to the market in the

[96] *Commercial Solvents*, supra note 23.

[97] V. Korah, 'The Interface between Intellectual Property Rights and Antitrust: The European Experience' 69(3) *Antitrust Law Journal* (2001) 801, 808.

[98] A. S. Pathak, 'Articles 85 and 86 and Anticompetitive Exclusion in EEC Competition Law: Part 1' 10(1) *European Competition Law Review* (1989) 74, 88.

[99] Eighth *Annual Report on Competition Policy* (1978).

[100] Ibid., 9.

[101] CSC was the US parent company and ICI was the Italian subsidiary. Under the single economic entity doctrine they were to be considered as one undertaking.

form of high costs and the complexity of the necessary equipment. From 1966 to November 1969, Zoja got its aminobutanol, for its ethambutol production, from CSC/ICI. Due to a price increase for aminobutanol, Zoja found alternative suppliers for aminobutanol. These suppliers used aminobutanol for paint, not for pharmaceuticals. In 1970, these alternative suppliers would no longer supply Zoja as CSC had required them not to supply Zoja.[102] When Zoja tried to obtain supplies from other suppliers, Zoja was told that CSC had either ceased to deliver or forbidden the suppliers from selling the raw material for pharmaceutical use.[103] Zoja, which used to be the main customer of ICI, returned to ICI for supply, but ICI then refused to supply it.

In considering the question of abuse, the ECJ found that the evidence showed that, in 1970, ICI started manufacturing its own product based on aminobutanol. To facilitate its own access to the downstream market for that product, CSC decided not to supply Zoja when it reapplied for supply.[104] CSC was able to leverage its market power on the upstream market to eliminate Zoja on the downstream market. By 'cutting off' the supply to Zoja, CSC improved ICI's position and indirectly its own position in Europe on the downstream market. The latter was a market with extremely low supply-side substitutability. Thus, the court specifically rejected claims that other nascent technologies in the trial stage were substitutes for CSC's raw materials.[105] Instead, the court held that the refusal to supply risked eliminating all competition on the part of Zoja:[106]

> [A]n undertaking being in a dominant position as regards the production of raw material and therefore able to control the supply to manufacturers of derivatives cannot, just because it decides to start manufacturing these derivatives (in competition with its former customers), act in such a way as to eliminate their competition which, in the case in question, would have amounted to eliminating one of the principal manufacturers of ethambutol in the common market ... [A]n undertaking which has a dominant position in the market in raw materials and which, with the object of reserving such raw material for manufacturing its own derivatives, refuses to supply a customer, which is itself a manufacturer of these derivatives, and therefore *risks* eliminating all competition on the part

[102] E. Fox, 'Monopolization and Dominance in the United States and the European Community: Efficiency, Opportunity, and Fairness' 61 *Notre Dame Law Review* (1986) 981, 994.

[103] V. Korah, '*Istituto Chemioterapico Italiano SpA and Commercial Solvents Corporation v. Commission of the European Communities*' 11 *Common Market Law Review* (1974) 248, 249.

[104] *Commercial Solvents*, supra note 23, para. 24.

[105] Ibid., para. 15.

[106] Ibid., para. 25. Emphasis added.

> of this customer, is abusing its dominant position within the meaning of Article 86 [Article 82].

In essence the court was saying that refusal to supply Zoja – a customer dependent on supply from ICI and a potential competitor of ICI in the downstream market – was harmful, as it eliminated all competition on the part of Zoja. The latter was economically dependent on ICI and had no other sufficient and reasonable possibilities of finding another supplier. This was particularly so as CSC had banned its customers in the paint market from supplying Zoja.

Unlike in *Oscar Bronner*, where the ECJ found that not all competition was eliminated by the refusal to give access, the court found that all competition was eliminated on the part of Zoja. If the aim of the case is to protect the economic freedom of Zoja then it would have made sense to find an abuse where Zoja is eliminated. However, if the aim is consumer welfare, then the court ought to have explained how the elimination of Zoja would harm consumers (tuberculosis patients). Perhaps the court assumed that Zoja's elimination would harm tuberculosis patients, because it relied on the counterfactual that in the absence of the refusal to supply Zoja, both Zoja and CSC/ICI would have been present in the downstream market. This would mean more competition in the downstream market, to the benefit of consumers. If this was the court's counterfactual, arguably consumer welfare would have increased in the form of more choice. However, there was no examination of the likelihood of CSC/ICI's successful entrance on the downstream market while supplying Zoja. The court pointed out that CSC/ICI's conduct had been adopted to reserve the raw material to itself,[107] which could indicate that CSC/ICI would have been unable to enter the downstream market if it was still supplying Zoja. There was no examination of the likelihood of consumer harm following the conduct. Would consumers be harmed by CSC/ICI *replacing* Zoja in the downstream market? That depends on CSC/ICI's efficiency in the downstream market.

The assumed counterfactual also relied on the hope that Zoja would have been able to compete with CSC/ICI in the downstream market. This is far from certain. The situation could easily have been that the vertical integration of CSC/ICI in the downstream market would have forced Zoja to leave the market if CSC/ICI was more efficient than Zoja. Is it likely that CSC/ICI would have been more efficient than Zoja? Presumably yes, as CSC/ICI would probably have been able to obtain aminobutanol more

[107] Ibid., para. 25.

cheaply than Zoja as supplies came from its parent company. In this case, Zoja's exit from the market would not have been because of the refusal to supply, but due to lack of efficiency. Arguably, it is the *artificial* hindrance of competition that concerned the court. Presumably the court would not have cared about Zoja's exit from the market if it had been due to CSC/ICI's efficiency, as competition would have selected the best competitors to stay in the market. However, the court pointed out that CSC/ICI's conduct had been adopted to reserve the raw material to itself, a possibility that existed due to its market power in the upstream market. The court focused on the market power on the upstream market to conclude that CSC/ICI thereby reserved to itself the downstream market, without considering whether CSC/ICI's final product was sufficiently insulated from competition to give it power in the downstream market. This does not go far enough if the objective to be met is consumer welfare. Unless CSC/ICI's vertical integration itself raised barriers to entry, the price charged to consumers after this integration was likely to be no higher than the price to consumers before the integration.[108] According to the Commission's decision, there were high barriers to entry in the form of high costs and the complexity of the necessary equipment and industry know-how.[109] These barriers however were not established because of the vertical integration, but existed already before the integration. The most likely hindrance caused by CSC/ICI's refusal to supply Zoja would have been that Zoja and presumably other trading parties were unable to get the essential raw material to produce ethambutol; they were dependent on CSC/ICI.

Perhaps the court did believe that consumers would be harmed by CSC/ICI's conduct, but why did the court not talk about consumer welfare if that was what it was really concerned about? The court appears to have aimed at protecting the economic freedom of Zoja, and it did not analyse how the elimination of Zoja would harm consumers. It is clear that if – and that is a big if – both Zoja and CSC/ICI had been in the downstream market, consumers would have had more choice, but more choice does not necessarily increase consumer welfare, as will be discussed in chapter 5.

In addition to freedom to participate in the marketplace, the Community Courts have been concerned with freedom to choose sources of supply. In the *Hoffmann-La Roche* case, the ECJ held that Hoffmann-La Roche – a pharmaceutical company that, among other things, supplied

[108] Fox, supra note 102, 1002.

[109] OJ [1972] L299/51 *Istituto Chemioterapico Italiano SpA and Commercial Solvents Corporation.*

vitamins – had abused its dominant position by entering into exclusive purchasing agreements with some customers in return for loyalty rebates.[110] The court stated that if a dominant undertaking 'ties purchasers ... to obtain all or most of their requirements exclusively from [the dominant undertaking]' then that is an abuse under Article 82, 'whether the obligation in question is stipulated without further qualification or whether it is undertaken in consideration of the grant of a rebate'.[111] It condemned Hoffmann-La Roche's rebates, stating that 'they are not based on an economic transaction which justifies this burden or benefit but are designed to deprive the purchaser of or restrict his possible choices of sources of supply and to deny other producers access to the market'.[112] The court condemned the rebates as they were designed to deprive or restrict the purchaser of his possible choice of source of supply. Arguably, purchasers were not forced to get their supply from Hoffmann-La Roche, but wanted to do so due to the rebate. Some argue that the court is willing to find an abuse even where the customers are not *obliged* to obtain all their supplies from the dominant undertaking, but are *induced* to take supply by means of fidelity rebates.[113] The court's view was that an exclusivity agreement in conjunction with the rebate restricts customers' freedom of action in the market by preventing them from getting supplies from other suppliers. Moreover, competitors' freedom of action was also limited by the conduct, which foreclosed their access to the customer base.

Similarly in *Michelin I*, the ECJ said that 'the discounts tend to remove or restrict the buyer's freedom to choose his sources of supply, [and] to bar competition from access to the market'.[114] In *BPB Industries*, the CFI opined that the prevention of another market player from obtaining supplies from its competitors was an abuse where the purpose was to weaken already fragile competition further. The court said that 'the application by a supplier who is in a dominant position, and upon whom as a result the customer is more or less dependent, of any form of loyalty rebate through which the supplier endeavours, by means of financial advantages, to prevent its customers from obtaining supplies from competitors constitutes an abuse'.[115] In *Irish Sugar*, the CFI held that the Irish Sugar company

[110] *Hoffmann-La Roche*, supra note 24.
[111] Ibid., para. 89. [112] Ibid., para. 90.
[113] E. White, 'Some Important Aspects of the *Hoffmann-La Roche* Judgment' 77 *Law Society's Gazette* (1980) 246.
[114] *Michelin I*, supra note 24, para. 73.
[115] Case T-65/89 *BPB Industries and British Gypsum v. Commission* [1993] ECR II-389, para. 120.

had committed an abuse by operating a system of sugar export rebates, granted on the sales of industrial sugar to companies exporting to other Member States. Similar to the approach taken in *Hoffmann-La Roche*, the CFI referred to the abusive nature of loyalty rebates and stated that 'a rebate granted by an undertaking in a dominant position ... without that rebate being capable or being regarded as a normal quantity discount ... constitutes an abuse of that dominant position, since such a practice can only be intended to tie the customers to which it is granted and place competitors in an unfavourable competitive position'.[116]

The concern with refusal to supply, as well as rebates, is the element of foreclosure, which will be discussed in chapter 5.

6. Conclusion

This chapter discussed what objectives are considered important in the application of Article 82 and why some of them are pursued. It found that Article 82 is part of a system designed, amongst other things, to safeguard competition in the common market from distortion. Undistorted competition must be protected to achieve the broader aims of the Treaty. The courts have made clear that Article 82 is not intended only or primarily to protect the immediate interests of individual competitors or consumers, but to protect the structure of the market, which is weakened by the very presence of the dominant undertaking on the market. As a result of that weakness, the dominant company has a special responsibility towards competition in the market.

Besides the overall aim of protecting undistorted competition, market integration has been, and still is, considered an important objective. It was discussed whether market integration is a means to an end of other objectives. There are different views on this. Some cases appear to favour market integration and freedom at the expense of consumer welfare, whereas other cases take the reverse position. In addition to market integration, there are some traces of consumer welfare in the Article 82 case law, although the Community Courts do not use that terminology directly. Some policy statements support the consumer welfare objective, but it is more vaguely pronounced in jurisprudence. Despite the Commission's focus on consumer welfare, Article 82 cannot be reduced to consumer welfare only, as Article 82 has pursued a variety of other objectives. Given

[116] Case T-228/97 *Irish Sugar v. Commission* [1999] ECR II-2969, para. 213.

this, the Commission appears to give a disproportionate amount of attention to consumer welfare.

Finally, the chapter found that Article 82 pursues an objective of economic freedom. This is in order to protect individual market players' access to and participation in the market, and is therefore closely linked to foreclosure.

The main and overarching objective in Article 82 is undistorted competition. This is important if there is a need for balancing different conflicting objectives as undistorted competition will be the benchmark against which to balance. Undistorted competition, as compared to market integration, must be the overarching objective, as market integration is a means to an end of other objectives. The next chapter considers whether there is a conflict between the objectives of economic freedom and consumer welfare.

4

The legitimacy of the consumer welfare goal in Article 82

1. Introduction

Following the review of Article 82, consumer welfare has been given primacy. Whether this is legitimate depends on at least three factors, which will be discussed in this chapter. The first is whether a potential conflict exists between economic freedom (freedom of competition)[1] and consumer welfare. Only if there is no potential tension between these two objectives, or where economic freedom is a means to an end for consumer welfare, is it acceptable for the Commission to give priority to consumer welfare. In case of a conflict, the Commission can only give priority to consumer welfare in the hierarchy of the different objectives pursued by Article 82 if the conflict is recognised and resolved by the ECJ in favour of consumer welfare.

The second consideration is whether economic freedom is considered a fundamental right. Even if there is no conflict between the two goals, consumer welfare cannot be given primacy if economic freedom is considered a fundamental right. A fundamental right requires that it be protected as a right of a higher rank. If economic freedom has status as a fundamental right, then giving priority to the utilitarian goal of consumer welfare would undermine the Community legal order, as it would prioritise a utilitarian approach over a fundamental rights-based approach. This would have to be properly debated and would require support from the Community Courts. If the latter do not favour consumer welfare, the Commission can lobby for a change, but the Commission's decisions would have to follow ECJ case law. Consumer welfare is a utilitarian rule, so the scenario is not that the Commission is giving priority to one fundamental right over another fundamental right in the normative hierarchy of laws. Economic freedom could be considered a fundamental right in

[1] Freedom of competition and economic freedom are used interchangeably in this chapter, as they both mean that the economic system should allow all individuals the freedom to participate in the marketplace unimpaired by the power of others.

two situations: first, if the Treaty is based on the ordoliberal economic constitution (which protects freedom of competition as a fundamental right); or second, if economic freedom is considered in itself a fundamental right in the Community legal order.

The third factor is whether the phrase 'thereby placing them [the other trading parties] at a competitive disadvantage' in Article 82(2)(c) refers to consumers. A negative answer could mean that consumer welfare cannot be given priority. These three factors will be discussed respectively in sections 2, 3 and 4. Section 5 concludes.

2. Economic freedom and consumer welfare

Whether the Commission's priority of consumer welfare is legitimate depends in part on whether there is a conflict between economic freedom and consumer welfare.[2] Section 2.1 highlights the potential conflict. Section 2.2 adopts chapter 2's definition of consumer welfare and examines how consumer welfare and economic freedom protect the process of competition, in order to consider whether economic freedom is a means to an end for consumer welfare. Section 2.3 provides a summary.

2.1 The potential conflict

A potential and serious conflict can arise between economic freedom and consumer welfare in at least two situations. The first is where competition amongst rivals is protected but does not benefit consumer welfare, for example, 'competitors that are not (yet) as efficient as the dominant company' are protected in the short term[3] or less efficient competitors are protected.[4] This may mean that there are more firms in the market and potentially more competition. This may lead to consumer welfare in the long run, if those protected competitors become efficient over time. However, one needs to be careful not to conclude that the larger the

[2] This section of the chapter partly relies on an article the author wrote in 2007: L. Lovdahl Gormsen, 'The Conflict between Economic Freedom and Consumer Welfare in the Modernisation of Article 82 EC' 3(2) *European Competition Journal* (2007) 329–44.

[3] DG COMP, *Discussion Paper on the Application of Article 82 of the Treaty to Exclusionary Abuses* (December 2005) ('*Discussion Paper*') para. 67. Available at: http://ec.europa.eu.int/comm/competition/antitrust/others/discpaper2005.pdf.

[4] OJ [2009] C45/7 *Guidance on the Commission's Enforcement Priorities in Applying Article 82 EC Treaty to Abusive Exclusionary Conduct by Dominant Undertakings ('Guidance Paper')* para. 23.

number of firms the higher the welfare.[5] If less efficient firms are protected or subsidised, it may prevent market competition from selecting the best firms. By protecting a competitor by curtailing the power of a dominant supplier, the consumer may benefit through increased choice and a reallocation of profits from the dominant supplier to competing suppliers. As these competitors will probably not have the ability to reap monopoly profits, these profits would be expected to be passed back to the consumer through reduced prices. If these effects outweigh the value of any above-cost discount offered by the dominant supplier, consumers gain from overall price reductions. While the move to protect competitors to the dominant supplier *may* increase choice and potentially improve allocative efficiency through lower prices,[6] this is not guaranteed. Nor is it guaranteed that dynamic movements towards productive and dynamic efficiency will be best facilitated in this way.[7] In some circumstances, it is plausible that the protected market players will become efficient over time.[8] However, it is also possible that the most productive way of supplying customers will be through fewer suppliers, particularly when economies of scale are great. Depending on which of these effects is the greatest, the consumer could gain or lose from such measures.[9]

The second potential conflict situation is where an exclusion of some small and medium-sized companies, which may lack economies of scale, would not harm consumer welfare if these companies were unable to guarantee consumer welfare in the form of lower prices, better quality and an effective choice. However, it would harm the excluded or impaired companies' economic freedom as they would no longer be able to participate in the market.

In the case of a conflict between economic freedom and consumer welfare, the Community Courts must make a choice as to whether they favour economic freedom at the expense of consumer welfare or vice versa. A way of examining this is by assessing how Article 82 protects the process of competition.

[5] M. Motta, *Competition Policy: Theory and Practice* (Cambridge University Press, 2004) 51.

[6] Allocative efficiency refers to the way in which resources are allocated to the production of the goods and services that society (consumers) most values, as defined in chapter 2.

[7] Productive efficiency refers to the effective use (produced at the lowest cost) of resources and dynamic efficiency refers to the extent to which a company introduces new products or new processes of production, as defined in chapter 2.

[8] J. Seon Hur, 'The Evolution of Competition Policy and its Impact on Economic Development in Korea' in UNCTAD Report on *Competition, Competitiveness and Development: Lessons from Developing Countries* (2004) 227–49.

[9] See J. Vickers, 'Abuse of Market Power' 115 *Economic Journal* (2005) F244, F250.

2.2 *Protecting the competitive process as a means to an end or an end in itself*

'[A]ntitrust law is designed to protect and facilitate the competitive process itself, and the only way to do that effectively is to understand what one is trying to protect or facilitate.'[10]

This is hardly a new insight, but nonetheless important. Whether the process of competition is protected in itself or as an outcome for what it brings is an essential distinction, as the former does not allow any restriction on the process of competition whereas the latter enables the competitive process to be restricted to achieve an outcome that the process could not itself provide. Some argue that protecting the competitive process intrinsically has heavily influenced the Community's conception of competition law.[11] Ordoliberals consider that the process of competition has intrinsic value, as the process needs to be protected in itself to preserve the freedom of the individual in that process. This approach has been linked to Kantian philosophy.[12] This is a philosophy preferring the protection of human dignity and the fight against the instrumentalisation of human nature rather than a neo-classical position. Freedom of competition is so important that the process should be protected even where competition is inefficient.[13] Ordoliberals would prefer a state of inefficiency coupled with freedom, rather than an efficient but totalitarian state.[14] That said, ordoliberals saw economic efficiency as a generic term for growth and for the encouragement and development of technical progress, and for allocative efficiency. However, they considered efficiency as an indirect goal

[10] D. P. Wood, 'The Role of Economics and Economists in Competition Cases' 1(1) *OECD Journal of Competition Law and Policy* (1999) 82, 83.

[11] O. Odudu, *The Boundaries of EC Competition Law: The Scope of Article 81* (Oxford University Press, 2006) 15.

[12] E. J. Mestmäcker, 'Bausteine zu einer Wirtschaftsverfassung: Franz Böhm in Jena', reprinted in Mestmäcker, *Wirtschaft und Verfassung in der Europäischen Union* (Baden-Baden: Nomos Verlagsgesellschaft, 2nd edn, 2006) 123–7.

[13] W. Eucken and H. Grossman-Doerth, 'What Kind of Economic and Social System?' in H. Willgerodt and A. Peacock (eds.), *Germany's Social Market Economy: Origins and Evolution* (Basingstoke: Macmillan, 1989) 34–7; D. Hildebrand, *The Role of Economic Analysis in the EC Competition Rules* (The Hague: Kluwer Law International, 2nd edn, 2002) 153–62; R. Van den Bergh and P. D. Camesasca, *European Competition Law and Economics: A Comparative Perspective* (Antwerp: Intersentia, 2001) 136–7; D. Gerber, *Law and Competition in Twentieth Century Europe: Protecting Prometheus* (Oxford: Clarendon Press, 1998) 37.

[14] C. Watrin, 'Germany's Social Market Economy' in Alastair Kilmarnock (ed.), *The Social Market and the State* (London: Social Market Foundation, 1999) 91–5.

derived from individual freedom.[15] Ordoliberalism cannot be ignored as its competition policy has had a profound influence on EU competition law[16] and on the case law of the Community Courts and the Commission's decisional practice.[17]

Consumer welfare, as it was defined in chapter 2, is explicitly concerned with consumer gain in the form of lower prices, higher-quality products, a wider selection of goods and services and innovation. Consumer welfare takes a neo-classical position which values welfare without any consideration of the position of individuals in its utilitarian calculus.[18] According to the utilitarian majoritarian view of consumer welfare,[19] safeguarding competition to protect individual economic freedom is not a relevant consideration unless it benefits consumers.[20] The competitive process is a product of demand and supply and must be protected against distortion to safeguard the outcome flowing from an undistorted process of competition. In this view, the process of competition must be protected instrumentally to guarantee the best outcome for consumers.

The analysis of case law in previous chapters shows that Article 82 has prohibited conduct which endangered the freedom of market participants by altering the competitive market structure. Prohibiting conduct where

15 W. Möschel, 'Competition Policy from an Ordo Point of View' in H. Willgerodt and A. Peacock (eds.), *German Neo-liberals and the Social Market Economy* (London: Macmillan, 1989) 146.

16 D. Evans, 'Roundtable Discussion about the US Supreme Court's Decision in *Verizon v. Trinko*' 7(2) *Global Competition Review* (2004) 26; B. Hawk, 'Article 82 and Section 2' in OECD, *Paper on Competition on the Merits*, DAF/COMP(2005)27, 253; D. Gerber, 'Constitutionalizing the Economy: German Neo-liberalism, Competition Law and the "New" Europe' 42 *American Journal of Comparative Law* (1994) 25, 73.

17 P. Lowe, 'Consumer Welfare and Efficiency: New Guiding Principles of Competition Policy?', 27 March 2007, the Thirteenth International Conference on Competition and Fourteenth European Competition Day, 2.

18 Möschel, supra note 15, 148–9.

19 The rule of utility is that the measure of good is whatever brings the greatest happiness to the greatest number of people. Since utilitarians judge all actions by their ability to maximise good consequences, any harm to one individual can always be justified by a greater gain to other individuals. This is true even if the loss for the one individual is large and the gain for the others is marginal, as long as enough individuals receive the small benefit. Some critics reject utilitarianism on the basis that it seems to be incompatible with human rights. For example, if slavery or torture is beneficial for the population as a whole, it could theoretically be justified by utilitarianism. Utilitarian theory thus seems to overlook the rights of the individual: see J. Waldron, 'Rights' in R. E. Goodin and P. Pettit (eds.), *A Companion to Contemporary Political Philosophy* (Oxford: Blackwell Publishing, 1995) 581.

20 Such benefits to consumers however do not include consumers gaining separate utility from, for example, preferring small corner shops to bigger supermarkets.

firms are seeking to use their economic power to undermine the market's competitive structures, without considering whether such behaviour is likely to harm consumer welfare, may be viewed as nothing more than protecting smaller competitors from aggregation of economic power.[21] Damage to the competitive market structure is imbued in the very definition of abuse, articulated by the ECJ in *Hoffmann-La Roche*.[22] In general, by protecting the structure of competition, priority is given to the process, and not necessarily to the outcome of competition. If, by protecting the process of competition, consumers are indirectly protected, then that is a bonus, but not the main aim. This belief is supported by Advocate General Kokott in her Opinion in *British Airways*:[23]

> Article 82 EC … is not designed only or primarily to protect the immediate interests of individual competitors or consumers, but to protect the structure of the market and thus competition as such (as an institution), which has already been weakened by the presence of the dominant undertaking on the market. In this way, consumers are also indirectly protected. Because where competition as such is damaged, disadvantages for consumers are also to be feared.

This replicates ordoliberal thinking, where the benefit of competition is a market characterised by a desirable process. Under the ordoliberal model, the aim of competition policy is 'the protection of individual economic freedom of action as a value in itself, or vice versa, the restraint of undue economic power'.[24] Thus, 'the protection of competition against restrictions is intended to safeguard competition as an institution or to guarantee the freedom of the individual'.[25] This philosophy also underpins Kokott's Opinion, in particular her reference to competition as an 'institution'.[26] Some argue that a focus on competition as an institution does not imply insensitivity to economic efficiency, as protecting an

[21] G. Amato, *Antitrust and the Bounds of Power* (Oxford: Hart Publishing, 1997) 69; E. M. Fox, 'Monopolization and Dominance in the United States and the European Community: Efficiency, Opportunity, and Fairness' 61 *Notre Dame Law Review* (1986) 981.

[22] Case 85/76 *Hoffmann-La Roche & Co. AG v. Commission* [1979] ECR 461, para. 91.

[23] Opinion of Advocate General Kokott in Case C-95/04P *British Airways plc v. Commission* [2007] ECR I-2331, delivered on 23 February 2006, para. 68.

[24] W. Möschel, 'The Proper Scope of Government Viewed from an Ordoliberal Perspective: The Example of Competition Policy' 157 *Journal of Institutional and Theoretical Economics* (2001) 3.

[25] A. Deringer, *The Competition Law of the European Economic Community: A Commentary on the EEC Rules of Competition (Articles 85 to 90) Including the Implementing Regulations and Directives* (New York: Commerce Clearing House, 1968) 14.

[26] Opinion of Advocate General Kokott, supra note 23, para. 69.

undistorted competitive process will generally tend to maximise wealth and consumer welfare, at least in the medium term.[27] Although Kokott does not believe that the aim of protecting the process of competition is to protect consumer welfare, she believes that consumers are indirectly protected if the structure of competition is protected. According to Kokott, priority is given to the process of competition, and if this 'indirectly' protects consumers, then this is a bonus, but not an aim. Priority is given to the process of competition, not the outcome. This approach favours economic freedom at the expense of consumer welfare.

DG Competition's Director General Philip Lowe disagrees. For him, consumer welfare must come at the expense of economic freedom, because the competitive process should not be protected intrinsically, but instrumentally:[28]

> [C]onsumer welfare and efficiency are the new guiding principles of EU competition policy. Whilst the competitive process is important as an instrument, and whilst in many instances the distortion of this process leads to consumer harm, its protection is not an aim in itself. The ultimate aim is the protection of consumer welfare, as an outcome of the competitive process.[29]

According to Lowe, the competitive process is protected instrumentally to safeguard the outcome, which is consumer welfare. If the competitive process is not to be protected in itself, it conflicts with the ordoliberal belief that individual economic freedom must be protected as a value in itself,[30] where *all* individuals should be allowed to participate in the competitive process unhampered by the economic power of others.[31] A focus on the process of competition in the long run rather than competition's short-term results would ensure that the remaining competitors in the market are not prevented from competing on the merits.[32] If ensuring

[27] T. Eilmansberger, 'How to Distinguish Good from Bad Competition under Article 82 EC: In Search of Clearer and More Coherent Standards for Anticompetitive Abuses' 42 *Common Market Law Review* (2005) 129, 135.

[28] Lowe, supra note 17, 2.

[29] Unlike Lowe, Eilmansberger argues that the protection of the competitive process is a goal in itself: see T. Eilmansberger, 'Dominance – the Lost Child? How Effects-based Rules Could and Should Change Dominance Analysis' *European Competition Journal* (July 2006) 15, 18.

[30] This is supported by Möschel, supra note 24.

[31] G. Monti, *EC Competition Law* (Cambridge University Press, 2007) 23. Emphasis added.

[32] P. Lowe at the Thirteenth Annual Conference on International Antitrust and Policy, 23 October 2003, the Fordham Antitrust Conference in Washington, 5. Available at: http://ec.europa.eu/competition/speeches/text/sp2003_040_En.pdf.

competition in the long run promotes consumer welfare, it could be argued that economic freedom provides consumer welfare. Adams and Brock believe that efficiency and consumer welfare are expected to flow from a system of economic freedom: 'The primary purpose of antitrust is to perpetuate and preserve a system of governance for a competitive, free enterprise economy. Efficiency and consumer welfare constitute ancillary benefits that are expected to flow from a system of economic freedom.'[33] Brodley argues that there can be unity between economic efficiency and the goal of economic freedom.[34] This is supported by Elzinga, who argues that economic efficiency and equity goals are not always mutually exclusive.[35] However, Lowe does not seem to believe that economic freedom is a means to the end of consumer welfare. Instead, he appears to believe that consumer welfare and efficiency are *new* guiding principles. If they are *new* principles, then they must replace some *old* principles. If economic freedom were considered to be an *old* principle and believed to be a means to an end of consumer welfare, there would be no need to 'replace' freedom of competition with consumer welfare. Whether Lowe considers economic freedom to be an *old* principle is uncertain, but he has acknowledged its influence within the jurisprudence:[36]

> The case-law of the European courts and also the decisional practice of the Commission were initially influenced by ordoliberal thought which has its origin in the so-called Freiburg School ... Competition was understood as a process of economic coordination on the basis of freedom of action. The protection of individual economic freedom – as a value in itself – was regarded as the primary objective of competition policy.

Some decisional and judicial practice of Article 82 takes a long-term perspective with an emphasis on rivalry, but there is no enquiry into relative efficiency. This reflects the ordoliberal approach.[37] Where there is no analysis of what efficiencies rivalry may bring, it becomes very difficult to know whether the aim of protecting the process of competition is to promote consumer welfare. Protecting rivalry (or competition) among market players is all very well, but rivalry can serve several desirable ends, including economic freedom and consumer welfare, and these ends may or may

[33] W. Adams and J. W. Brock, 'Antitrust and Efficiency: A Comment' 62 *New York University Law Review* (1987) 1116.

[34] J. F. Brodley, 'The Economic Goals of Antitrust: Efficiency, Consumer Welfare and Technological Progress' 62 *New York University Law Review* (1987) 1020, 1021.

[35] K. G. Elzinga 'The Goals of Antitrust: Other than Competition and Efficiency, What Else Counts?' 125 *University of Pennsylvania Law Review* (1977) 1191, 1193.

[36] Lowe, supra note 17, 2. [37] Hawk, supra note 16, 253.

not conflict with each other. Thus, protecting rivalry without looking at what it brings is nothing more than protecting the process of competition intrinsically. To avoid this, Monti encourages a focus on the outcome: '[t]o judge whether there is a distortion of competition it is more helpful to look to see whether the ends are met rather than whether firms are rivals, because it provides a more precise method to determine whether there is a market failure'.[38] Posner also sees competition as a means of achieving something else – efficiency – rather than as an end in itself. He argues that there is a danger in protecting competition as an end in itself, because the elimination of even a tiny rival would diminish competition.[39]

A focus on what competition may bring in the long term seems to be at the root of DG COMP's approach in protecting a 'not yet as efficient competitor'[40] and the Commission focus on 'less efficient competitors'.[41] Protecting less efficient competitors or 'not yet as efficient competitors' is taken to mean that there will be more firms in the market, which potentially could mean more competition in the long run, driving prices down and increasing allocative efficiency to the benefit of consumers. This is not necessarily a bad idea. However, it would require price regulation.[42] In this author's view, it may even be a good idea when liberalising a market dominated by a former state monopoly. In such a market, the former state monopoly will undoubtedly have a huge market share and it may take several years for other competitors to gain a foothold in the market. For example, state monopolies in certain sectors have established themselves in the market through the benefit of taxpayers' money and gained 'first mover advantages' from benefits that no other company has. Thus, when liberalising a market it may seem sensible to keep a 'not yet as efficient competitor' alive in the market. However, a practical problem with protecting less efficient competitors or 'not yet as efficient competitors' is that it would require competition authorities to produce a timeframe for the period they are willing to protect these competitors as well as a strategy for the various ways of doing it.[43] Besides the practical issue, it is questionable whether less efficient competitors will actually generate any efficiency to the benefit of consumer welfare, in the form of innovation

38 Monti, supra note 31, 22.

39 R. Posner, *Antitrust Law* (University of Chicago Press, 2nd edn, 2001) 28–9.

40 *Discussion Paper*, supra note 3, para. 67.

41 *Guidance Paper*, supra note 4, para. 23.

42 A. S. Edlin, 'Stopping Above-Cost Predatory Pricing' 4 *Yale Law Journal* (2002) 941, 991.

43 Not only, however, is this a complicated analysis, but the concept 'not yet as efficient competitor' also gives the competition authority huge discretion in assessing whether and when a company will be 'as efficient' as the dominant company.

for example. If they do not innovate it may not only be detrimental for consumers, but also harmful to the incumbent's incentive to innovate. Moreover, protecting less efficient competitors may involve a loss of economies of scale, which is productively inefficient.[44]

This author recommends the Commission to develop a framework for examining relative efficiencies in the long term if the Commission wants to protect competition in order to promote consumer welfare. This is because, when trying to protect the freedom of the market participants to promote consumer welfare, there is a real risk that the result is protection of competitors. It becomes extremely difficult to know when the protection of economic freedom benefits consumer welfare, and when it protects competitors under the consumer welfare standard. Competitors should be protected only to the point where it benefits consumers, but this principle is excluded where the process of competition is of intrinsic value. In welfare terms, if less efficient firms are protected or subsidised, it can prevent market competition from selecting the best firms, which will actually result in higher prices and lower welfare.[45] If the Commission is only willing to promote economic freedom for the benefit of consumers, then it will have to protect the competitive process instrumentally and not intrinsically. In this way, consumer welfare should be read in conjunction with harm to the process of competition,[46] but not by relying on assumptions of harm to consumers from harm to the structure of competition. This point will be discussed in detail in chapter 5.

In conclusion, if the process of competition is protected instrumentally to bring consumer welfare, freedom to participate in the marketplace may be restricted. Sometimes promoting consumer welfare means harming freedom of competition and vice versa. Where the process of competition is protected intrinsically, the freedom to be part of the competitive process is protected, but consumer welfare may be harmed. Economic freedom and consumer welfare only seem to co-exist where an intrinsic protection of the process of competition also benefits consumer welfare, or where an instrumental protection of the competitive process does not sacrifice economic freedom.

[44] F. M. Scherer, 'Antitrust, Efficiency, and Progress' 63 *New York University Law Review* (1987) 998, 1002–3.

[45] Motta, supra note 5, 51.

[46] This argument does find some support: see V. Mertikopoulou 'DG Competition's Discussion Paper on the Application of Article 82 of the EC Treaty to Exclusionary Abuses: The Proposed Economic Reform from a Legal Point of View' 28(4) *European Competition Law Review* (2007) 241, 242.

2.3 Summary of section 2

This section has highlighted the potential conflict between economic freedom and consumer welfare. It has outlined different views of protecting the competitive process. The latter can be protected either intrinsically or instrumentally. Some believe that competition is best protected by safeguarding the freedoms inherent in the process, whereas others believe competition is best protected by promoting the outcomes it can bring. The Commission sends opaque signals as to whether it prefers to protect the process of competition in itself or for what it brings. On the one hand, it seems keen to move away from protecting the process in itself, but on the other hand, it wants to protect less efficient competitors in the hope that it may bring consumer welfare in the long term, but until this is the case it protects the freedom of these less efficient market participants. There are no significant signs either that consumer welfare is favoured at the expense of economic freedom or that economic freedom is a means to an end of consumer welfare, as no framework or timeframe is provided for how best to protect less efficient competitors to the benefit of consumers. If the Commission is serious about protecting the process of competition, including less efficient competitors, in the long term to promote consumer welfare, this author recommends the Commission to develop a framework for examining relative efficiencies in the long term.

3. Freedom of competition

The previous section concluded that there is a potential conflict between the objectives of economic freedom and consumer welfare. Where the objectives conflict, the Community Courts must make a choice as to whether they favour economic freedom or consumer welfare. The balance has in general been in favour of the former, not the latter, as the competitive process has been protected intrinsically. However, the Commission seems keen to change this to a focus on protecting the process of competition instrumentally in order to increase consumer welfare. With that in mind, this section considers whether freedom of competition is considered a fundamental right. If it is, giving priority to consumer welfare would be giving precedence to a utilitarian-based approach over a fundamental rights-based approach. Some argue that the Community Courts' legal order is based on the ordoliberal economic constitution. This raises two questions. First, is economic freedom considered a fundamental right in the ordoliberal economic constitution? And second, is the Community legal order based on the ordoliberal economic constitution? If the answers are affirmative, the Community legal order ought to protect freedom of competition as a fundamental right. A fundamental right requires that it be protected as a right of a higher rank. The Commission cannot give priority to a utilitarian goal of consumer welfare over a fundamental rights-based approach, as that would undermine the Community legal order, unless it has been properly debated and has achieved support from the Community Courts. Section 3.1 discusses whether economic freedom, which traces its roots to ordoliberalism, is considered a fundamental right in the ordoliberal economic constitution. Section 3.2 considers whether the Community legal order is founded on the ordoliberal economic constitution. Section 3.3 questions whether freedom of competition aims at safeguarding economic freedom as a fundamental right in the Community legal order. Section 3.4 provides a summary.

3.1 The ordoliberal economic constitution and freedom of competition

For ordoliberals freedom of competition was represented as constitutional in scope.[47] A core element of the ordoliberal constitutional message was that the economic constitution should respect the interdependence of undistorted competition, individual economic freedoms and the rule of law, and protect these principles and rights from discretionary politics.[48]

As described in chapter 2, ordoliberals advocated a social market economy, which became the actual economic system created by Ludwig Erhard in (the then) West Germany.[49] The social market economy represented the ordoliberal vision of society, where individual economic freedom and competition were sources of political freedom, and represented the 'economic constitution' of society. Competition law was the main pillar of the social market economy and was as said represented as constitutional in scope.[50] The primary goal of ordoliberal competition policy was freedom of competition to protect individual economic freedom in the interest of a free and fair political and social order.[51] Individual economic freedom

[47] Gerber, supra note 13, 277 and 282.

[48] C. Joerges, 'What is Left of the European Economic Constitution?' EUI Working Paper Law No. 13 (2004) 13. This paper is also published in a shorter version in 30(4) *European Law Review* (2005) 461.

[49] N. Goldsmith and A. Berndt, 'Leonhard Miksch (1901–1950): A Forgotten Member of the Freiburg School', Walter-Eucken-Institute, Freiburg Discussion Papers on Constitutional Economics No. 3 (2002).

[50] Gerber, supra note 13, 277 and 282.

[51] Möschel, supra note 15, 146.

could be achieved by limiting and/or controlling economic power, or at least its harmful effects.[52] Competition policy was embedded in the economic order of a free and open society.[53] It was shaped by the rule of law rather than by *ad hoc* political decision-making. The state retained a strong role in protecting the basic parameters of the system of competition. Competition within the economy provided the basis for the economic order envisioned by ordoliberals: a free market economy.[54] The free market has to be liberated from economic power, otherwise only a system of anarchic welfare would prevail.[55] To avoid economic power, complete competition should be achieved through competition on both the supply and the demand sides of the market.[56] Having competition on both sides of the market would require that no market player, on either the supply or the demand side, was restricted by foreclosure. It was therefore imperative to protect individuals' freedom to compete, so that no firm had the power to coerce other firms.[57] The competitive order of complete competition was to be protected by the economic constitution.

The ordoliberal competitive order connected competition law with fundamental rights by making individual economic freedom and competition the backbone of the economic constitution of society. Ordoliberals believed that freedom of competition needs to be protected by law as it is the most 'ingenious instrument of deprivation of power in history'.[58] For them, competition is a process whereby market actors participate in the economy without being disproportionately constrained by either private or public power. Individual economic freedom is an essential accompaniment to political freedom and competition is necessary for the economic liberty of the individual.[59] A competitive order would ensure a prosperous and humane society which guaranteed individual economic freedom

[52] Gerber, supra note 13, 251. [53] Möschel, supra note 15, 142.

[54] Ordoliberals defined the free market economy as an economic system that dispenses with any official control and instead entrusts control of the interplay of economic forces to a mechanism (the market price system) which discharges its control functions automatically: F. Böhm, 'Democracy and Economic Power' in *Cartel and Monopoly in Modern Law* (Karlsruhe: C. F. Muller, 1961) 25.

[55] Ibid., 30.

[56] W. Eucken, 'Die Wettbewerbsordnung und ihre Verwirklichung' 2 ORDO 1949 1. (An English translation of this article can be found in 2(2) *Competition Policy International* (2006) 219.)

[57] Möschel, supra note 15, 157 footnote 16.

[58] C. Ahlborn and C. Grave, 'Walter Eucken and Ordoliberalism: An Introduction from a Consumer Welfare Perspective' 2(2) *Competition Policy International* (2006) 196, 200.

[59] F. A. Hayek, *New Studies in Philosophy, Politics, Economics and the History of Ideas* (University of Chicago Press, 1978) 179–90.

and price stability.[60] Economic freedom was necessary both to prevent the accumulation of private economic power and to sustain economic development.[61] Price stability was seen as essential for a society where long-term contracts would act as the cement for civil society.

The economic constitution should include basic principles to counteract any tendencies that could neutralise competition.[62] It should regulate and limit, for example, the emergence of private economic power by prohibiting cartels, the growth of single-firm market power and contracts that create unjustified limits on the competitive autonomy of firms. The economic constitution should decide the legal structure of the economic system guaranteeing individual freedom and competition as fundamental rights. The economic constitution should, amongst other things, protect the process of competition. However, it is important to recognise that, as emphasised by one of the founding fathers of ordoliberalism, Franz Böhm, '[t]he real motives behind the enactment of antitrust law were … not economic efficiency and the effectiveness of economic control, but social justice and civil liberties which were held to be threatened by monopolies'.[63] Competition needed to be protected to guarantee equality of individuals and protect civil liberties:[64]

> Competition policy [ordoliberal competition policy] serves to protect the evolutionary process of competition as such, and to prevent the concentration of private power to the detriment of the competitive and the political processes. Consequently, competition constitutes a value in its own right, which goes well beyond efficiency considerations. In this view, the [ordoliberal] economic constitution serves, first, to guarantee the basic equality of individuals as economic subjects; second, to back up the private law society by public authority; and third, to protect civil liberties.

Ordoliberals wanted to protect freedom of competition in order to protect humanistic values rather than efficiency or other purely economic concerns. This does not mean that economic theory did not play a role in ordoliberal competition policy. Ordoliberalism used economics as a means to develop a free order (*Ordnung*).[65] The free order

[60] See W. Eucken, *Grundsätze der Wirtschaftspolitik* (Berne, 1952).

[61] R. Barrell and K. Dury, 'Choosing the Regime: Macroeconomic Effects of UK Entry into EMU' NIESR Discussion Paper No. 168 (2000) 5.

[62] Individual rights set out in the economic constitution were directly enforceable: see W. Sauter, *Competition Law and Industrial Policy in the EU* (Oxford: Clarendon Press, 2003) 47.

[63] Böhm, supra note 54, 28.

[64] Sauter, supra note 62, 47.

[65] An '*Ordnung*' provides a framework for a functional free-market mechanism, which not only accommodates development and change, but also ensures human dignity and freedom.

should liberate humanitarian values from being overpowered by chaotic, anarchic and collectivistic forces.[66] Ordoliberalism tried to combine open markets and individual economic freedom with social justice. It is distinct from traditional liberalism in two respects. First, ordoliberalism believed that an unregulated free market is *not* the most efficient means of allocating resources. Adam Smith's 'laissez faire' economy does not necessarily ensure a competitive economy. In such an unregulated economy, monopolistic practices, interventionism and distortions of price relationships may arise. Therefore, ordoliberals believed that structural and regulating principles should facilitate a functionally competitive economy with a compatible social policy, characterised by a flexible price mechanism and stable policies.[67] Second, individual economic freedom needs to be protected from both political power and the misuse of private economic power. Traditional liberalism maintains that the rule of law is mainly to protect the individual against government coercion (political power).[68] However, ordoliberalism attached equal importance to safeguarding individual economic freedom from private undertakings' economic power.

The aim of the ordoliberal economic constitution was economic freedom for all through the limitation of public and private power in the market. There should be no intrusion upon individual freedom and private autonomy; private autonomy should be enhanced through contracts being protected and private competition being safeguarded. The economic constitution should protect these fundamental rights, which could not be 'captured' by private interests, as articulated by Böhm.

3.2 The Community legal order and the ordoliberal economic 'constitution'

Section 2 established that Community competition law has been influenced by ordoliberalism and the previous section discussed some of the fundamental rights of the ordoliberal economic constitution. This section asks whether the Community legal order is based on the ordoliberal economic constitution. If it is, freedom of competition ought to be protected as a fundamental right.

[66] See L. Miksch, 'Walter Eucken' 4 *Kyklos* (1950) 279.

[67] S. Karsten, 'Eucken's "Social Market Economy" and its Test in Post-war West Germany. The Economist as Social Philosopher Developed Ideas that Paralleled Progressive Thought in America' 44(2) *American Journal of Economics and Sociology* (1985) 169.

[68] See B. Leoni, *Freedom and the Law* (Indianapolis: Liberty Fund, 3rd edn, 1991).

There has been some debate as to whether the EC Treaty is based on the ordoliberal economic constitution and even whether it constitutes the constitution of Europe. As for the latter, this is because the EU is neither a federal state nor similar to one.[69] It has no independent sovereignty and is not self-sufficient, but complements the Member States.[70] The EU is a supranational[71] organisation authorised by the Member States and it gains its legitimacy by validation – ratification by its Member States rather than by its people.[72] Yet, the Treaty does have important elements which are to be found in a constitution defined in the broader sense as 'the basic principles and laws of a nation, state, or social group that determine the powers and duties of the government and guarantee certain rights to the people'.[73] The EU has exclusive competence in a wide range of matters and the EU institutions do have functions comparable to those of a government.[74] The EU institutions are limited by the rule of law, which is a basic idea of constitutionalism. Moreover, the ECJ has helped to constitutionalise the EU by establishing the supremacy of EU law in fundamental cases such as *Costa v. ENEL*,[75] *Simmenthal*[76] and *Factortame*.[77] The court has also established the direct effect of EU law in *Van Gend en Loos*.[78] Both the doctrine of supremacy and that of direct effect are keystones of European constitutionality.[79]

As for the debate about whether the Treaty is based on the ordoliberal economic constitution, Mestmäcker, an ordoliberal scholar advising the Commission in the 1970s, has argued that the Community legal order is founded on the ordoliberal economic constitution, because open markets

[69] H. Rasmussen, *EU-Ret i Kontekst* (Copenhagen: GadJura, 3rd edn, 1998) 365 ff.

[70] E. T. Swaine, 'Subsidiarity and Self-interest: Federalism at the European Court of Justice' 41 *Harvard International Law Journal* (2000) 1, 10.

[71] Supranational means government above, or beyond, the state level of government where states do not wield individual vetoes in all areas.

[72] J. Weiler, 'The Transformation of Europe' 100 *Yale Law Journal* (1991) 2403, 2423 and 2433.

[73] D. M. Walker, *The Oxford Companion to Law* (Oxford: Clarendon Press, 1980).

[74] S. Douglas-Scott, *Constitutional Law of the European Union* (Harlow: Pearson Education, 2002) 516.

[75] Case 6/64 *Costa Flaminio v. ENEL* [1964] ECR 585.

[76] Case 106/77 *Amministrazione delle Finanze dello Stato v. Simmenthal SpA* [1978] ECR 629.

[77] Case C-213/89 *R v. Secretary of State for Transport, ex parte Factortame Ltd* [1990] ECR I-2433.

[78] Case 26/62 *Van Gend en Loos v. Administratie der Belastingen* [1963] ECR 1.

[79] Douglas-Scott, supra note 74, 517: Joerges disagrees: he thinks it is insufficient to point to direct effect and supremacy as core elements of EU law to characterise the system as constitutional: supra note 48, 9.

and competition are guiding principles of the Community's economic constitution.[80] Mestmäcker argued that to ensure the establishment of a common market and economic rights and fundamental freedoms,[81] barriers to trade had to be abolished and undistorted competition ensured.[82] The competition rules became a tool to protect the results flowing from eradicating barriers to the markets within the common market. It was understood that the elimination of barriers would not be achieved if private agreements or economically powerful firms were permitted to manipulate, or not prevented from manipulating, the flow of trade within the common market.[83] In this way, the free movement rules and the competition rules become the cornerstone of the European Constitution and the source of its legitimacy.[84] Some would agree that the fundamental freedoms and competition, which are ensured through directly applicable treaty provisions, must have constitutional status.[85] However, not everybody shares this view[86] and some argue that 'the normative hierarchy of national constitutional rights, international and European conventions on human rights, and the economic freedoms which form the foundation of the Community, has become confused and ambiguous'.[87]

Maduro argues that the *Keck* decision[88] demonstrates that no such concept of a European Economic Constitution has been adopted by

[80] E. J. Mestmäcker, 'Sur Anwendung der Wettbewerbsregeln auf die Mitgliedstaaten und auf die Europäischen Gemeinschaft' in J. F. Baur, P.-C. Müller-Graff and M. Zuleeg (eds.), *Europarecht, Energierecht, Wirtschaftsrecht: Festschrift für Bodo Borner sum 70. Geburtstag* (Cologne: Carl Heymanns Verlag, 1992).

[81] Articles 28, 39, 43 and 49 of the EC Treaty.

[82] This is very much inspired by the Spaak Report: *Rapport des Chefs de Délégation aux Ministres des Affaires Étrangères* (in English: *Report of the Heads of Delegation of the Governmental Committee*) set up by the Messina Conference, named after Paul-Henri Spaak, then the Belgian prime minister. Spaak was the chairman of the preparatory committee in charge of its preparation. The Report was presented on 21 April 1956 and led to the Treaty of Rome of 1957, which came into force on 1 January 1958.

[83] E. Mestmäcker, 'Die Beurteilung von Unternehmenszusammenschlüssen nach Artikel 86 des EWG-Vertrags', reprinted in Mestmäcker, *Wirtschaft und Verfassung in der Europäischen Union* (Baden-Baden: Nomos Verlagsgesellschaft, 2nd edn, 2006) 597, 606.

[84] E. J. Mestmäcker, 'On the Legitimacy of European Law' 58 *Rabels Zeitschrift für Ausländisches und Internationales Privatrecht* (1994) 615.

[85] J. B. Cruz, *Between Competition and Free Movement: The Economic Constitutional Law of the European Community* (Oxford: Hart Publishing, 2002) 79.

[86] 'It is largely thanks to Germany, therefore, that the EEC attached so much importance to competition from the outset, to the point where it became almost a constitutional principle.' K. Van Miert, 'The Future of European Competition Policy', 17 September 1998, the Ludwig Erhard Foundation in Bonn (speech/98/1351). Available at: http://ec.europa.eu/competition/speeches.

[87] B. Hepple, 'Social Values and European Law' 48 *Current Legal Problems* (1995) 39, 46.

[88] Joined Cases C-267 and C-268/91 *Keck and Mithouard* [1993] ECR I-6097.

the ECJ.[89] Moreover, ordoliberal economic constitutional concepts are not reflected predominantly in the text, or even the genesis, of the Treaty.[90] Others rely on the argument that only a few lawyers outside Germany have systematically used the concept of economic constitution.[91] They even argue that a majority of scholars of constitutional law and administrative law in Germany have not taken the ordoliberal constitutionalisation of the economy seriously.[92] Importantly, they point out that the German Federal Constitutional Court (*Bundesverfassungsgericht*) has held that economic liberalism does not have constitutional status in Germany.[93] The Constitutional Court is not the only one to reject the concept of the economic constitution, others have rejected it too.[94] Some even argue there is not much left of the economic constitution anyway whether it is ordoliberal or not.[95] This, in conjunction with the ECJ's dictum in *Van Gend en Loos* that 'the Community constitutes a new legal order of international law for the benefit of which the States have limited their sovereign rights',[96] makes this author conclude that it is probably unlikely that the Treaty is based on the ordoliberal economic constitution. Despite this, aiming to protect freedom of competition as a value in its own right[97] cannot be ignored as ordoliberal competition policy has had a profound influence on EU competition law.[98] Thus, before reaching a final conclusion, it is necessary to examine whether the Community Courts have taken a view on this specifically in relation to competition.

3.3 *Freedom of competition as a fundamental right in the Community legal order*

This section examines whether the Community Courts have considered freedom of competition to be a fundamental right. Although the previous section found that the Community legal order is unlikely to be based on the ordoliberal economic 'constitution', the status of economic freedom

89 M. P. Maduro, 'Reforming the Market or the State? Article 30 and the European Constitution: Economic Freedom and Political Rights' 3(1) *European Law Journal* (1997) 55, 65.

90 Ibid., 65.

91 Sauter, supra note 62, 30; C. Joerges, 'The Law in the Process of Constitutionalising Europe' EUI Working Paper Law No. 4 (2002) 6.

92 Joerges, supra note 91, 13.

93 W. Sauter, 'The Economic Constitution of the European Union' 4 *Columbia Journal of European Law* (1998) 27, 48–9.

94 Cruz, supra note 85, 28.

95 Joerges, supra note 48, 8.

96 *Van Gend en Loos*, supra note 78.

97 Möschel, supra note 15, 148–9.

98 See the views referred to above, supra note 16.

as fundamental cannot be rejected or accepted before analysing some Community jurisprudence. A fundamental right requires that it be protected as a right of a higher rank.[99] If freedom of competition is a fundamental right, it is of higher rank than a non-fundamental right. Therefore in case of conflict, it is likely that a fundamental right would trump a non-fundamental right.

The original EC Treaty did not contain any explicit reference to basic fundamental rights and values, but in the *Stauder* case[100] the ECJ recognised that it might have to protect fundamental rights.[101] As for freedom of competition, the ECJ said in *Procureur de la République v. Association de Défense des Brûleurs d'Huiles Usagées,* 'it should be borne in mind that the principles of free movement of goods and freedom of competition, together with freedom of trade as a fundamental right, are general principles of community law of which the Court ensures observance'.[102] The court acknowledged that freedom of competition is a general principle.[103] The general principles include, but are not limited to, human rights principles.[104]

[99] J. Coppel and A. O'Neill, 'The European Court of Justice: Taking Rights Seriously?' 29 *Common Market Law Review* (1992) 669, 682.

[100] Case 29/69 *Stauder v. City of Ulm* [1969] ECR 419, para. 7.

[101] One commentator has said: 'the European Court of Justice deserves immense credit for pioneering the protection of fundamental human rights within the legal order of the Community when the Treaties themselves were silent on this matter. It has been the Court that has put in place the fundamental principles of respect for human rights which underlie all subsequent developments': see 'The European Union and Human Rights: Final Project Report on an Agenda for the Year 2000', cited by A. Arnull, *The European Union and its Court of Justice* (Oxford University Press, 1999) 223.

[102] Case 240/83 *Procureur de la République v. Association de Défense des Brûleurs d'Huiles Usagées* [1985] ECR 531, para. 9.

[103] The most established general principles are those that protect fundamental (human) rights, legal certainty, including the concept of legitimate expectations, proportionality and equality in the form of non-discrimination, but administrative principles such as the right to a fair hearing and transparency are also part of the general principles. For a discussion of the evolution of the general principles of EU law, see T. C. Hartley, *The Foundations of European Community Law* (Oxford University Press, 5th edn, 2003) and P. Craig and G. De Búrca, *EU Law: Text, Cases and Materials* (Oxford University Press, 3rd edn, 2003).

[104] Jacobs has said: 'confusion can be caused here by the concept of "general principles of law". Different general principles may have different functions, they may have different effects, and they may differ in their scope. While the ECJ made a great advance years ago by including the protection of fundamental rights within the scope of general principles of law, and thus ensuring such protection in the absence of any Treaty provisions, the time may now have come to recognise the very diverse character and scope of the different general principles'. F. G. Jacobs, 'Human Rights in the European Union: The Role of the Court of Justice' 26(4) *European Competition Law Review* (2001) 331, 337.

Specifically in relation to Article 82, the ECJ held in *Michelin I* that freedom of competition is a fundamental principle of the EC Treaty:[105]

> [A]part from the extra bonus granted in 1977, the discount system had an adverse effect on free competition within the common market, which is a fundamental principle of the Treaty, even though the variation in the discount was relatively slight and it has not been proved that the system was applied in a discriminatory manner.

Although the court characterised free competition as a fundamental right, there may be times when one fundamental right clashes with another fundamental right. In case of such conflict, some believe the two rights must be balanced against each other to decide which of the two rights is of higher rank. This author takes the view that a right labelled as a fundamental right cannot be balanced against a non-fundamental right as the latter is of lower 'rank' and therefore not commensurable. However, two fundamental rights can be balanced against each other.[106] In Article 82, the Community Courts appear to balance freedom of competition with other rights. For example, in the *Magill* case, which concerned a conflict between the protection of an intellectual property right, on the one hand, and the protection of free competition, on the other hand, the CFI held:[107]

> [I]n order to resolve the conflict ... between copyright on the one hand and the rules on, inter alia, freedom of competition on the other, the proper approach is ... to identify in each particular case the 'specific subject-matter' of the intellectual property right, which alone merits special protection within the Community legal order and thereby justifies certain encroachments on the Community rules.

According to the court, an intellectual property right enjoys special protection within the Community legal order. Despite this, the court

105 Case 322/81 *Nederlandsche Banden-Industrie Michelin NV v. Commission* [1983] ECR 3461, para. 113.

106 This chapter does not go into this discussion, however interesting, but the reader is referred to Coppel and O'Neill, supra note 99, 690, who argue: 'The invocation of the idea of fundamental rights by the European Court does not set essential limits to lawful executive action, because executive action which has as its object the promotion of the four market freedoms is itself, in the vocabulary of the European Court, instantiating a fundamental right. A claim to violation of certain fundamental human rights, hence, ceases to be a trump-card against executive action. It is no longer possible to speak of a validation of a lower norm by a higher norm. Instead two norms of equal qualitative significance are balanced against the other.'

107 Case T-76/89 *Independent Television Publications Ltd v. Commission* [1991] ECR II-575, para. 28.

concluded that the intellectual property right, in this case a copyright, could not qualify for special protection:[108]

> [A]lthough the programme listings were at the material time protected by copyright as laid down by national law, which still determined the rules governing that protection, the conduct at issue [denial of access to the basic information which is indispensable for the compilation of a TV guide] could not qualify for such protection within the framework of the necessary reconciliation between intellectual property rights and the fundamental principles of the Treaty concerning the free movement of goods and freedom of competition. The aim of that conduct was clearly incompatible with the objectives of Article 86 [Article 82].[109]

The Community Courts seem to balance freedom of competition against other rights. This is also clear from the *IMS Health* case[110] where the ECJ balanced the protection of the intellectual property right and free competition. The ECJ was only willing to give priority to freedom of competition if consumers would otherwise be harmed. If freedom of competition requires the likelihood of consumer detriment to 'trump' an intellectual property right, then freedom of competition does not appear to have the status of a fundamental right. Despite this, it is too early to conclude that the Commission's priority of consumer welfare is legitimate, as this not only depends on free competition being a fundamental right, but also on whether consumer welfare conflicts with the wording of the Treaty. This will be considered in section 4 below.

3.4 Summary of section 3

This section found that ordoliberals saw competition as the main pillar of the social market economy. For ordoliberals, freedom of competition was constitutional in scope. The ordoliberal economic 'constitution' aimed to protect complete competition to facilitate freedom to participate in the marketplace as a fundamental right. The section considered whether the position is similar in the Community legal order. It discovered that the Treaty is unlikely to be based on the ordoliberal economic constitution and that the Community Courts do not treat freedom of competition as a fundamental right (a fundamental right being one which automatically takes priority over other

[108] Ibid., para. 60.

[109] This was upheld on appeal by the ECJ, Case C-241/91P *RTE and ITP v. Commission* [1995] ECR I-743, para. 31.

[110] Case C-418/01 *IMS Health GmbH & Co. OHG v. NDC Health GmbH & Co. KG* [2002] ECR I-3401.

rights). Instead the Community Courts engage in a balancing of different rights. Before concluding whether the Commission's commitment to consumer welfare is legitimate, it is necessary to analyse the expression 'thereby placing them [the other trading parties] at a competitive disadvantage' in Article 82(2)(c). This phrase appears to prioritise economic freedom, rather than consumer welfare, unless the reference to trading parties refers only to consumers. This will be discussed in the following section.

4. Protecting other trading parties in Article 82(2)(c)

The Commission has the freedom to decide its enforcement policy. However, it cannot ignore the wording of the Treaty. Although, strictly speaking, the Commission's commitment to consumer welfare only applies to exclusionary abuses, which could exclude Article 82(2)(c), in practice however, discriminatory practices may have an exclusionary effect.[111] Therefore, it is relevant to examine Article 82(2)(c). Section 4.1 outlines the three conditions in Article 82(2)(c) and engages in a brief discussion of the first two conditions. Section 4.2 discusses the third condition of Article 82(2)(c) to examine whether the phrase 'thereby placing them [the other trading parties] at a competitive disadvantage' refers to consumers. Section 4.3 concludes.

4.1 The three conditions of Article 82(2)(c)

Three conditions have to be fulfilled before Article 82(2)(c) is violated:

(i) there must be dissimilar conditions, which
(ii) are applied to equivalent transactions, and
(iii) other trading parties must be placed at a competitive disadvantage.

Before considering the third condition, the first two conditions will be discussed briefly. These two conditions make it necessary to determine whether two transactions are equivalent and thus comparable, and whether they are treated dissimilarly. Some argue that the Commission and the Community Courts generally assume dissimilar conditions are applied to equivalent transactions without much analysis.[112] An example is *Hoffmann-La Roche*.[113] Hoffmann-La Roche had entered into about

[111] *Discussion Paper*, supra note 3, para. 53.
[112] D. Geradin and N. Petit, 'Price Discrimination under EC Competition Law: The Need for a Case-by-Case Approach' GCLC Working Paper (July 2005), 8; I. Van Bael and J. F. Bellis, *Competition Law of the European Community* (The Hague: Kluwer Law International, 4th edn, 2005) 915 and 917.
[113] *Hoffmann-La Roche*, supra note 22.

thirty contracts with twenty-two large purchasers of vitamins under which the purchasers contracted to buy all or most of their requirements of vitamins or of certain vitamins from Hoffmann-La Roche in return for a rebate. The ECJ said:[114]

> [T]he effect of fidelity rebates is to apply dissimilar conditions to equivalent transactions with other trading parties in that two purchasers pay a different price for the same quantity of the same product depending on whether they obtain their supplies exclusively from the undertaking in a dominant position or have several sources of supply.

The court argued that the rebate offered by Hoffmann-La Roche had a discriminatory effect as two purchasers would pay a different price for the same quantity of the same product. Arguably, however, such transactions are not equivalent. The purchasers who buy vitamins exclusively from Hoffmann-La Roche receive a rebate in return for exclusivity. The purchasers who prefer to buy vitamins from Hoffmann-La Roche as well as from other suppliers are not subject to an exclusivity contract and are therefore not offered a rebate. Some customers sign exclusivity contracts and others do not. This is not exactly an equivalent transaction. Despite this, the court said that this discrimination would place Hoffmann-La Roche's trading parties (its customers) at a competitive disadvantage. The court appears to be concerned with secondary-line discrimination,[115] which means discrimination imposed on one or several customers of the dominant firm as against one or several other customers.[116] This is in line with legal literature, which interprets Article 82(2)(c) to be directed at discrimination causing secondary-line injury.[117]

In *Portuguese Airports*, the Commission held that '[t]here must be an objective justification for any difference in treatment of its various clients

[114] Ibid., para. 90.

[115] As opposed to primary-line discrimination, which means discrimination used to expand or maintain a dominant position to the disadvantage of the competitors of the discriminator by applying different prices to its own customers. Fox, supra note 21, 1008.

[116] A. Jones and B. Sufrin, *EC Competition Law* (Oxford University Press, 2nd edn, 2004) 411.

[117] Ibid., 594; S. M. Lage and R. Allendesalazar, 'Community Policy on Discriminatory Pricing: A Practitioner's Perspective' in C. D. Ehlermann and I. Atanasiu (eds.), *What is an Abuse of a Dominant Position?* (Oxford: Hart Publishing, 2006) 341; D. Geradin and N. Petit, 'Price Discrimination under EC Competition Law: Another Antitrust Doctrine in Search of Limiting Principles?' 2(3) *Journal of Competition Law and Economics* (2006) 479, 487; M. Waelbroeck, 'Price Discrimination and Rebate Policies under EU Competition Law' in B. Hawk (ed.), *International Antitrust Law and Policy: Fordham Corporate Law 1995* (New York: Juris Publishing, 1996) 160.

by an undertaking in a dominant position'.[118] Hoffmann-La Roche argued that even customers bound by an exclusivity clause were free to obtain supplies from other suppliers if Hoffmann-La Roche was unable to offer prices more favourable than its competitors. This is a so-called English clause. The ECJ held that 'the English clause does not remove the discrimination resulting from the fidelity rebates between purchasers in similar circumstances depending on whether or not they reserve their freedom to choose their suppliers'.[119]

In addition to establishing that two transactions are equivalent and treated dissimilarly, the wording of Article 82(2)(c) requires that other trading parties are placed at a competitive disadvantage. If 'trading party' does not include consumers, this provision could exclude discrimination of consumers from the scope of subparagraph (c), which could undermine the priority of consumer welfare.

4.2 Other trading parties must be placed at a competitive disadvantage

This section discusses whether the third condition of Article 82(2)(c) includes consumers. The Commission's decision in *Deutsche Post AG* engaged in a discussion of who was considered a trading partner of Deutsche Post.[120] The case concerned interception of cross-border mail by the German public postal operator, which was intercepting mail originating from the British Post Office (BPO). Deutsche Post argued in favour of a narrow interpretation of trading parties by holding that 'the persons that deliver the mailings for posting with the BPO' are not trading partners of DPAG [Deutsche Post AG]. The only trading partner of DPAG in this case is the BPO.'[121] Although the Commission held that the term 'trading partner' must be given a slightly different interpretation because Deutsche Post held a monopoly in Germany, it considered Deutsche Post to be a trading partner of both the UK senders, contracting with the BPO, and of BPO directly:[122]

> [d]ue to the existence of the postal monopoly in Germany, the term trading partner – which normally refers to a voluntary commercial relationship between two undertakings – must be given a slightly different interpretation. The postal monopoly imposes upon foreign senders a commercial

[118] OJ [1999] L69/31 *Portuguese Airports*, para. 27.

[119] *Hoffmann-La Roche*, supra note 22, para. 106.

[120] OJ [2001] L331/40 *Deutsche Post AG*.

[121] Ibid., para. 123.

[122] Ibid., para. 130.

> if not directly contractual relationship with DPAG. The sender in the UK that contracts with the BPO to have his mailings sent to Germany knows beforehand that the mail will be delivered by DPAG to German addressees. The actions of DPAG in the German market for incoming cross-border letter mail directly affect the commercial activities of the UK senders. At the very least, there is an indirect relationship between the UK senders contracting with the BPO and DPAG. Under these circumstances, the Commission finds that the senders must be regarded as trading partners of DPAG within the meaning of Article 82 (c).

In its assessment, the Commission referred to the ECJ's judgment in *Deutsche Post AG v. GZS and Citicorp*.[123] There, the ECJ concluded that discriminatory treatment of different mail categories may constitute an abuse under Article 82 without addressing the question whether the sender was a trading partner of Deutsche Post AG or not. By referring to *Deutsche Post AG v. GZS and Citicorp* it is not entirely clear whether the Commission considered it unnecessary to examine whether trading parties are placed at a competitive disadvantage. If it did, then the Commission is basically saying that it is not necessary to apply the conditions imposed by Article 82(2)(c) strictly.[124] Advocate General Van Gerven took this approach in his Opinion in *Corsica Ferries Italia Srl v. Corpo dei Piloti del Porto di Genova*:[125]

> It appears implicitly from the Community case-law … that the Court does not interpret that phrase [other trading parties, thereby placing them at a competitive disadvantage] restrictively, with the result that it is not necessary, in order to apply it, that the trading partners of the undertaking responsible for the abuse should suffer a competitive disadvantage against each other or against the undertaking in the dominant position.

If it is not necessary to apply the conditions imposed by Article 82(2)(c) strictly, it means that subparagraph (c) can be applied to dominant firms' pricing practices even where trading parties are not placed directly at a competitive disadvantage. One commentator suggests the use of 'thereby' in subparagraph (c) implies that it is presumed that a competitive disadvantage to trading parties flows from the application of 'dissimilar conditions'.[126]

123 Joined Cases C-147-148/97 *Deutsche Post AG v. Gesellschaft für Zahlungssysteme mbH and Citicorp Kartenservice GmbH* [2000] ECR I-825.

124 Lage and Allendesalazar, supra note 117, 339–42.

125 Opinion of Advocate General Van Gerven in Case C-18/93 *Corsica Ferries Italia Srl v. Corpo dei Piloti del Porto di Genova*, delivered on 9 February 1994, para. 34.

126 M. Furse, *Competition Law of the EC and UK* (Oxford University Press, 5th edn, 2006) 307.

The Commission confirmed that in *Deutsche Post AG*, even in the absence of direct negative effects on trading parties, subparagraph (2)(c) of Article 82 was violated, as Deutsche Post's behaviour had direct negative effects on consumers.[127] In other words, where there is direct harm to consumers, there is no need to show trading parties are directly disadvantaged despite trading parties being directly mentioned in Article 82(2)(c). This is in line with the way Article 82(2)(b) has been interpreted. In the absence of direct effects on consumers, Article 82(2)(b) is violated where there is significant harm to the structure of the market. It is not necessary to show direct harm to consumers despite 'consumers' being mentioned directly in subparagraph (b). Where there is direct harm to consumers, however, there is then no need to show effects on the competitive structure.[128]

In the *British Airways* case,[129] British Airways argued that the Commission had not done enough to show that trading parties (travel agents) were placed at a competitive disadvantage as a result of the reward schemes.[130] The ECJ held:[131]

> [I]n order for the conditions for applying subparagraph (c) of the second paragraph of Article 82 EC to be met, there must be a finding not only that the behaviour of an undertaking in a dominant market position is discriminatory, but also that it tends to distort that competitive relationship, in other words to hinder the competitive position of some of the business partners of that undertaking in relation to the others.
>
> In that respect, there is nothing to prevent discrimination between business partners who are in a relationship of competition from being regarded as being abusive as soon as the behaviour of the undertaking in a dominant position tends, having regard to the whole of the circumstances of the case, to lead to a distortion of competition between those business partners. In such a situation, it cannot be required in addition that proof be adduced of an actual quantifiable deterioration in the competitive position of the business partners taken individually.

According to the court, discrimination alone is not enough. It must be shown that the competitive position of the business partners is distorted to some extent, although this deterioration does not have to be quantified. It is enough to demonstrate that the reward schemes *tend* to lead to a distortion of competition between travel agents, and additional proof of an actual

[127] *Deutsche Post AG*, supra note 120, para. 134.
[128] OJ [2000] L5/55 *1998 Football World Cup*, para. 100.
[129] *British Airways*, supra note 23, para. 142.
[130] Ibid., para. 142. [131] Ibid., paras. 144–5.

quantifiable deterioration is not required. This indicates that Article 82(2)(c) may be violated also where there is an indirect competitive disadvantage to trading parties. This gives competition authorities and courts a direct route to condemn discrimination where it hinders the competitive position of business partners. Thus, Article 82(2)(c) cannot be said to protect only consumers. This has led some to argue that 'the self-made Commission/Court abridged version of Article 82(2)(c) might best be seen in terms of an underlying tendency to seek to preserve an existing market structure, a kind of policy of protecting towards the distributor ... If so, this is not a policy that is connected with competition or consumer welfare.'[132]

4.3 Summary of section 4

Section 4 discussed the phrase 'thereby placing them [the other trading parties] at a competitive disadvantage' in Article 82(2)(c). This expression appears to protect the economic freedom of trading parties and not consumers, in which case giving primacy to consumer welfare would go against the wording of Article 82. The analysis showed that where there is direct harm to consumers, indirect harm to trading parties is assumed. However, where there is no direct harm to consumers, harm to trading parties cannot be assumed only by proving the first two conditions, i.e. dissimilar conditions to an equivalent transaction. It must be shown that the conduct in question tends to distort competition between the trading parties. It must be assessed whether there is harm to trading parties, although indirect harm to trading parties is enough. In this way, harm to the welfare of consumers is enough to establish that freedom of competition is distorted, However, a priority of consumer welfare would mean that Article 82(2)(c) would not apply, unless it could be shown that the allegedly discriminating conduct is harmful to consumers. This is contrary to the way in which this provision has been applied by the Community Courts. The case law shows that Article 82(2)(c) can apply where the economic freedom of the trading parties is distorted.

5. Conclusion

The main aim of this chapter was to examine whether the Commission priority of consumer welfare is legitimate, given that chapter 3 concluded

[132] B. Sher, 'Price Discounts and *Michelin 2*: What Goes Around, Comes Around' 23(10) *European Competition Law Review* (2002) 482, 487–8.

that freedom of competition is considered a valid objective in the application of Article 82. The legitimacy of consumer welfare depends on various factors, two of which were discussed in this chapter. The first is whether economic freedom is a means to an end of consumer welfare. The second is whether economic freedom is considered a fundamental right in the Community legal order.

This chapter found that consumer welfare and economic freedom have a different normative foundation. It concludes that there is a potential conflict between economic freedom and consumer welfare. Economic freedom and consumer welfare only seem to co-exist where an intrinsic protection of the process of competition also benefits consumer welfare, or where an instrumental protection of the competitive process does not sacrifice economic freedom. Because of the conflict, a balancing act needs to be carried out to examine which of these two objectives should take priority over the other. An examination of the way in which the Commission and Community Courts have protected the process of competition reveals that they are keen to protect the process of competition intrinsically, which favours freedom of competition. Despite this, the Commission seems eager to protect the process of competition instrumentally for what it brings to consumers. At the same time the Commission wants to protect less efficient competitors in the hope that it may bring consumer welfare in the long term. However, the Commission has not provided a framework or a timeframe for how best to protect less efficient competitors to the benefit of consumers. This author believes that without such a framework, the Commission is still protecting the process of competition in order to guarantee economic freedom, but not necessarily to the benefit of consumer welfare. The Commission will have to explain carefully how protecting inefficient competitors promotes consumer welfare. This must be based on either evidence or well-documented theory indicating how consumers are likely to be harmed, otherwise it appears to be nothing more than a protection of economic freedom. If the Commission and the Community Courts never intended to protect freedom of competition in itself, but only to the extent that it benefited consumer welfare, they must incorporate an analysis of efficiencies to show how consumers benefit. Otherwise, the legitimacy of decisions and judgments is undermined. If the Commission wants to change, this author recommends that it develop a framework for examining relative efficiencies in the long term.

Besides the potential conflict and the balancing of the objectives, the chapter had to examine whether freedom of competition is considered a fundamental right which would take priority over consumer welfare. It established that economic freedom, which traces its roots to ordoliberalism, is considered a fundamental right in the ordoliberal economic 'constitution'. Ordoliberal competition policy has had a profound influence on EU competition law, so it cannot be ignored. However, despite being influenced by ordoliberalism, it found that the Community legal order is unlikely to be founded on the ordoliberal economic constitution where freedom of competition is considered a fundamental right. This chapter also found that, according to the way in which Article 82 has been interpreted, freedom of competition is not considered a fundamental right in the Community legal order. Thus, the Community legal order does not make freedom of competition a right of a higher rank. This means that the Commission can prioritise consumer welfare over freedom of competition, but it cannot disregard economic freedom by making consumer welfare the only, or even main, goal of Article 82.

Finally, this chapter found that the expression in Article 82(2)(c), 'thereby placing them [the other trading parties] at a competitive disadvantage', sometimes means consumers, but not always. The consequence is that Article 82(2)(c) applies where there is a distortion or restriction of competition between trading parties. This prevents the Commission from postponing its intervention until consumer harm is likely. It will have to intervene already where an indirect harm to trading parties is likely.

5

The role of effects in Article 82

1. Introduction

Chapter 3 concluded that Article 82 aims at protecting many objectives, not just consumer welfare, and chapter 4 that there is a conflict between consumer welfare and economic freedom. Because of the conflict, this chapter examines whether the harmful effects of a restriction of economic freedom mean that consumer welfare is also harmed. It examines whether the prohibition in Article 82 requires harmful effects to be proven, and if so, whether the Commission examines effects on the market, competition, consumers, the structure of competition or competitors. A discussion of effects concerns the Commission's methodology, but is linked to a discussion of Article 82's goals.[1] Whether it is necessary to show effects on consumers in order to prohibit exclusionary conduct depends on whether consumer welfare is the objective in a specific case. If Article 82 aims at achieving consumer welfare,[2] harm to consumers is an important element. Objectives and methodology are sometimes intertwined and changing the underlying purpose of a provision may sometimes require a change of methodology as well, although this is not always the case. However, it does not alter the fact that they are two different things.[3] In relation to the objectives of consumer welfare and economic freedom, the methodology is different in that economic freedom is concerned with the effects on *the structure of competition* whereas consumer welfare is concerned with the effects on *consumers*. That said, adopting an effects-based approach may not always be necessary to achieve the objective. For example, if the aim is consumer welfare, there is no need to examine harmful effects on consumers if economic theory shows that consumers are almost always harmed when a dominant undertaking engages in certain

[1] EAGCP Report on *An Economic Approach to Article 82 EC* (July 2005) 8.

[2] The Commission seems to think that consumer welfare is important: see OJ [2009] C45/7 *Guidance on the Commission's Enforcement Priorities in Applying Article 82 EC Treaty to Abusive Exclusionary Conduct by Dominant Undertakings* (*Guidance Paper*) para. 19.

[3] L. Lovdahl Gormsen, 'Article 82 EC: Where Are We Coming From and Where Are We Going To?' 2(2) *Competition Law Review* (2005) 5.

kinds of behaviour. Where a practice is very rarely beneficial, for example horizontal price fixing, it makes sense to prohibit the whole category even with knowledge that this will condemn some beneficial instances.[4]

In the quest for a 'more economic approach' to Article 82 during the modernisation process, the EAGCP Report said that such an approach 'requires a careful examination of how competition works in each particular market in order to evaluate how specific company strategies affect consumer welfare', 'focusing on the effects of company actions rather than on the form that these actions may take'.[5] If the definition is adopted, an economic approach to Article 82 would require the Commission to measure effects on consumers. This is not only a question of objectives but also one of methodology. However, as noted, consumer welfare can be promoted without adopting an effects-based approach if economic theory supports it.

This chapter examines, first, the nature of effect: *actual* or *likely* effect, and whether Article 82 aims at examining effects on the market, competition, consumers, market structure or competitors. This may provide an answer as to which objective is actually adopted when applying Article 82. The chapter also considers, second, whether certain kinds of exclusionary conduct are presumed to have anticompetitive foreclosure effects and, if so, what the Commission is trying to achieve by relying on these presumptions. By answering that question, it becomes possible to assess whether the current presumptions are in need of a change. Before discussing these two points, it is necessary to define the term 'anticompetitive foreclosure', as it differs depending on which aim Article 82 is pursuing.

Section 2 defines what it meant by anticompetitive foreclosure effects when pursuing an objective of consumer welfare and when pursuing a goal of economic freedom. Section 3 examines whether the Commission and the Community Courts require effects to be shown and, if so, on what. Section 4 examines two assumptions of abuse to analyse whether they reflect the objective being pursued. Section 5 concludes.

2. Anticompetitive foreclosure

Exclusionary conduct can lead to either partial or full foreclosure. Whether exclusionary conduct leading to foreclosure is unacceptable

4 F. H. Easterbrook, 'The Limits of Antitrust' 63 *Texas Law Review* (1984) 1.

5 EAGCP Report, supra note 1, 2.

depends on which objective Article 82 is trying to achieve in a specific case. If Article 82 aims at promoting consumer welfare, foreclosure impairing customers and/or competitors' ability to compete on the merits is only considered objectionable if it leads to consumer harm. The harmful effects are higher prices, lower quality or reduced choice to consumers. However, if Article 82 aims at protecting market participants' economic freedom, foreclosure is unacceptable if it restricts the economic freedom of market participants on the horizontal and/or the vertical level. Whether foreclosure of competitors and customers can be assumed to be harmful also to end consumers is questionable and will be considered in this section.

Economic freedom of market participants on the horizontal level, i.e. competitors, is restricted if a dominant undertaking's conduct forecloses competitors' access to the customers in the market. Economic freedom of market participants on the vertical level, i.e. customers, is restricted if a dominant undertaking's conduct forecloses customers' access to other suppliers in the market. The harmful effects of horizontal and vertical foreclosure are competitors' reduced choice of customers and customers' reduced choice of suppliers. This shows that foreclosure is problematic when pursuing both a consumer welfare objective and an economic freedom objective, but with the important difference of who is considered harmed by the foreclosure. Whether the exclusionary conduct is considered to be anticompetitive foreclosure and therefore prohibited in Article 82 depends on which objective is pursued and who it harms: consumers, competitors and/or customers.

2.1 Foreclosure and consumers

The *Guidance Paper* states that the Commission will prioritise cases where foreclosure leads to consumer harm.[6] In other words, it will prioritise cases where foreclosure is anticompetitive. The *Guidance Paper* links foreclosure to consumer harm and yet it defines anticompetitive foreclosure as a situation 'where *effective* access of actual or potential competitors to supplies or markets is hampered or eliminated as a result of the conduct of the dominant undertaking whereby the dominant undertaking is likely to be in a position to profitably increase prices to the detriment of consumers'.[7] The test for anticompetitive foreclosure is whether effective competition is eliminated, so that the dominant undertaking is in a

[6] *Guidance Paper*, supra note 2, para. 19. [7] Ibid., para. 19. Emphasis added.

position where it can exploit consumers. Whether or not consumers are actually exploited does not matter, what matters is whether the dominant undertaking is in a position where exploitation is a possibility. However, as chapter 2 explained, if the aim is consumer welfare, what matters is not whether access is effectively foreclosed or not, but whether the conduct is harmful to consumers. The Commission does not have the resources to examine whether the conduct in question actually harms consumers in every case. Instead, it assumes consumers are harmed where foreclosure is *effective*, which excludes foreclosure which is insignificant and unlikely to have any harmful effects on the competitive process.[8] However, prohibiting exclusionary conduct under a consumer welfare standard already where there is a *risk* of exploitation is the same as prohibiting dominance, as the likelihood of exploitation is arguably implicit in the very definition of dominance:[9]

> Article 86 [now Article 82] prohibits any abuse by an undertaking of a dominant position … The dominant position thus referred to relates to a position of economic strength enjoyed by an undertaking which enables it to prevent effective competition being maintained on the relevant market by affording it the power to behave to an appreciable extent independently of its competitors, its customers and ultimately of the consumers.

According to this definition, dominance is found where an undertaking is able to behave to an appreciable extent independently of its competitors, its customers and ultimately the consumers. If a dominant undertaking is able to behave independently, it must be able to set its prices high and exploit customers and consumers without competitors being able to impose a restraint upon it.

It is clear that the Commission found inspiration for its definition of anticompetitive foreclosure in the *Guidance Paper* from its *Guidelines on the Assessment of Non-horizontal Mergers*.[10] The latter describe anticompetitive foreclosure as

> any instance where actual or potential rivals' access to supplies or markets is hampered or eliminated as a result of the merger, thereby reducing

[8] Case T-65/98 *Van den Bergh Foods Ltd v. Commission* [2003] ECR II-4653, upheld on appeal in Case C-552/03P *Unilever Bestfoods (Ireland) Ltd v. Commission* [2006] ECR I-9091.

[9] Case 27/76 *United Brands Company v. Commission* [1978] ECR 207, para. 65; Case 85/76 *Hoffmann-La Roche AG v. Commission* [1979] ECR 461, para. 38; Case T-30/89 *Hilti AG v. Commission* [1991] ECR I-1439, para. 90.

[10] OJ [2008] C265/6 *Guidelines on the Assessment of Non-horizontal Mergers under the Council Regulation on the Control of Concentrations Between Undertakings*.

> these companies' ability and/or incentive to compete. As a result of such foreclosure, the merging companies – and, possibly, some of [their] competitors as well – may be able to profitably increase the price charged to consumers. These instances give rise to a significant impediment to effective competition and are therefore referred to hereafter as 'anti-competitive foreclosure'.[11]

However, despite being drafted as recently as 2008, these guidelines appear to be written as if they relate to the old Merger Regulation[12] where the substantive test was a dominance test.[13]

Because dominant undertakings' competition on the merits may foreclose competitors but also benefit consumers, DG COMP's Director General Lowe has acknowledged that 'not all foreclosure is a concern under Article 82: what the Commission's enforcement should target is conduct that results in anticompetitive foreclosure'.[14] Because both competition on the merits and anticompetitive conduct can lead to foreclosure, enforcement authorities need to be careful not to condemn foreclosure in itself if the aim is consumer welfare, but only to prohibit foreclosure which harms consumers. However, the distinction between foreclosure and anticompetitive foreclosure remains somewhat blurred as long as harmful effects on consumers are assumed from harm to economic freedom. It is acceptable that the distinction is not clear where the objective is economic freedom, as foreclosure in itself is a problem, as opposed to anticompetitive foreclosure.

2.2 *Foreclosure and customers and competitors*

According to Advocate General Kokott in her Opinion in *British Airways*, whether the foreclosure in question is abusive depends on whether dominant undertakings 'are capable of making it difficult or impossible for the *competitors* of the dominant undertaking to have access to the market and for the *business partners* of the dominant undertaking to choose between various sources of supply'.[15]

[11] Ibid., para. 18.

[12] OJ [1990] L257/13 Council Regulation 4064/89 on *Control of Concentrations Between Undertakings*.

[13] This matter will not, however interesting, be discussed in this book.

[14] P. Lowe, 'The European Commission Formulates its Enforcement Priorities as Regards Exclusionary Conduct by Dominant Undertakings', Global Competition Policy (February 2009) 1, 6.

[15] Advocate General Kokott's Opinion in C-95/04P *British Airways plc v. Commission* [2007] ECR I-2331, delivered on 23 February 2006, para. 42. Emphasis added.

An example is the *Michelin I* case.[16] Michelin had set annual sales targets for each specific customer and granted a variable discount conditional upon the customer's reaching its annual sales targets for truck, van and car tyres. Unlike in *Hoffmann-La Roche*, Michelin did not require its dealers to purchase all or most of their requirements from Michelin. However, the ECJ held that 'any system under which discounts are granted according to the quantities sold during a relatively long reference period has the inherent effect, at the end of that period, of increasing pressure on the buyer to reach the purchase figure needed to obtain the discount'.[17] This meant that the discount system put the dealers under considerable pressure, especially towards the end of the year, to attain Michelin's sales targets, or else lose the discount. Competitors would not easily be able to make offers that would compensate for this loss of discount, which 'limit[ed] the dealers' choice of supplier and [made] access to the market more difficult for competitors'. The court said that 'neither the wish to sell more nor the wish to spread production more evenly can justify such a restriction of the *customer's* freedom of choice and independence'.[18]

Conduct likely to foreclose players on the horizontal and/or the vertical level of the market must be prohibited to safeguard their economic freedom. Prohibiting such conduct arguably restricts the dominant undertaking's economic freedom. However, on a balance between protecting the economic freedom of customers and competitors versus the dominant undertaking's economic freedom, the former will take priority because the latter has a special responsibility towards residual competition in the market.[19] A dominant undertaking cannot adopt any conduct risking the elimination of that residual competition.

Such a strict approach to dominant undertakings' conduct is closely related to the ordoliberals' dislike of market power. According to them, the hindrance of other market players' performance was structurally inconsistent with the competitive order of complete competition.[20] Ahlborn and Grave have argued that 'due to the huge impact ordoliberalism had on EC competition policy, many of the ordoliberal concepts have been hard-wired into the system ... During the discussion about

[16] Case 322/81 *Nederlandsche Banden-Industrie Michelin NV v. Commission* (*Michelin I*) [1983] ECR 3461.

[17] Ibid., para. 81.

[18] Ibid., paras. 84–6. Emphasis added.

[19] Ibid., para. 57.

[20] See chapter 2.

the modernization of Article 82 EC these ordoliberal concepts … have frequently been the focus of the debate.'[21]

Inducing customers to take supply from the dominant undertaking can lead to exclusion or impairment of competing suppliers. Such inducement limits access to the dominant supplier's customer base, and thereby restricts competitors' freedom to participate in the market. It can also prevent buyers from having freedom to choose their sources of supply. The question is whether, by preventing such practices, consumer welfare is promoted. This goes back to the question of whether foreclosure of competitors and customers can be assumed to be harmful also to end consumers. For example, would safeguarding competitors from being excluded or competing vigorously in the market not only protect their freedom to participate in the market, but also provide consumers with some welfare in the form of choice?[22] This question is addressed in the following section.

2.3 Choice

As noted above, when trying to achieve economic freedom in the market, the harmful effects of foreclosure are considered to be competitors' reduced choice of customers and customers' reduced choice of suppliers. Reduced choice restricts their economic freedom and therefore is unacceptable. Choice must be available so that customers can move from one supplier to another, even though they would not necessarily use that choice, but at least it would be available to them. Similarly, competitors should have access to customers although they may not actually supply them. This shows that conduct which restricts a *hypothetical* customer choice, as opposed to an *actual* choice, is enough. Thus, where a dominant undertaking offers its customers a loyalty rebate, there is no need to demonstrate that absent the rebate a significant number of customers would have chosen to buy their products from competing suppliers and therefore the rebate alters customers' choice.[23] There is no need to show what would have happened to customer demand in the absence of the rebate,

[21] C. Ahlborn and C. Grave, 'Walter Eucken and Ordoliberalism: An Introduction from a Consumer Welfare Perspective' 2(2) *Competition Policy International* (2006) 196, 206.

[22] According to the Commission, squeezing competitors out of the market will deprive consumers of choice, seventeenth *Annual Report on Competition Policy* (1988) 77.

[23] Indeed, why would the dominant undertaking offer a rebate if customers would get their supplies from it anyway?

it is sufficient that there is a restriction of hypothetical customer choice. This is confirmed in *Michelin I*, where the ECJ held that 'the discount *tends* to remove or restrict the buyer's freedom to choose his sources of supply'.[24] The ECJ adopted a similar position in *Hoffmann-La Roche*, where the court stated that it constitutes an abuse when an undertaking in a dominant position directly or indirectly ties its customer by a supply obligation, since this deprives the customer of the ability to choose freely his sources of supply and denies other producers access to the market.[25] In this way, a discussion of choice is linked to the discussion of foreclosure. Although customers may not make use of their choice, it is not even available to them if alternative suppliers are foreclosed from accessing the market.

Actual choice, as opposed to hypothetical choice, appears to be relevant in relation to coercion in tying cases. For example, in the tying part of the *Microsoft* decision, choice was discussed in relation to both coercion and foreclosure.[26] In relation to the coercion, the Commission argued that 'customers are not given the choice of acquiring the tying product without the tied product'. The 'Original Equipment Manufacturers' (OEMs), who assemble computers, could not license the Windows operating system without the Windows Media Player (WMP) pre-installed, as Microsoft did not offer a licence which would cover Windows without WMP.[27] In relation to foreclosure, the Commission appeared – like in rebate cases – to be concerned with hypothetical choice. The Commission said that the tying of WMP meant that WMP became the 'choice' of media player and that in turn *risked* foreclosing the market.[28] Where there is foreclosure, there may not be any, or may be very little, alternative choice (depending on the percentage of foreclosure). Whilst customers and consumers would not necessarily make use of their choice, it would not even be available to them because of the foreclosure. By protecting the structure of competition, hypothetical choice is protected.

By protecting hypothetical choice, consumers may have more options between different suppliers at the intermediate level, or choice between differentiated variants of a product at the retail level. This may increase aggregate consumer surplus. However, choice is only valued if consumers value the option such choice gives them, e.g. increased bargaining power

24 *Michelin I*, supra note 16, para. 73. Emphasis added.

25 *Hoffmann-La Roche*, supra note 9, paras. 90, 98 and 111.

26 COMP/C-3/37.792 *Microsoft*.

27 Ibid., para. 827. 28 Ibid., para. 842.

and range of quality. Mars bars bought in a shop offering many different types of chocolate may give consumers more happiness than Mars bars bought in a shop with no choice – even holding price constant. Yet some consumers buy Mars bars regardless of the alternatives, so choice does not add anything to these consumers' welfare, it may even create inertia and result in less happiness to them. If choice is about increasing utility for consumers, a set of choices may add little to consumer welfare as not all choices have the same value for consumers. From a welfare point of view, choice is only valued if it leads to a better and more efficient outcome for consumers in the form of lower prices and better quality. If choice does not have these benefits, then consumer welfare is not concerned with choice. Choice is not valued in itself. For example, in a market which is characterised by a natural monopoly there would be no choice. If the natural monopoly is the most efficient supply structure and thus leads to the best outcome for consumers, then it would be totally acceptable from a consumer welfare perspective.

Due to the overlap between consumer welfare and economic freedom when it comes to choice, the Commission and the Community Courts must explain – if they aim at promoting consumer welfare – how reduced choice harms consumers. The ECJ did not do that in, for example, *Commercial Solvents*,[29] as illustrated in chapter 3.

3. Effects in relation to structure of the market or to consumers

Section 3.1 discusses the nature of the effects required: *actual* or *likely* effects. This is essential in relation to presumptions, which will be discussed in section 4, as a requirement of actual effects would mean that assumptions cannot be made. Section 3.2 considers which part of the market an analysis of effects relates to: competition, competitors, consumers, the structure or the market itself. It illustrates that economic freedom is concerned with the effects on *the structure of competition* whereas consumer welfare is concerned with the effects on *consumers*. This is important for the main aim of this chapter, which is whether harmful effects of a restriction of economic freedom can be used to assume that consumer welfare is also harmed. It uses the Commission's decision in *Microsoft* to analyse whether the Commission was protecting consumer welfare, as it claimed to have done following the decision. It shows how the

[29] Case 6–7/73 *Istituto Chemioterapico Italiano SpA and Commercial Solvents Corporation v. Commission* [1974] ECR 223.

Commission adopted an analysis of effects; not on consumers, but on the structure of competition. This clearly shows that the Commission believes that harm to economic freedom is harm to the welfare of consumers. This ignores the conflict between the two objectives. Examining which parts of the market the Commission cares about can tell one something about which objective the Commission is aiming to achieve. Section 3.3 asks what the Commission is hoping to achieve by looking at the structure of competition.

3.1 Actual or likely effects

In *Michelin II*, the defendant, Michelin, argued:[30]

> [In order to] establish an infringement of Article 82 EC, the Commission is required to prove that the rebates are likely in due course to undermine the competitive structure of the market and ultimately to permit the undertaking concerned to abuse the consumer. Since the specific aim of competition law is to encourage price competition, the applicant maintains that a rebate system can be described as an abuse only if it has a foreclosure effect or, in other words, if it weakens competition in the longer term and enables the undertaking in a dominant position to recover the costs generated by its rebate policy.

Michelin also argued, with reference to paragraph 91 of *Hoffmann-La Roche*,[31] that for Article 82 to apply 'it is essential that the practice in issue had an effect' and that 'the Commission did not examine the actual economic effect of the criticised conduct'.[32] The CFI stated that '[u]nlike Article 81(1) EC, Article 82 EC contains no reference to the anticompetitive aim or anticompetitive effect of the practice referred to. However, in the light of the context of Article 82 EC, conduct will be regarded as abusive only if it restricts competition.'[33] The court does not deny the

[30] Case T-203/01 *Manufacture Française des Pneumatiques Michelin v. Commission* (*Michelin II*) [2003] ECR II-4071, para. 53.

[31] *Hoffmann-La Roche*, supra note 9, para. 91 reads: 'the concept of abuse is an objective concept relating to the behaviour of an undertaking in a dominant position which is such as to influençe the structure of a market where, as a result of the very presence of the undertaking in question, the degree of competition is weakened and which, through recourse to methods different from those which condition normal competition in products or services on the basis of the transactions of commercial operators, has the effect of hindering the maintenance of the degree of competition still existing in the market or the growth of that competition'.

[32] *Michelin II*, supra note 30, paras. 235–6.

[33] Ibid., para. 237.

relevance of effects, but specifies that the effect referred to in *Hoffmann-La Roche* 'does not necessarily relate to the actual effect of the abusive conduct complained of. For the purposes of establishing an infringement of Article 82 EC, it is sufficient to show that the abusive conduct of the undertaking in a dominant position *tends* to restrict competition or, in other words, that the conduct is *capable* of having that effect.'[34] Moreover, 'for the purposes of applying Article 82 EC, establishing the anticompetitive object and the anticompetitive effect are one and the same thing ... If it is shown that the object pursued by the conduct of an undertaking in a dominant position is to limit competition, that conduct will also be liable to have such an effect.'[35]

This shows that the Commission is not required to postpone intervention until it can show *actual* effects, but can intervene in the market where exclusionary conduct is *likely* to have adverse effects.[36] This is acceptable, otherwise the Commission would be unable to rely on presumptions.

As will be demonstrated in section 4 below, the Commission relies on assumptions of harmful effects. Where effects are assumed, the criterion cannot be actual effects as that would exclude reliance on assumptions. Assumptions are very useful and necessary to make enforcement administrable and efficient. This author does not criticise the reliance on assumptions, but questions, in the following section, what part the market analysis of effects relates to: competition, competitors, consumers, the structure or the market. This is important for deciding which assumptions the Commission should rely on in order to achieve its objectives.

3.2 *Effects on which part of the market?*

The explicit wording of Article 82 does not refer to effects. Unlike Article 81, there is no requirement of the conduct having as its object or effect the prevention, restriction or distortion of competition within the common market. Article 82 merely prohibits 'any abuse by one or more undertakings of a dominant position ... insofar as it may affect trade between Member States'.[37] However, Competition Commissioner Kroes confirms

[34] Ibid., para. 239. Emphasis added.

[35] Ibid., para. 241; Case T-340/03 *France Télécom v. Commission* [2007] ECR II-107, para. 195.

[36] *Guidance Paper*, supra note 2, para. 19.

[37] See wording of Article 82 in chapter 1, p. 9.

'[t]he exercise of market power must be assessed essentially on the basis of its effects on the market'.[38] This is all very well, but what does 'effects on the market' mean? Does it mean effects on the structure of competition or on consumers? Given Kroes' emphasis on consumer welfare in other policy statements,[39] she presumably means effects on consumers. This section examines whether the Commission is analysing effects on consumers. Former Competition Commissioner Monti says, in his foreword to the Commission's *Annual Report on Competition Policy* in 2000, that effects on consumers are often neglected:[40]

> While it is generally understood that competition policy improves overall economic efficiency, it is surprising that its most evident effect, that on consumers, is often neglected. Consumers should be better informed of, more closely taken into account and more directly involved in competition matters. In turn, this helps competition policy to focus more clearly on actions, which are ultimately beneficial to consumers' interests.

Some argue that neither the actual nor the potential effects of conduct on consumer welfare are considered in the case law of the Community Courts;[41] whereas others consider that they are sometimes dealt with but in an inconsistent way.[42]

This section examines whether the Commission and Community Courts analyse effects and on what. The latter is important for the question of which objective they are aiming at protecting. Aiming at promoting consumer welfare does not require an assessment of the effect of an undertaking's behaviour on the *structure of competition* in a given market, but requires an analysis of the effects of an undertaking's behaviour on *consumers*. Because chapter 4 found that economic freedom is

38 N. Kroes, 'The Commission's Review of Exclusionary Abuses of Dominant Position', 26/27 June 2006, the Fourth Annual Bilateral Meeting organised by the Korean Competition Forum, 5.

39 For example, N. Kroes, 'Preliminary Thoughts on Policy Review of Article 82', 23 September 2005, Fordham Corporate Law Institute New York; N. Kroes, 'European Competition Policy in a Changing World and Globalised Economy: Fundamentals, New Objectives and Challenges Ahead', 5 June 2007, GCLC/College of Europe Conference on '50 years of EC Competition Law', Brussels.

40 Thirtieth *Annual Report on Competition Policy* (2000) 1.

41 P. Marsden and P. Whelan, ' "Consumer Detriment" and its Application in EC and UK Competition Law' 27(10) *European Competition Law Review* (2006) 569, 584.

42 R. O'Donoghue and A. J. Padilla, *The Law and Economics of Article 82 EC* (Oxford Hart Publishing, 2006) 217; J. Temple Lang, 'Panel Discussion on Non-Pricing Abuses' in C. D. Ehlermann and I. Atanasiu (eds.), *European Competition Law Annual 2003: What is an Abuse of a Dominant Position?* (Oxford: Hart Publishing, 2006) 477.

not a means to an end of consumer welfare, it is hard to see how one can assume that consumers are harmed merely by demonstrating harm to the structure of competition, i.e. harm to economic freedom.

Some cases reveal that the Commission and the Community Courts do engage in an analysis of effects. For example, in *Van den Bergh Foods*, the CFI concluded that Article 82 also applies to *de facto* exclusivity.[43] This finding was based upon the effect of the exclusivity clause, which was preventing the retailers from selling other brands of ice cream and thus preventing competing manufacturers from gaining access to the relevant market.[44] Whilst the CFI examines effects, it is not effects on consumers. In *Microsoft*,[45] the Commission argued it had adopted an effects-based approach.[46] Whilst the Commission analysed the effects, it was effects on the structure of competition. This goes back to the point introduced above that a methodology based on effects does not necessarily mean the Commission is aiming at protecting consumer welfare. Beside *Microsoft*, there are other cases decided under Article 82 where effects have been considered in the light of the facts of the case, but they all consider effects on the structure of competition.[47]

3.3 *Tying part of the* Microsoft *case as an illustrative example of effects on the structure of competition*

In the tying part of the Commission's decision in *Microsoft*,[48] the Commission argued that Microsoft did not give customers the choice of obtaining the Windows operating system without Windows Media Player (WMP). According to Microsoft, consumers did not have to pay extra for having the WMP as they got it for free.[49] This is a good argument if the aim of Article 82 is consumer welfare, as consumers are not exploited (at least) in the form of a higher price. The Commission rejected this argument by referring to the fact that the wording of Article 82(2)(d) does not include

[43] *Van den Bergh Foods*, supra note 8. [44] Ibid., para. 160.

[45] *Microsoft*, supra note 26.

[46] IP/08/1877 of 3 December 2008, 'Antitrust: Consumer Welfare at Heart of Commission Fight Against Abuses by Dominant Undertakings'.

[47] For example, OJ [2001] L331/40 *Deutsche Post AG*, paras. 37 ff.; Case T-65/89 *BPB Industries plc and British Gypsum Ltd v. Commission* [1993] ECR II-389, paras. 65–6; upheld on appeal in Case C-310/93P *BPB Industries plc and British Gypsum Ltd v. Commission* [1995] ECR I-865; see also P. Akman, ' "Consumer Welfare" and Article 82 EC: Practice and Rhetoric' 32(1) *World Competition* (2009) 71.

[48] *Microsoft*, supra note 26, paras. 793 ff. [49] Ibid., para. 830.

a reference to 'paying'. Moreover, limiting tying abuses to where there is payment would restrict the application of Article 82 to tying cases where customers had to buy something extra. The Commission referred to the ECJ's judgment in *Hoffmann-La Roche*[50] to show that the court found that the rebate scheme offered by Hoffmann-La Roche constituted an abuse even where Hoffmann-La Roche did not contractually force its customers to purchase anything extra. According to the Commission, such an interpretation suggests the absence of competitive harm if customers do not have to spend money for the tied product, and that would conflate the coercion and foreclosure of competition elements of tying.[51] In relation to the latter point, the Commission said:[52]

> that the harmful effects on consumers from tying WMP (also) derive from undermining the structure of competition in media players which is liable to result in deterrence of innovation and eventual reduction in choice of competing media players.
>
> In particular, it will be shown that inasmuch as tying risks foreclosing competitors, it is immaterial that consumers are not forced to 'purchase' or 'use' WMP. As long as consumers 'automatically' obtain WMP – even if for free – alternative suppliers are at a competitive disadvantage.

This clearly shows that the Commission relies on an assumption of consumer harm where there is harm to the structure of competition. The Commission argued that Microsoft's tying of WMP foreclosed competition in the market for media players. It explained that foreclosure would undermine the structure of competition and discourage innovation and reduce choice. As shown above, reduced choice is not necessarily unacceptable from a welfare point of view. To justify its lack of analysis on how Microsoft's behaviour is likely to harm consumers, the Commission simply referred to CFI's judgments in *Michelin II*[53] and *British Airways*[54] to stress that foreclosure effects do not have to be *concrete* foreclosure effects.[55]

The Commission said in paragraph 841 of *Microsoft*:

> There are indeed circumstances relating to the tying of WMP which warrant a closer examination of the effects that tying has on competition in this case. While in classical tying cases, the Commission and the Courts considered the foreclosure effect for competing vendors to be

[50] *Hoffmann-La Roche*, supra note 9. [51] *Microsoft*, supra note 26, para. 831.
[52] Ibid., paras. 832–3. [53] *Michelin II*, supra note 30.
[54] Case T-219/99 *British Airways plc v. Commission* [2003] ECR II-5917.
[55] *Microsoft*, supra note 26, para. 838.

> demonstrated by the bundling of a separate product with the dominant product, in the case at issue, users can and do to a certain extent obtain third party media players through the Internet, sometimes for free. There are therefore indeed good reasons *not* to assume without further analysis that tying WMP constitutes conduct which by its very nature is liable to foreclose competition.

The Commission acknowledged that tying WMP to the Windows operating system could not automatically be assumed to foreclose competition, and went on to examine if foreclosure of competitors led to anticompetitive effects. It found that the universal distribution of WMP in Windows would oblige content providers to program their content in Windows Media format. This would have the effect of excluding competing media players from the market and indirectly compelling consumers to use only WMP.[56] This assumes that a restriction of competitors' economic freedom will harm consumers indirectly, which would be a fair assumption to make if harm to economic freedom equals harm to consumers. However, chapter 4 showed that this is not always the case. The Commission acknowledged that such anticompetitive effects may be outweighed where there are objective justifications.[57]

One of the efficiencies advanced by Microsoft was the lowering of transaction costs for consumers, reducing time and confusion by having a set of default options in a personal computer.[58] The reduction of transaction costs consisted in the economies made by a tied sale of two products, which saved resources otherwise spent on maintaining a separate distribution system for the second product. The Commission rejected the possibility of distributive efficiency by stating that such costs are insignificant in software licensing.[59] Another efficiency advanced by Microsoft was that the WMP is indispensable for simplifying the work of applications developers.[60] This argument was also rejected. The Commission said that Microsoft had not submitted adequate evidence that tying WMP was objectively justified by pro-competitive effects that would outweigh the distortion of competition caused by it.[61] Thus, it concluded that Microsoft's tying of its WMP to its Windows operating system was not indispensable for the developer and consumer benefits; it artificially reduced competitors' incentives to develop competing software;[62] and therefore competition in the media player market was considerably weakened.[63]

[56] Ibid., paras. 843–76. [57] Ibid., para. 955. [58] Ibid., para. 956.
[59] Ibid., para. 958. [60] Ibid., para. 962. [61] Ibid., para. 970.
[62] Ibid., para. 983. [63] Ibid., para. 984.

The Commission rejected Microsoft's efficiencies arguments based on lack of evidence. However, whatever efficiency arguments Microsoft advanced they would have been rejected, because the Commission did not interpret Article 82 in the light of consumer welfare. This is clear from its analysis on effects. Chapter 2 showed that efficiencies are only relevant where the aim is consumer welfare. Chapter 3 showed that Article 82 aims at protecting many objectives, not only consumer welfare. Thus, it would have been preferable if the Commission had clarified, at the beginning of its investigation, that Article 82 would be interpreted in the light of economic freedom. This would have saved Microsoft's and taxpayers' money by avoiding a long, painful investigation, because the Commission would not have accepted any efficiency arguments anyway. The Commission could have justified its position by arguing that pursuing economic freedom is preferable in a market where a company approaches a monopoly and where preference is given to the process of rivalry over possible pro-competitive efficiency gains. The *Discussion Paper* acknowledges that the Commission will give preference to the process of rivalry over possible pro-competitive efficiency gains where the undertaking in question is approaching a monopoly.[64]

On appeal, Microsoft claimed that the Commission's decision was based on a speculative foreclosure theory, which normally is not taken into consideration when analysing tying.[65] The CFI said that 'while it is true that neither the provision nor, more generally, Article 82 EC as a whole contains any reference to the anticompetitive effect of bundling, the fact remains that, in principle, conduct will be regarded as abusive only if it is capable of restricting competition'.[66] The court rejected Microsoft's argument:[67]

> [T]he applicant cannot claim that the Commission relied on a new and highly speculative theory to reach the conclusion that a foreclosure effect exists in the present case. As indicated at recital 841 to the contested decision, the Commission considered that, in light of the specific circumstances of the present case, it could not merely assume, *as it normally does in cases of abusive tying*, that the tying of a specific product and a dominant product has by its nature a foreclosure effect. The Commission therefore examined more closely the actual effects which

64 DG COMP's *Discussion Paper on the Application of Article 82 of the Treaty to Exclusionary Abuses* (December 2005) (*Discussion Paper*) para. 91.

65 Case T-201/04 *Microsoft Corp. v. Commission* [2007] ECR II-3601, para. 846.

66 Ibid., para. 867.

67 Ibid., para. 868. Emphasis added.

> the bundling had already had on the streaming media player market and also the way in which that market was likely to evolve.

The CFI confirmed that the Commission did not merely assume that the tying of WMP and the Windows operating system had *by its nature* a foreclosure effect, but had explained why such effects were capable of being present in the case. But again, if the aim is consumer welfare, it would have had to explain how the tying behaviour was capable of harming *consumers* in the specific market. Instead of focusing on consumers, the court referred to the Commission's explanation that Microsoft benefited from an 'unparalleled advantage with respect to the distribution of its product' that 'inevitably had significant consequences for the structure of competition' on the streaming media player market.[68] The ubiquity of WMP as a result of its tying with Windows was capable of having 'an appreciable impact on content providers and software designers' because of the significant 'indirect network effects' that existed in the WMP market.[69] The ubiquity of WMP on Windows PCs 'secured Microsoft a competitive advantage unrelated to the merits of its products' and erected a barrier to entry to new 'contenders' not only on the media players market, but also on other adjacent markets, such as media players on wireless information devices, set-top boxes, DRM solutions and on-line music delivery.[70] The court found that the evolution of the market consistently pointed to a trend in favour of WMP and Windows Media formats to the detriment of the main competing media players.[71]

If the Commission believes it pursued an objective of consumer welfare by adopting an effects-based approach, it is mistaken. The *Microsoft* case illustrates that the Commission did indeed adopt an analysis of effects, but instead of examining whether Microsoft's behaviour was harmful to consumers, it examined whether its conduct was harmful to the structure of competition.

By prohibiting conduct which harms the structure of competition the Commission may protect inefficient competitors. Protecting *inefficient* competitors against elimination goes beyond protecting an efficient competitive process.[72] The emphasis is on 'efficient' because significant harm to effective competition normally requires that the foreclosed competitors play a sufficiently important role in the competitive

[68] Ibid., para. 1054. [69] Ibid., para. 1061.

[70] Ibid., para. 1076. [71] Ibid., para. 1078.

[72] R. Joliet, *Monopolization and Abuse of Dominant Position* (University of Liège, 1970) 250–1.

process.[73] Likewise, an alteration of the competitive structure in itself is not objectionable and may even follow from a natural selection of the best competitors. It only becomes unacceptable where the alteration of the market structure is so significant that it harms consumers. However, looking at the structure of competition only may not tell one anything about consumer welfare. For example, in dynamic markets even a monopoly may be the necessary market structure that ensures that consumers benefit from firms' willingness to innovate.[74] In such markets, firms compete *for* the market rather than *in* the market.[75] These markets are characterised by expensive R&D (in the form of high fixed costs) and low marginal costs of production. It is necessary to price substantially above marginal cost to cover total costs.[76] Thus, it is important to have the 'first mover advantage' to earn monopoly profits.[77] In dynamic markets, competition to obtain a monopoly is an important form of competition.[78] Assessing the structure of competition only and not taking a step further to examine *how* the harm to the structure of competition in a specific market is likely to either harm or benefit consumers is not enough if the aim is consumer welfare. Some argue that even insignificant changes in the market structure have become associated with harmful effects on consumers, and therefore have been caught by Article 82.[79] This begs the question what the Commission is hoping to achieve by examining the structure of competition. This is discussed in the following section.

3.4 What is the Commission hoping to achieve by examining the structure of competition?

Showing effects on consumers requires economic evidence, which may be difficult/expensive/slow to obtain, or even impossible to obtain. There is a danger of intervention being too late. Such type II errors occur

[73] *Guidelines on the Assessment of Non-horizontal Mergers*, supra note 10, para. 48.

[74] S. Bishop and M. Walker, *The Economics of EC Competition Law: Concepts, Application and Measurement* (London: Sweet & Maxwell, 2nd edn, 2002) 37.

[75] Ibid., 36. [76] O'Donoghue and Padilla, supra note 42, 607.

[77] Bishop and Walker, supra note 74, 37.

[78] M. Motta, *Competition Policy: Theory and Practice* (Cambridge University Press, 2004) 64.

[79] E. Rousseva, 'Modernizing by Eradicating: How the Commission's New Approach to Article 81 EC Dispenses with the Need to Apply Article 82 EC to Vertical Restraints' 42 *Common Market Law Review* (2005) 587, 592.

where competition authorities do not intervene due to lack of evidence although intervention would have been justified.[80] Instead of postponing intervention, the Commission relies on an assumption of consumer harm where there is harm to the structure of competition. Perhaps the Commission is hoping that consumer welfare may be promoted in the long run by protecting the structure of competition. This appears to be DG COMP's reason for protecting 'not yet as efficient competitors' as this may mean there will be more firms in the market,[81] which could potentially lead to more competition in the long run, driving prices down and increasing allocative efficiency to the benefit of consumers. The *Guidance Paper* believes that even less efficient competitors may exert a constraint on the dominant undertaking.[82] However, as chapter 4 explained, this would require the Commission to enforce price regulation,[83] as inefficient consumers are unlikely to be able to stay in the market without such regulation.

Despite these possible reasons, the Commission ought to show how the dominant undertaking's conduct is likely to harm the specific consumer group otherwise competition on the merits may be mistaken for anticompetitive exclusionary conduct. Whilst case law acknowledges that only conduct through means other than competition on the merits is prohibited,[84] competition on the merits is not defined in the Treaty and its content is not self-evident. Because it is often difficult to distinguish competition on the merits from conduct with long-term anticompetitive effects, legitimate competition from which consumers benefit can be mistakenly treated as exclusionary conduct. Such type I errors, where competition authorities intervene in circumstances where intervention is not justified, may harm consumers by chilling legitimate conduct wrongly found to be exclusionary.[85] Adopting a methodology by which competition authorities have to prove that the conduct in question is likely to have

[80] See chapter 1. [81] *Discussion Paper*, supra note 64, para. 67.

[82] *Guidance Paper*, supra note 2, para. 23.

[83] A. S. Edlin, 'Stopping Above-Cost Predatory Pricing' 4 *Yale Law Journal* (2002) 941, 991. He argues that consumers often need inefficient entrants and explains how these can be protected by an initial price freeze until the smaller entrant has established itself in the market.

[84] *Hoffmann-La Roche*, supra note 9, para. 91, according to which Article 82 requires 'recourse to methods different from those which condition normal competition' otherwise it is not an abuse; Case 62/86 *AKZO Chemie BV v. Commission* [1991] ECR I-3359, para. 70, according to which Article 82 prohibits conduct 'by using methods other than those which come within the scope of competition on the basis of quality'.

[85] See chapter 1.

anticompetitive effects on consumers would have a less chilling effect on competition. In addition, it is hoped that it would not discourage innovation and risk-taking from which consumers derive great benefits over the long term. Aggressive but legitimate competition may make it more difficult for inefficient competitors to stay in the market or even compete vigorously in the market, but unless such conduct has an effect on consumers, it should not be prohibited under a consumer welfare standard.

This section is not suggesting that the Commission should not rely on assumptions of consumer harm, but concludes that the Commission cannot automatically assume that consumers are harmed where there are harmful effects to the structure of competition, if it is trying to achieve consumer welfare. Whether assumptions of consumer harm are acceptable depends on theory, economic evidence and the experience underpinning the assumption. The following section examines some of the assumptions the Commission and the Community Courts have relied upon over the years. Whether an assumption is considered acceptable depends on what the Commission is trying to achieve by relying on the assumption. Assumptions which may be acceptable where the aim is economic freedom may be objectionable under the consumer welfare standard.

4. Some case-law-developed assumptions

In some cases neither the Commission nor the Community Courts explain *how* the conduct in question is likely to have harmful effects on the structure of competition and/or on consumers. Instead, the conduct is *assumed* to be abusive. There are various assumptions of abuse. One assumption is where the object of the conduct is to restrict competition, abuse is assumed where evidence of intent is found.[86] Intent is used as a 'proxy' for proof of abuse.[87] Another assumption of abuse is where there is a risk of competition being eliminated. Whether these are good assumptions depends on whether they reflect reality and what the aims of the assumptions are. In general, assumptions can make administrative enforcement efficient and are to be welcomed if they are supported by a

[86] *Michelin II*, supra note 30, para. 241; Case T-228/97 *Irish Sugar plc v. Commission* [1999] ECR II-2969, para. 170, upheld on appeal in Case C-497/99P *Irish Sugar plc v. Commission* [2001] ECR I-5333.

[87] The Community Courts sometimes use the terminology of object and sometimes that of aim or intent. Object and aim will be used interchangeably in this chapter.

good theory on how consumers are harmed, if the aim is consumer welfare; or, how the structure of competition is harmed, if the aim is economic freedom. However, assumptions should not be adopted just to increase efficient enforcement if they sacrifice the right outcome, unless efficiency of the administrative rule outweighs the chances of a good outcome.[88]

4.1 *Intent as a proxy for abuse*

In *Michelin II*, abuse was found on the basis that the object of the conduct was to limit competition.[89] The conduct in question was an annual rebate, a service bonus and a progress bonus, all capable of both foreclosing competitive entry/expansion and enhancing efficiencies.[90] Thus, it is not certain from the nature of the conduct that it restricts competition.[91] The CFI reached its conclusion by referring to the presumptions established in *AKZO*.[92]

The first presumption in *AKZO* is that prices below average variable costs (AVC)[93] are to be regarded as abusive in themselves.[94] *Tetra Pak II* confirms this presumption,[95] as well as establishing that additional proof of intention to eliminate competitors is not necessary where prices are below average variable costs.[96] This is because 'there is no conceivable economic purpose other than the elimination of a competitor, since each item produced and sold entails a loss for the undertaking'.[97] This presumption is not unobjectionable in principle.[98] Only part of the variable costs is

[88] Easterbrook, supra note 4. [89] *Michelin II*, supra note 30.

[90] See D. Spector, 'Loyalty Rebates: An Assessment of Competition Concerns and a Proposed Structured Rule of Reason' 1(2) *Competition Policy International* (2005) 88.

[91] Without a theory based on the real market conditions on how the rebate system harms consumers – assuming that consumer welfare is the main objective – the Commission runs the risk of prohibiting efficient conduct and committing a type I error (prohibiting conduct that is not harmful – false positive). This is one of the main issues fuelling the criticism of the application of Article 82, in particular, in the context of rebates.

[92] *Michelin II*, supra note 30, para. 242.

[93] *Guidance Paper*, supra note 2, footnotes 18 and 40 explain that in most cases, AVC and average avoidable costs (AAC) will be the same, as it is often only variable costs that can be avoided. AAC is the average of the costs that could have been avoided if the company had not produced a discrete amount of (extra) output.

[94] *AKZO*, supra note 84, para. 71.

[95] Case C-333/94P *Tetra Pak International SA v. Commission* (*Tetra Pak II*) [1996] ECR I-5951, para. 41.

[96] Ibid., para. 42. [97] Ibid., para. 41.

[98] B. Allan, 'Article 82: A Commentary on DG Competition's Discussion Paper' 2(1) *Competition Policy International* (2006) 42, 57.

covered and none of the fixed costs are covered. The eliminatory nature – the risk of eliminating a competitor – of such pricing is presumed.[99] Where the conduct in itself is abusive, subjective intent as well as the awareness of illegality is irrelevant.[100] Abuse can occur in the absence of fault.[101]

The second presumption in *AKZO* is that prices above AVC but below average total costs (ATC)[102] are considered abusive where they are determined as part of a plan for eliminating a competitor.[103] Evidence of intent, such as documents from the dominant undertaking showing a clear predatory strategy, is taken into consideration when examining pricing below ATC.[104] Variable costs are covered, but only part of the fixed costs is covered. Thus, an additional element of intent is necessary as the eliminatory nature of the conduct cannot automatically be presumed.[105] There may be a legitimate reason for not covering all fixed costs. By adding intent as a necessary element, the Commission and the Community Courts must believe that the likelihood of elimination of a competitor is greater where there is intent than where there is no such intent.[106] In the specific case, AKZO argued that selling off stock below total cost is better than not selling anything in order to recover some fixed costs.[107] The Commission rejected this argument, because it found clear evidence that AKZO had the intention of selectively targeting its competitor ECS's customers to force ECS to abandon those customers or to match a loss-making price in order to retain those customers.[108] Intent assisted the Commission and

[99] *France Télécom*, supra note 35, para. 227.

[100] A. Jones and B. Sufrin, *EC Competition Law* (Oxford University Press, 3rd edn, 2007) 324.

[101] Case 6/72 *Europemballage Corporation and Continental Can Co. Inc. v. Commission* [1973] ECR 215, para. 27; *Hoffmann-La Roche*, supra note 9, para. 91; T. Eilmansberger, 'How to Distinguish Good from Bad Competition under Article 82 EC: In Search of Clearer and More Coherent Standards for Anticompetitive Abuses' 42 *Common Market Law Review* (2005) 129, 146; L. Gyselen, 'Rebates: Competition on the Merits or Exclusionary Practice?' in Ehlermann and Atanasiu, supra note 42, 293.

[102] The *Guidance Paper*, supra note 2, footnote 18 explains that ATC and long-run average incremental cost (LRAIC) are good proxies for each other, and are the same in the case of single-product undertakings.

[103] *AKZO*, supra note 84, para. 72.

[104] *Tetra Pak II*, supra note 95, paras. 151 and 171; *France Télécom*, supra note 35, paras. 198–215.

[105] *Tetra Pak II*, supra note 95, para. 41.

[106] From a philosophical point of view, an anticompetitive outcome is more likely found where a dominant undertaking intended to achieve such an outcome than where it did not have such intent: see A. Kenny, 'Intention and Purpose' 63 *Journal of Philosophy* (1966) 642, 649–51.

[107] *AKZO*, supra note 84.

[108] Ibid., para. 9.

the ECJ in discovering whether the object of AKZO's conduct was to cover some fixed costs, which is legitimate, or to force ECS out of the market or prevent it from competing vigorously in the market, which is anticompetitive. In the specific case there was clear evidence that the pricing was not to sell off stock, but to impair ECS.

Returning to *Michelin II*, the CFI referred to the second presumption in *AKZO*.[109] Depending on the specific rebate scheme, rebates can be predatory as they are low marginal prices on some (marginal) incremental units. Low prices at the margin and low prices per unit can be predatory. However, the point of referring to the presumption in *AKZO* was not to decide whether the pricing practice was predatory, but to emphasise that conduct 'cannot be allowed if its *purpose* is to strengthen that dominant position and thereby abuse it'.[110] A similar position is taken in *British Airways*.[111] The legal presumption based on intent established in *AKZO* also seems to apply in rebate cases. Where the purpose of a rebate is anticompetitive, it is not necessary to consider the actual effects or even foreseeable effects on customers or competitors, but only that the rebates are *capable* of having these effects on any potential customer or competitor.[112] Likely effects on customers or competitors are assumed where intent to abuse is found. This is a presumption of harm to economic freedom where intent is found.

Instead of considering whether the rebate system in *Michelin II* was likely either to lead to higher prices for heavy goods vehicle tyres in France, or to prevent prices from decreasing, the CFI was confident that the Commission had proven that the purpose of Michelin's rebate system was to tie its customers to it.[113] It is the eliminatory effects dominant undertakings intend to achieve through their conduct which restrict competition.[114] The court assumed that Michelin's loyalty-enhancing rebate schemes were likely to make it more difficult for Michelin's competitors to access the relevant market.[115] This shows that the court was aiming at protecting economic freedom and not at promoting consumer

[109] *Michelin II*, supra note 30, para. 242. [110] Ibid., para. 243. Emphasis added.

[111] *British Airways*, supra note 54, para. 241.

[112] Ibid., para. 293; *Michelin II*, supra note 30, para. 239.

[113] *Michelin II*, supra note 30, para. 244.

[114] J. Faull and A. Nikpay, *The EC Law of Competition* (Oxford University Press, 2nd edn, 2007) 349.

[115] *Michelin II*, supra note 30, para. 244. Market access is linked to market integration, and Article 82 becomes a tool to protect the results flowing from eradicating barriers to the markets within the common market. The competition rules are after all linked to the establishment of a common market to ensure competition is undistorted so economic

welfare. If the objective is economic freedom, having a dominant position in conjunction with the intent to restrict competition is enough to trigger the prohibition in Article 82. By using intention to make a potentially 'good' act 'bad',[116] dominant undertakings have no ability to defend themselves, as claiming lack of intention does not constitute a defence.[117] According to case law, dominant undertakings can only advance objective justifications purely based on objective factors beyond the control of undertakings and on public policy considerations where there is a need to provide efficient service to the public.[118] As chapter 2 explained, when protecting economic freedom the standard is complete competition and dominant undertakings must conduct themselves 'as if' they are faced with 'complete competition'. It is clear from the special responsibility imposed upon dominant undertakings[119] that they are required to act as if they are faced with complete competition.[120]

Exclusionary conduct will always harm economic freedom, but not always consumer welfare. If the aim is to promote consumer welfare, it is essential to distinguish between exclusionary conduct which is beneficial to consumers and exclusionary conduct which is harmful to consumers. Thus, relying on intent as a proxy for abuse is dangerous, because the very object of competing is to strengthen market power to defeat competitors and thereby increase market share and turnover in the market. Because it is very difficult to disassociate the normal desire to increase turnover and market share from the motive to defeat competitors, some argue that intent is an unreliable criterion[121] or even an unsatisfactory test:[122]

> Whenever a competitor competes he intends to take business away from rivals, which involves excluding them. If he were completely successful

rights and freedoms in the form of the freedom to provide services, free movement of goods and freedom of establishment are ensured. This aim would be defeated if private agreements or economically powerful firms were allowed to re-establish barriers to trade or make access to the market difficult.

116 To the extent that there is a tendency to criminalise European competition enforcement there is a question mark over whether intent ought to be a necessary criterion in all cases. This question will not be answered here. Criminalisation of European competition enforcement in general has been considered by W. Wils, *Efficiency and Justice in European Antitrust Enforcement* (Oxford: Hart Publishing, 2008) 155, in particular 164 ff.

117 Faull and Nikpay, supra note 114, 349.

118 E. Rousseva, 'The Concept of "Objective Justification" of an Abuse of a Dominant Position: Can it Help to Modernise the Analysis under Article 82 EC?' 2(2) *Competition Law Review* (2006) 27, 71.

119 *Michelin I*, supra note 16, para. 57.

120 Lovdahl Gormsen, supra note 3, 10.

121 R. Posner, *Antitrust Law* (University of Chicago Press, 2nd edn, 2001) 214.

122 R. Bork, *The Antitrust Paradox: A Policy at War with Itself* (New York: Free Press, 1993) 39.

> in the market, he would thereby exclude them completely, and he would have intended to do so. Some test other than an intent to exclude must be framed, one that distinguishes exclusion through efficiency from exclusion by means unrelated to efficiency.

Bork argues that undertakings will always deliberately intend to exclude other competitors so intent cannot be the test. Fox suggests using intent by asking whether the undertaking would have pursued the same strategy if the market would remain as competitive after the challenged conduct as before the conduct. If the answer is negative, then the purpose of the conduct is almost surely to strengthen market power, and the purpose is a proxy for probable effect. If the answer is affirmative, then the purpose was probably not to strengthen market power.[123] This section does not consider the advantages and disadvantages of Fox's suggested test, as it argues that intent to eliminate a competitor ought not to be used as a proxy for abuse in the first place *if* the aim is consumer welfare. This is not to say that the Commission can never rely on intent, but that it depends on what the Commission is trying to achieve. Reliance on intent, as a proxy for abuse, is acceptable if pursuing an objective of economic freedom, but such presumption does not sit well with the goal of consumer welfare. This point was elaborated in *Syfait I*[124] and *Sot. Lelos*,[125] which are discussed in the following section.

4.2 *Intent and consumer welfare*

In his Opinion in *Syfait*,[126] Advocate General Jacobs warned against relying on a presumption of abuse even where anticompetitive intent is proven.[127] In the *Syfait I* case, GlaxoSmithKline (GSK) refused to supply its wholesalers, the aim being to prevent parallel imports. Jacobs opines that the ECJ should not rely on a presumption of partitioning of the market *even* where there is intent to partition the market, because partitioning of the market is an inevitable consequence of attempting to

[123] E. Fox, 'Monopolization and Dominance in the United States and the European Community: Efficiency, Opportunity, and Fairness' 61 *Notre Dame Law Review* (1986) 981, 1001.

[124] Case C-53/03 *Synetairismos Farmakopoion Aitolias & Akarnanias and others v. GlaxoSmithKline AEVE* (*Syfait I*) [2005] ECR I-4609.

[125] Joined Cases C-468/06 to C-478/06 *Sot. Lelos kai Sia EE and others v. GlaxoSmithKline AEVE* (*Sot. Lelos*) [2008] ECR I-7139.

[126] Advocate General Jacobs' Opinion in *Syfait I*, supra note 124, delivered on 28 October 2004.

[127] Ibid., para. 72.

protect a legitimate interest. For Jacobs the important question is whether the dominant undertaking's conduct is justified, not whether the dominant firm had the intention to restrict competition by partitioning the market. Intent should not sidetrack the focus where partitioning of the market is a consequence of the characteristics of the market and not the primary intention.[128] Instead, Jacobs suggests making objective justifications a part of the overall assessment of conduct.[129] Where there is an objective justification, an abuse ought not to be found in the first place, regardless of intent. He argues that the usual benefits of parallel trade, such as intra-brand competition and reduced prices in the state of import to the benefit of consumers, may not apply in the pharmaceutical sector.[130] In some Member States, the price of pharmaceuticals is regulated, so consumers may not benefit from parallel trade. It is clear that Jacobs is trying to challenge intent, because he thinks the goal is consumer welfare and that there is no/little impact on consumers. Having a goal of consumer welfare requires evidence of how consumers are likely to be harmed in the specific case, and not how consumers are generally likely to be harmed by a restriction of parallel trade. Jacobs argued that the usual presumption of harm to consumers where parallel trade is restricted ought not to apply in pharmaceutical markets where there is price regulation, but, as will be discussed below, the ECJ did not pursue a consumer welfare goal.

It is unknown whether the ECJ would have followed Advocate General Jacobs' Opinion. The ECJ rejected the case based on inadmissibility by finding that the Hellenic Competition Commission (*Epitropi Antagonismou*) is not a court or tribunal within the meaning of Article 234 EC.[131] The case returned to Greece where litigation started in the administrative court of appeal of Athens (*Dioikitiko Efeteio Athinon*) and before the court of first instance of Athens (*Polymeles Protodikeio Athinon*). A reference to the ECJ was made under Article 234 in *Sot. Lelos kai Sia EE.*[132] The Greek court asked whether it is an abuse of a dominant position contrary to Article 82 'if a pharmaceuticals company [in the specific case GlaxoSmithKline] occupying such a position on the national market for certain medicinal products refuses to meet orders sent to it by wholesalers on account of the fact that those wholesalers are involved in parallel exports of those products to other Member States'.[133] Before the ECJ had

[128] Ibid., para. 71. [129] See chapter 2.
[130] Advocate General Jacobs' Opinion in *Syfait I*, supra note 124, para. 74.
[131] *Syfait I*, supra note 124, para. 37. [132] *Sot. Lelos*, supra note 125, para. 68.
[133] Ibid., para. 28.

the opportunity to answer the question, Advocate General Ruiz-Jarabo Colomer delivered his Opinion in *Sot. Lelos*.[134]

Colomer also acted as the Advocate General in *Tetra Pak II*, where he opined that predatory pricing is in itself abusive.[135] Colomer takes a different view from Jacobs. Colomer argues that GSK never denied that its real objective was to eliminate parallel exports:[136]

> It is evident that the intention of GSK is contrary to the objectives of the Treaty, since it affects freedom of trade between Member States to an extent which might harm the attainment of a single market, as this is understood in the case-law and in Article 3(1)(g) EC, since it undoubtedly partitions national markets and impairs the structure of competition within the common market.
>
> In summary, the foregoing analysis shows that GSK has committed a serious infringement of the Treaty, which *would* merit being treated as an abuse per se, *since it is difficult to identify any economic motive other than the elimination of the parallel trade of its competitors*, the Greek wholesalers.

Colomer says that GSK has committed a grave violation of the Treaty that would deserve the label of an abuse *per se* given that the basis of the behaviour has no other economic motive than the *intention* of eliminating parallel trade from its competitors. Despite this, he rejects any suggestion of *per se* abuse because 'if certain conduct always gives rise to a legal presumption that an abuse has occurred, dominant undertakings would be deprived of their right to defend themselves'.[137] Moreover, developing *per se* rules would, from a purely economic perspective, be too form-based.[138] Colomer concludes that 'Article 82 EC does not provide a basis for attributing conduct which is abusive *per se* to undertakings in a dominant position, even when the circumstances of the case show that there is intent and an anticompetitive effect caused by that conduct.' Despite this, he goes on to say that '[t]he refusal of an undertaking holding a dominant position to meet fully the orders sent to it by pharmaceutical wholesalers by reason of its *intention* to limit their export activity and, thereby, the harm caused to it by parallel trade constitutes an abuse within the

[134] Advocate General Colomer's Opinion in *Sot. Lelos*, supra note 125, delivered on 1 April 2008.

[135] Advocate General Colomer's Opinion in *Tetra Pak II*, supra note 95, delivered on 27 June 1996, para. 78.

[136] Advocate General Colomer's Opinion in *Sot. Lelos*, supra note 125, paras. 53–4. Emphasis added.

[137] Ibid., para. 69. [138] Ibid., para. 72.

meaning of Article 82 EC'.[139] There was evidence that consumers in the importing states would not benefit from parallel trade, but Colomer was not concerned with the consumers in the specific case. Instead, he refers to the harm caused to the pharmaceutical wholesalers by restricting the parallel trade. Restriction of trade must be avoided, as it restricts parallel importers' freedom to participate in the market.

In the aftermath of the Opinion, the ECJ had to consider whether it was willing to abandon its normal position on protecting parallel trade. GSK admits that its refusal to supply *aims* at restricting competition, but tries to justify its behaviour by arguing that in Greece the price is regulated by the Greek state whereas in other Member States there is no such regulation. If it does not prevent parallel imports, it will not earn its monopoly rent, which it is entitled to because of its investment in R&D. Moreover, parallel trade in pharmaceuticals would not have an impact on final consumers in any event because the state pays for the pharmaceuticals. This is not an irrelevant argument *if* the main objective of Article 82 is consumer welfare. GSK is asking the court to abandon its normal (strict) position on parallel trade, because parallel trade in the pharmaceutical market does not give the final consumers a lower price.[140] In other words, despite its intention to restrict competition, it has no effects on final consumers and so should not be prohibited under Article 82.[141]

Whilst the ECJ acknowledged that the final consumer in the importing Member State may not necessarily benefit from parallel trade in the form of a lower price,[142] it found that 'the attraction of the other source of supply which arises from parallel trade in the importing Member State lies precisely in the fact that that trade is *capable* of offering the same products on the market of that Member State at a lower price than those applied on the same market by pharmaceuticals companies'.[143] Where there is harm to free trade due to restriction of parallel exports, it does not matter that consumers in the importing Member State are actually not harmed. By safeguarding parallel trade, by protecting undistorted competition and

[139] Ibid., para. 123. Emphasis added. [140] *Sot. Lelos*, supra note 125, para. 31.

[141] It is interesting to compare the following Article 81 cases: Case C-199/92P etc. *Huls AG v. Commission* [1999] ECR I-4287, para. 163, and Case C-51/92P etc. *Hercules Chemicals NV v. Commission* [1999] ECR I-4235, stating that a concerted practice is caught by Article 81(1) even in the absence of anticompetitive effects on the market, with Case T-25/95 etc. *Cimenteries CBR SA v. Commission* [2000] ECR II-491, para. 1865, where the CFI says that there would be no infringement of Article 81 if the parties can prove that there are no anticompetitive effects.

[142] *Sot. Lelos*, supra note 125, para. 54. [143] Ibid., para. 55. Emphasis added.

the integration of national markets, it is believed that consumers are also protected.[144] This is the usual presumption, which Jacobs tried to challenge in his Opinion by arguing that the pharmaceutical sector is different, in that there is price regulation. Despite consumers being unlikely to be harmed in terms of pricing changes, the court found that preventing parallel imports is unacceptable. This may be a good standpoint if the court is pursuing an aim other than consumer welfare, as the lack of actual consumer harm may not necessarily mean that the undertaking is not abusing its dominant position.

The ECJ said that without any objective justifications, refusal to supply existing customers constitutes an abuse.[145] The court refered to the *United Brands* case to argue that a dominant undertaking is allowed to defend its legitimate interest, but not if the *purpose* of defending its legitimate interest is to strengthen its dominant position and abuse it.[146] It rejected GSK's argument that preventing parallel exports has little impact on the final consumer by saying that GSK 'cannot base its arguments on the premise that the parallel exports which *it seeks to limit* are of only minimal benefit to the final consumers'.[147] The court made an analogy with Article 81 to argue that some agreements, which are *aimed* at restricting parallel exports, are considered to restrict competition by object.[148] Following the analogy, it explained that practices of an undertaking in a dominant position aimed at avoiding all parallel exports from one Member State to another cannot escape the scope of Article 82.[149] The fact that Greece is subject to price regulation is exactly what creates the opportunity for parallel trade.[150] However, the court said that GSK has a legitimate interest in preventing abnormal parallel trade, but it must not deviate from normal commercial trading. Whilst GSK is not obliged to supply abnormal quantities, it cannot refuse to supply ordinary requests for supply.[151] Whether the quantity of supply ordered by its wholesalers is ordinary or not is for the national court to decide. The ECJ finished by explaining that even in situations where 'parallel trade would effectively lead to a shortage of medicines on a given national market, it would not be for the undertakings holding a dominant position but for the national authorities to resolve the situation, by taking appropriate and proportionate steps'.[152]

[144] Ibid., para. 68. [145] Ibid., para. 34. [146] Ibid., para. 50.
[147] Ibid., para. 57. Emphasis added. [148] Ibid., para. 65. Emphasis added.
[149] Ibid., para. 66. [150] Ibid., para. 67.
[151] *United Brands*, supra note 9, para. 182. [152] Ibid., para. 75.

The market integration objective is apparent in *Syfait I* and *Sot. Lelos* but as chapter 3 explained, this objective is an intermediate objective of an ultimate objective, which can either be efficiency or freedom to participate in the market. *Sot. Lelos* showed that economic freedom takes priority over consumer welfare in the name of market integration.

The following section will discuss another presumption developed through case law, which is the presumption of abuse where there is a risk of competition being eliminated. Again, this is to consider whether this is an acceptable presumption if the goal is either consumer welfare or economic freedom.

4.3 Risk of elimination of competition as a proxy for abuse

Parallel trade is not the only kind of conduct capable of restricting a source of supply; predatory pricing and rebates, for example, can have a similar effect.[153] If the regulatory aim is freedom of competition, then it is acceptable to prohibit conduct capable of restricting a source of supply. However, if the aim is consumer welfare, it needs to be examined whether the restriction harms consumers by balancing the pro- and anticompetitive effects of the conduct. The traditional view when examining exclusionary conduct, such as rebates or predatory pricing, has been to assume abuse where there is a *risk* of competition being eliminated. Such a presumption does not sit well with an objective of consumer welfare, because not even where effective competition *is* eliminated can it automatically be assumed that consumers are harmed. This is true, in particular, in dynamic markets, discussed above in section 3.2.

The presumption has become relevant again with Advocate General Mazák's Opinion in *France Télécom*, also know as the *Wanadoo* case,[154] because of the old discussion of the necessity of recoupment within the area of predatory pricing. Whether recoupment is a requirement depends on which objective is being pursued. If the Commission believes that economic freedom must be protected, then it is enough to protect the structure of competition. In this case, there is no need to examine whether the dominant undertaking is able to recoup; predatory pricing is

[153] For example, *Hoffmann-La Roche*, supra note 9, para. 90, notes that rebates 'are not based on an economic transaction which justifies this burden or benefit but are designed to deprive the purchaser of or restrict his possible choices of sources of supply and to deny other producers access to the market'. Similarly *Michelin I*, supra note 16, para. 73; *BPB Industries*, supra note 47, para. 120.

[154] Case C-202/07P *France Télécom SA v. Commission.*

found to be abusive where there is a risk of eliminating competition. This is illustrated in the *France Télécom* case. The CFI argued that Article 82 'must be applied where there is a risk of eliminating competition, without having to wait for the object of driving out competition to be achieved'.[155] 'Where an undertaking in a dominant position actually implements a practice whose object is to oust a competitor, the fact that the result hoped for is not achieved is not sufficient to prevent that being an abuse of a dominant position within the meaning of Article 82 EC.'[156]

France Télécom presumably thought (wrongly) that the Commission was aiming at promoting consumer welfare and therefore argued that the Commission had erred in law by maintaining that it was not necessary to prove recoupment.[157] The CFI disagreed and held that the Commission was 'right to take the view that proof of recoupment of losses was not a precondition to making a finding of predatory pricing'.[158] The court justified its position by relying on the ECJ's judgment in *Tetra Pak II*:[159]

> [I]t would not be appropriate, in the circumstances of the present case, to require in addition proof that Tetra Pak had a realistic chance of recouping its losses. It must be possible to penalise predatory pricing whenever there is a risk that competitors will be eliminated ... The aim pursued, which is to maintain undistorted competition, rules out waiting until such a strategy leads to the actual elimination of competitors.

The *Tetra Pak II* case does not reject recoupment in general, but 'in the circumstances of the present case', because a risk that competitors will be eliminated *was already found* in that case. This indicates that additional proof of exploitation in the form of recoupment is not necessary *where* evidence shows that there is a risk that a competitor will be eliminated. Such a risk can be presumed automatically where 'there is no conceivable economic *purpose* other than the elimination of a competitor, since each item produced and sold entails a loss for the undertaking'.[160]

Advocate General Colomer's Opinion in *Tetra Pak II* supports this: 'recouping losses is the result sought by the dominant undertaking'.[161] This view is also supported in *AKZO* where the ECJ explains that '[a] dominant undertaking has no interest in applying such prices except that of eliminating competitors so as to enable it *subsequently to raise its prices*

[155] Ibid., para. 193. [156] Ibid., para. 196. [157] Ibid., paras. 219–22.
[158] Ibid., para. 228. [159] Ibid., para. 226.
[160] *Tetra Pak II*, supra note 95, para. 41. Emphasis added.
[161] Advocate General Colomer's Opinion in *Tetra Pak II*, supra note 95, para. 78.

by taking advantage of its monopolistic position'.[162] In line with this, Advocate General Fennelly says, in his Opinion in *Compagnie Maritime Belge Transport*, '[t]he reason for restraining dominant undertakings from seeking to hinder the maintenance of competition by, in particular, eliminating a competitor is that they would thus be enabled to charge abusively high prices'.[163] Thus, the reason why *additional* proof of recoupment is not necessary is not because recoupment is not part of the test of predatory pricing, but because recoupment is implied where there is a risk of elimination of a competitor. That recoupment is implied where prices are below AVC is also Fennelly's reading of *AKZO*: '[i]t is implied in the first paragraph of the quotation from AKZO'.[164] The risk of elimination of a competitor follows automatically where the dominant undertaking prices below AVC. Where such a risk exists, there is also a danger that exploitation will occur at a later stage. In this way, recoupment is inherent in the risk of elimination of competitors. This view relies on a belief that companies are rational and engage in behaviour only to profit-maximise. No undertaking has an interest in engaging in pricing below costs unless there is a possibility of recouping the losses at a later stage. It does not make any business sense, as every unit of production is sold at a loss. It is the possible exclusion of competitors which allows the possible exploitation of customers and consumers to be assumed. In this way, there is a correlation between the exclusion of competitors and the possibility of exploitation of customers and consumers. Recoupment is inherent in the risk of elimination of competitors. However, as argued above, this risk of elimination, from which recoupment is assumed, already exists where an undertaking is dominant.[165] If proof of dominance is sufficient to establish likelihood of recoupment or any other form of exploitation, dominant undertakings have no other defence than proving that they are not dominant. This would be paradoxical, as Article 82 does not even come into consideration unless the undertaking is dominant. Moreover, in *United Brands*, the ECJ says that the dominant undertaking is allowed to defend its commercial interests, but not to engage in conduct whose 'actual purpose is to strengthen this dominant position *and* abuse it'.[166]

[162] *AKZO*, supra note 84, para. 71. Emphasis added.

[163] Advocate General Fennelly's Opinion in Joined Cases C-395 and 396/96P *Compagnie Maritime Belge Transport v. Commission* [2000] ECR 1365, delivered on 29 October 1998, para. 136.

[164] Ibid. [165] See section 2.1.

[166] *United Brands*, supra note 9, para. 189. Emphasis added. The CFI has upheld this position in other cases involving exclusionary conduct, for example, *BPB Industries*, supra note 47,

Only conduct through means other than competition on the merits is prohibited,[167] but without proving likely effects it becomes very difficult to distinguish between competition on the merits and abusive behaviour.

The presumption has been subject to much criticism,[168] the latest being from Advocate General Mazák, who challenges the presumption that dominance helps show recoupment.[169] Like Advocate General Jacobs in *Syfait I*, Mazák challenges the presumption, because he thinks the goal is consumer welfare. He argues: 'I consider that the Court of First Instance's, and for that matter the Commission's, interpretation of the Court's case-law [that recoupment is not necessary] is incorrect. In my view that case-law requires the possibility of recoupment of losses to be proven.'[170] He supports this argument by referring to *Tetra Pak II*, where he argues that the ECJ did not reject a requirement of recoupment in general, but rejected recoupment in the specific case due to the circumstances of the case.[171] Mazák takes the view that '[u]nless there is a possibility of recoupment, the dominant undertaking is probably engaged in normal competition'.[172] He supports this by referring to paragraph 136 of Advocate General Fennelly's Opinion in *Compagnie Maritime Belge Transport*:[173]

> The sharing of loss of revenues prompts me to revert briefly to the possible need to establish an intention or a possibility of recoupment. The process of sharing revenue losses is in essence a form of recoupment. The strategic purpose of the fighting rates carries with it the unspoken implication that rates will not be reduced for any sailings, current or future, where that is not necessary to meet competition. Furthermore, once the competitor was eliminated, they would clearly no longer be justified. Thus, to the extent that it is necessary, I believe that the present case passes the test of recoupment. At the same time, I would say that some such requirement [of recoupment] should be part of the test for abusively low pricing by dominant undertakings. It is implied in the first paragraph of the quotation from *AKZO* … It is inherent in the *Hoffmann-La Roche* test … The reason for restraining dominant undertakings from seeking to hinder the

para. 69; *Compagnie Maritime Belge*, supra note 163, para. 107; *British Airways*, supra note 54, para. 243.

167 *Hoffmann-La Roche*, supra note 9, para. 90; *AKZO*, supra note 84, para. 70.

168 For example Allan, supra note 98, 56–7; O'Donoghue and Padilla, supra note 42, 254; Bishop and Walker, supra note 74, 236; OECD, *Predatory Foreclosure* DAF/COMP(2005)14, 8 ff. Available at: www.oecd.org/dataoecd/26/53/34646189.pdf.

169 Advocate General Mazák's Opinion in Case C-202/07P *France Télécom SA v. Commission*, delivered on 25 September 2008, para. 76.

170 Ibid., para. 69. 171 Ibid., para. 70. 172 Ibid., para 73.

173 Advocate General Fennelly's Opinion, supra note 163, para. 136.

> maintenance of competition by, in particular, eliminating a competitor is that they would thus be enabled to charge abusively high prices. Thus, an inefficient monopoly would be reinstated and consumers would benefit only in the short run. If that result is not part of the dominant undertaking's strategy it is probably engaged in normal competition.

Fennelly says that '[i]f that result [higher prices] is not part of the dominant undertaking's strategy it is probably engaged in normal competition'. This would require proof of how the dominant undertaking's strategy is likely to result in higher prices. He says that 'to the extent that it is necessary' he believes the case (*Compagnie Maritime Belge Transport*) passes the test for recoupment, because '[t]he strategic purpose of the fighting rates carries with it the unspoken implication that rates will not be reduced for any sailings, current or future, where that is not necessary to meet competition. Furthermore, once the competitor was eliminated, they would clearly no longer be justified.'

When the aim is promoting consumer welfare proof of likely recoupment would be required. This, however, would exclude the Commission from automatically assuming abuse where there is a risk of elimination of competition, which is a risk that arguably already exists where a company is dominant. This is acceptable if the objective is economic freedom, which goes back to ordoliberalism and its fear of market power, but not if the goal is consumer welfare. Mazák's Opinion concludes that the Commission cannot rely on the presumption of abuse where there is a risk competition will be eliminated in cases where the Commission decides that consumer welfare must take priority over economic freedom. On appeal the ECJ rejected that recoupment is a necessary precondition to establishing that predatory pricing is abusive.[174]

4.4 Consequences of these presumptions

Chapter 3 established that Article 82 is not only about consumer welfare. Thus, using Article 82 to prevent restrictive effects on the structure of competition from occurring in the first place is acceptable if the aim is economic freedom. In the specific case of recoupment, the *Guidance Paper* explains the rationale for not requiring actual recoupment: 'in general, as predation may turn out to be more difficult than expected at

[174] Supra note 154, Case C-202/07P *France Télécom SA v. Commission*, para. 110.

the start of the conduct, the total costs to the dominant firm of predating could outweigh its later profits and thus make actual recoupment impossible while it may still be rational to decide to continue with the predatory strategy that it started some time ago'.[175] The Community Courts have held in a number of cases that when an undertaking actually implements practices with the aim of restricting competition, the fact that the result sought is not achieved is not enough to avoid the application of Article 82.[176] Failure to abuse after attempting to do so is a function of chance rather than choice and unsuccessful attempts must be punished. However, that may penalise consumers as there is an argument that the attempt to eliminate a competitor by pricing below costs benefits consumers.[177] However, the presumptions make it difficult for dominant undertakings to defend themselves against a finding of abuse. Also, assuming abuse where intent is found does not help us to disassociate the normal desire to increase turnover and market share from the motive of defeating competitors. This makes intent an unreliable criterion. The problem with the presumptions is that they are presumptions of harm to economic freedom that are being used to assume harm to consumers.

5. Conclusion

This chapter aimed at examining whether harmful effects of exclusionary conduct on economic freedom can also be used to assume that consumers are harmed. Section 2 explained that the concern with exclusionary conduct in Article 82 is foreclosure on both the horizontal and the vertical levels. Whether foreclosure is considered anticompetitive depends on which objective is being pursued. If the objective is consumer welfare, foreclosure will be anticompetitive where it harms consumers. If the objective is economic freedom, foreclosure will be anticompetitive where it harms customers and competitors. The section explained that there is an overlap between economic freedom and consumer welfare when it

[175] *Guidance Paper*, supra note 2, footnote 46.

[176] *Irish Sugar*, supra note 86, para. 191; Joined Cases T-24-26 and 28/93 *Compagnie Maritime Belge Transport and others v. Commission* [1996] ECR II-1201, para. 149; *Michelin II*, supra note 30, para. 245; *British Airways*, supra note 54, para. 297; *France Télécom*, supra note 35, para. 196.

[177] The Supreme Court endorses this view in *Brooke Group Ltd v. Brown & Williamson Tobacco Corporation*, 509 US 209 (1993) 224: 'although unsuccessful predatory pricing may encourage some inefficient substitution toward the product being sold at less than its cost, unsuccessful predation is in general a boon to consumers'.

comes to choice, which is linked to foreclosure. However, it concluded that a consumer welfare objective does not value choice in itself, but only for what it brings to consumers; which is different from an objective of economic freedom, which values the hypothetical choice customers and competitors have in the marketplace. Competitors' reduced choice of customers, and customers' reduced choice of suppliers restrict their economic freedom and are unacceptable where the objective is economic freedom.

Section 3 found that the Commission is not required to postpone intervention until it can show *actual* effects, but can intervene in the market where exclusionary conduct is *likely* to have adverse effects. It concluded that this is acceptable, otherwise the Commission would be unable to rely on presumptions. It also found that an objective of economic freedom is concerned with the effects on *the structure of competition* whereas an objective of consumer welfare is concerned with the effects on *consumers*. Thus, adopting a methodology of effects does not necessarily mean pursuing an objective of consumer welfare. It used *Microsoft* as an illustration of the Commission's analysis of effects. It found that the Commission considers effects on the structure of competition, which shows that the Commission was concerned with economic freedom in that case. It discussed what the Commission is hoping to achieve by examining the structure of competition. The Commission may be trying to safeguard 'not yet as efficient competitors', but, as explained, this would require price regulation. It concluded that the Commission cannot automatically assume that consumers are harmed where there are harmful effects to the structure of competition if it is trying to achieve consumer welfare.

Section 4 considered two case-law-developed presumptions of abuse: one where the object of the conduct is to restrict competition, where evidence of intent is found; and the other where there is a risk of competition being eliminated. It concluded that intent to eliminate a competitor ought not to be used as a proxy for abuse in the first place, *if* the aim is consumer welfare. However, that reliance on intent, as a proxy for abuse, is acceptable if pursuing an objective of economic freedom. Similarly, relying on a presumption of abuse where there is a risk of competition being eliminated is acceptable where the objective is economic freedom, but not where the goal is consumer welfare. The problem with the presumptions is that they are presumptions of harm to economic freedom and they are used to assume harm to consumers. Thus, section 4 concluded that the Commission cannot rely on the presumption of abuse where there is a risk competition will be eliminated in cases where the Commission decides that consumer welfare must take priority over economic freedom.

The overall conclusion is that the Commission must avoid relying on assumptions of harm to consumers from harm to economic freedom in cases where it thinks consumer welfare is the appropriate objective to pursue.

6

Guidelines

1. Introduction

This chapter questions whether the *Guidance Paper*[1] clarifies the doubts in Article 82 highlighted in chapter 1: (i) What is the underlying purpose of Article 82? (ii) Is it necessary to demonstrate actual or likely anticompetitive effects in the market when applying Article 82 and what effects are relevant? and (iii) How can dominant undertakings defend themselves against a finding of abuse?[2] In general, it can hardly be said to be an aim of priority guidelines to clarify the uncertainties surrounding the substance of the law, but instead to establish what the Commission's priorities are. However, the *Guidance Paper* does go into the substance of the law, despite being labelled 'enforcement priorities', thus part of this chapter considers the Commission interpretation of the law in the *Guidance Paper.*

Chapter 3 attempted to examine what the underlying purpose of Article 82 is by discussing the objectives of Article 82. It found that Article 82 pursues a number of objectives, some of which may conflict. The overarching objective of Article 82 is distortion of competition, which is important in a balancing act between conflicting objectives. The chapter concluded that the Commission appears to give disproportionate attention to consumer welfare given that the provision also pursues other objectives. Chapter 4 found that economic freedom and consumer welfare may conflict. Protecting freedom of competition does not always lead to consumer welfare. Jurisprudence takes a long-term view with a focus on rivalry. If the Commission wants to focus on consumer welfare, it will have to safeguard the process of competition not just in itself, but instrumentally, for what it brings to consumers. This requires the Commission to develop a framework for examining relative efficiencies in the long term. Clarifying the doubts in Article 82 would

1 OJ [2009] C45/7 *Guidance on the Commission's Enforcement Priorities in Applying Article 82 EC Treaty to Abusive Exclusionary Conduct by Dominant Undertakings* ('*Guidance Paper*'). This chapter refers to the paragraphs of the version of the *Guidance Paper* published on DG COMP's website on 3 December 2008 in case the numbering is different from the version published in the Official Journal on 24 February 2009.

2 These uncertainties were discussed in more detail in chapters 3, 4 and 5.

not only provide greater legal certainty to undertakings and help national courts and competition authorities to apply Article 82 in a consistent manner, but would also help the European Union to achieve its goals.

Chapter 5 found that the Commission and the Community Courts do not always consider it necessary to demonstrate effects on consumers. This is acceptable in cases where the aim is not consumer welfare. However, in some cases, harmful effects on consumers are assumed where the object of the conduct is anticompetitive and where there is a risk of competition being eliminated. These assumptions support likely restriction of economic freedom, but not necessarily harm to consumers. The chapter concluded that where the Commission aims at promoting consumer welfare, it is not enough to examine whether the structure of competition is harmed. It will have to examine what effects harm to the structure of competition has on consumers. What is important is effects on consumers, not just effects on the structure of competition. This is acknowledged by the Commission in its 'questions and answers memo'.[3] Assumptions are to be welcomed where they are based on sound economic theory supporting the underlying goal, or where it is more important to have efficient administration overall than to obtain the right outcome in every case. However, the Commission cannot rely on assumptions of consumer harm by assuming harm to economic freedom, as this ignores the conflict between the two objectives. With that in mind, this chapter considers whether the *Guidance Paper* provides any clarity on these matters.

This chapter consists of two parts. Part I contains two sections: sections 2 and 3. Section 2 explains the general role of guidelines in terms of legal certainty and legitimate expectations. Section 3 examines the Commission's legal basis for issuing priority guidelines. It also considers the aim of the *Guidance Paper* and why the Commission 'had' to label it enforcement priorities. It questions whether it makes a difference that consumer welfare is a 'priority' as opposed to a 'rule of substance'. This depends on whether the *Guidance Paper* goes into the substance of the law. The framework of the *Guidance Paper* will be considered in order to answer that question. Because the Commission goes into the substance of the law, part II examines whether it actually clarifies the uncertainties surrounding the application of Article 82. Part II consists of three sections: section 4 considers whether the *Guidance Paper* clarifies the uncertainties

[3] 'Antitrust: Guidance on Commission enforcement priorities in applying Article 82 to exclusionary conduct by dominant firms – frequently asked questions, Memo 08/761 of 3.12.2008'.

surrounding the application of Article 82; section 5 examines the consequences of the remaining uncertainty; and section 6 suggests a way forward.

PART I

2. The role of guidelines

Before specifically analysing the *Guidance Paper*, this section examines the general role of guidelines. This is to be able to assess whether the *Guidance Paper* fulfils that function. In the EU context, guidelines are categorised as 'soft law'. Rawlinson points out that soft law is about finding a compromise between the rigidities of hard law and the uncertainties associated with a more discretionary approach.[4] The Community Courts make a clear distinction between soft and hard law and emphasise that notices or guidelines enacted by the Commission are not rules of law that the administration is always bound to apply, but 'rules of practice', in other words they are soft law rather than hard law.[5] This is supported by Snyder, who defined soft law as 'rules of conduct which, in principle, have no legally binding force but which nevertheless may have practical effects'.[6] However, Senden includes the possibility of soft law having indirect legal effects. She defines soft law as 'rules of conduct that are laid down in instruments which have not been attributed legally binding force as such, but nevertheless may have certain – indirect – legal effects, and that are aimed at and may produce practical effects'.[7] This view is adopted in the European Parliament Report *Institutional and Legal Implications of the Use of 'Soft Law' Instruments*.[8]

4 F. Rawlinson, 'The Role of Policy Frameworks, Codes and Guidelines in the Control of State Aid' in I. Harden (ed.), *State Aid: Community Law and Policy* (Cologne: Bundesanzeiger, 1993) 52.

5 Joined Cases C-189, 202, 205, 208 and 213/02 *Dansk Rørindustri and others v. Commission* [2005] ECR I-5425, para. 209; Case C-167/04 *JCB Service v. Commission* [2006] ECR I-8935, para. 207.

6 F. Snyder, 'Soft Law and Institutional Practice in the European Community' European University Institute Working Paper Law No. 93/5, 2.

7 L. Senden, 'Soft Law, Self-regulation and Co-regulation in European Law: Where Do They Meet?' 9(1) *Electronic Journal of Comparative Law* (2005) 1, 23.

8 European Parliament Report, *Institutional and Legal Implications of the Use of 'Soft Law' Instruments*, 28 June 2007, document number A6-0259/2007 1, 4 point K.

The general understanding is that soft law consists of rules of practice which, although they lack any legally binding effects,[9] may create effects (such as legitimate expectations of the way the Commission will behave) for both the Commission and undertakings.[10]

This chapter does not engage in a more in-depth discussion of the notion of soft law.[11] Instead, it takes the view that Commission guidelines are considered soft law and discusses what effects such guidelines may create. This view is based on soft law including (i) preparatory and informative instruments, e.g. Green Papers, White Papers, action programmes and informative communications; (ii) interpretive and decisional instruments, e.g. the Commission's communications, notices, guidelines and codes; and (iii) steering instruments, e.g. non-formal recommendations falling outside Article 249, resolutions and codes of conduct.[12]

The Community Courts have said in a number of cases that the Commission is obliged to respect its notices and guidelines due to the general principles of law, such as the respect of legal certainty, legitimate expectations or equality. This is a very important point in relation to the *Guidance Paper*, which states that it is not a statement of law.[13] It raises the question whether the Commission is trying to avoid creating legitimate expectations and, if so, whether this means that the Commission is not obliged to respect case law. This point will be discussed in more detail in the following sections.

[9] According to Article 249 EC only regulations, directives and decisions are legally binding measures in the EU.

[10] Snyder, supra note 6, 2; Advocate General Tizzano's Opinion in *Dansk Rørindustri*, supra note 5, delivered on 8 July 2004, para. 59.

[11] Some literature on the subject is K. Abbot and D. Sindal, 'Hard and Soft Law in International Governance' 54(3) *International Organization* (2000) 421; K. Wellens and G. Borchardt, 'Soft Law in European Community Law' 14(5) *European Law Review* (1989) 267; D. Trubek, P. Cottrell and M. Nance, ' "Soft Law", "Hard Law", and the EU Integration' in G. de Búrca and J. Scott (eds.), *Law and New Governance in the EU and the US* (Oxford: Hart Publishing, 2006) 65; O. A. Ştefan, 'European Competition Soft Law in the European Courts: A Matter of Hard Principles?' 14(6) *European Law Journal* (2008) 753; F. Beveridge and S. Nott, 'A Hard Look at Soft Law' in P. Craig and C. Harlow (eds.), *Lawmaking in the European Union* (The Hague: Kluwer Law International, 1998) 285; specifically in relation to competition law see H. Cosma and R. Whish, 'Soft Law in the Field of EU Competition Policy' 14(1) *European Business Law Review* (2003) 25.

[12] Senden, supra note 7, 23–4.

[13] *Guidance Paper*, supra note 1, para. 3.

2.1 *Legal certainty*

Legal certainty is connected to transparency and predictability. Transparency is an umbrella term. It refers to access to documents, knowledge of who makes decisions and how they are made, simplification of the legislative process, consultation, a duty to give reasons, and other elements. Such transparency enhances democracy and legitimacy and inspires public confidence in the European Union and its institutions.[14] Guidelines provide greater transparency and predictability in the form of legal certainty to undertakings and their advisers.[15] Guidelines acknowledge the general principle of legal certainty under Community law, which requires that firms should, to the greatest possible extent, be able to judge whether their conduct is legal or not before they decide to engage in it.[16] Legal certainty is important as it is vital for the undertakings in the market – dominant or not – to know the legal framework within which they can operate.[17] Decisions on innovation and investment involve business risks and undertakings are less likely to be willing to take these risks if they cannot calculate the risk of future legal sanctions. Enhancing legal certainty reduces the legal risks, facilitating innovation and investment.[18]

2.2 *Legitimate expectations and equality*

The Community Courts have recognised that guidelines produce legitimate expectations for undertakings.[19] The ECJ said in *Dansk*

[14] The legal recognition of transparency began in Declaration 17 at Maastricht to strengthen the democratic nature of the institutions and the public's confidence in the administration. Later, rules were laid down in 1993 in a non-binding Code of Conduct (CC) on public access to Council and Commission documents and more formally in European Commission, OJ [1993] L340/43 Council Decision of 20 December 1993 on *Public Access to Council Documents*.

[15] J. Temple Lang, 'Legal Certainty and Legitimate Expectations as General Principles of Law' in U. Bernitz and J. Nergelius (eds.), *General Principles of European Community Law* (The Hague: Kluwer Law International, 2000) 163–84.

[16] T. Tridimas, *The General Principles of EC Law* (New York: Oxford University Press, 1999) 165–6.

[17] Case T-51/89 *Tetra Pak Rausing SA v. Commission* [1990] ECR II-309, [1991] 4 CMLR 334, para. 36; Joined Cases 212/80 to 217/80 *Amministrazione delle Finanze dello Stato v. Srl Meridionale Industria Salumi and others; Ditta Italo Orlandi & Figlio and Ditta Vincenzo Divella v. Amministrazione delle finanze dello Stato* [1981] ECR 2417, para. 10; Cases 209/84 to 213/84 *Ministère Public v. Asjes and others* (*Nouvelles Frontières*), para. 64.

[18] OJ [2003] L1/1 Council Regulation No. 1/2003, *The Implementation of the Rules on Competition Laid Down in Articles 81 and 82 of the Treaty*, recital 38.

[19] *Dansk Rørindustri*, supra note 5; Case C-397/03 *Archer Daniels Midland v. Commission* [2006] ECR I-4429, para. 93.

Rørindustri: 'although those measures [the guidelines] may not be regarded as rules of law which the administration is always bound to observe, they nevertheless form rules of practice from which the administration may not depart in an individual case without giving reasons that are compatible with the principle of equal treatment'.[20] This means that the Commission cannot depart from its guidelines without giving reasons.

Guidelines also ensure transparency and objectivity and thereby limit the Commission's discretion and arbitrariness. Because of legitimate expectations, the Commission cannot depart from rules it has imposed upon itself[21] or from soft law instruments,[22] unless it gives adequate non-discriminatory reasons for doing so.[23] The limitation effect however does not seem to be absolute,[24] as guidelines do not take away the Commission's flexibility or discretion in its entirety. For example, the Commission 'enjoys a wide discretion as regards the method used for calculating fines and ... it can, in this respect, take account of numerous factors'.[25] The Commission also retains the freedom to choose the evidence and theory it finds most relevant in an individual case. The CFI said in *General Electric*:[26]

> [W]here the Commission expresses itself in a notice in terms which allow it the scope to choose, from the types of evidence or approaches which may in theory be relevant, those which are the most appropriate in the circumstances of a given case, it retains great freedom of action ... [I]t should be noted that the Commission did not undertake, in the notice on market definition, to use one particular specific method in the assessment of demand-side substitutability. Instead, it stated that the approach which it will take has to vary depending on the circumstances of each individual case and it retained a large part of its margin of assessment in order to be able to deal with each individual case in an appropriate way.

20 *Dansk Rørindustri*, supra note 5, para. 209.

21 Case 148/73 *Louwage v. Commission* [1974] ECR 81, para. 12; Case T-7/89 *Hercules Chemicals v. Commission* [1991] ECR II-1711, paras. 53 and 54, confirmed on appeal Case C-51/92P *Hercules Chemicals v. Commission* [1999] ECR I-4235.

22 Case T-23/99 *LR af 1998 A/S v. Commission* [2002] ECR II-1705, para. 245; Case T-31/99 *ABB Asea Brown Boveri v. Commission* [2002] ECR II-1881, para. 258.

23 *Dansk Rørindustri*, supra note 5, para. 209.

24 L. Senden, *Soft Law in European Community Law* (Oxford: Hart Publishing, 2004) 448.

25 See Case C-308/04 *SGL Carbon v. Commission* [2006] ECR I-5977, para. 46.

26 Case T-210/01 *General Electric v. Commission* [2005] ECR II-5575, para. 519.

The Community Courts do not consider themselves bound by the Commission guidelines,[27] but may use them as a point of reference.[28] They do not limit themselves to determining whether the Commission's decision was taken in accordance with its guidelines, but consider whether, for example, a fine is proportionate to the gravity and duration of the infringement.[29] This is similar for the national courts and competition authorities, which must apply Articles 81 and 82 in their entirety.[30] They cannot take decisions running counter to Commission decisions or Community case law.[31] The difficulty for the national courts and the national competition authorities is that the *Guidance Paper* may lead to some confusion, in that it discusses the substance of the case law and then prioritises consumer welfare, despite the fact that there is no consistent jurisprudence holding that consumer welfare is the primary objective of Article 82.

Section 2 above showed that guidelines fall within the umbrella term 'soft law'. The Commission's obligation to respect its own notices and guidelines does not come from these instruments themselves, but from the general principles of law, such as the need for legal certainty, legitimate expectations or equality. From the rule-maker's point of view it is important to know whether it will be bound by a self-imposed set of rules, as it creates legitimate expectations for undertakings. As seen, the Community Courts have notably answered this question in the affirmative.

3. The legitimacy of priority guidelines

The EC Treaty has entrusted the Commission with an extensive and general supervisory and regulatory task.[32] The Commission enjoys wide discretionary powers when it comes to the question whether investigations should be initiated. Article 85 of the Treaty confers upon the Commission an obligation to 'ensure the application of the principles laid down in Articles 81 and 82'. It explicitly states that the initiative to start investigations lies with the Commission. The Commission is an authority

[27] Case T-368/00 *General Motors Nederland and Opel Nederland v. Commission* [2003] ECR II-4491, para. 188; Advocate General Jacobs' Opinion in *JCB Service*, supra note 5, delivered on 15 December 2005, para. 141.

[28] Case C-310/99 *Italian Republic v. Commission* [2002] ECR I-2289, para. 52.

[29] Case T-49/02 *Brasserie Nationale v. Commission* [2005] ECR II-3033, para. 170.

[30] Regulation 1/2003, supra note 18, recital 4 and Articles 3, 5 and 6.

[31] Ibid., recital 22 and Article 16.

[32] Article 211 of the Treaty.

with limited resources and is not able to investigate every complaint it receives. It needs to prioritise. The Commission is allowed to determine its priorities within the limits of the law as the CFI confirmed in *Automec*:[33]

> [I]t should be observed that, in the case of an authority entrusted with a public service task, the power to take all the organizational measures necessary for the performance of that task, including setting priorities within the limits prescribed by the law 'where those priorities have not been determined by the legislature' is an inherent feature of administrative activity. This must be the case in particular where an authority has been entrusted with a supervisory and regulatory task as extensive and general as that which has been assigned to the Commission in the field of competition. Consequently, the fact that the Commission applies different degrees of priority to the cases submitted to it in the field of competition is compatible with the obligations imposed on it by Community law.

Whilst the Commission is entitled to decide not to open a case or to close a case based on administrative priorities, a decision to close a case can be appealed and made subject to judicial review by the Community Courts. The courts can review the legality of the Commission's reasons for deciding not to pursue a case.[34] It is clear that the Commission can adopt priority guidelines as long as they are within the limits of the law.

3.1 *The aim of the Guidance Paper*

The first 'unofficial' attempt to draft guidelines regarding Article 82 was the *Discussion Paper*.[35] As discussed in chapter 1, this was a staff paper, not published in the Official Journal, which was an unusual step compared to the Commission's normal practice of producing a green paper, and may hint at a disagreement within the Commission as to publishing guidelines at all. Since it was a staff paper, it did not produce any legal effects, and was meant only for consultation to allow interested parties to express their view on a text that might have become substantive guidelines later. Despite not being an authoritative source or even published in the Official Journal, the *Discussion Paper* was drafted as substantive guidelines,[36] which raised expectations of the Commission

33 Case T-24/90 *Automec v. Commission* [1992] ECR II-2223, para. 77.

34 Ibid., para. 85.

35 DG COMP's *Discussion Paper on the Application of Article 82 of the Treaty to Exclusionary Abuses* (December 2005) ('*Discussion Paper*').

36 Ibid., para. 7.

issuing substantive guidance in this area of law. Against expectations, the Commission issued priority guidelines. Perhaps the idea of substantive guidelines was abandoned because of the severe criticism of the *Discussion Paper* which the Commission received at its public hearing in June 2006.[37] This raised doubts about whether agreement on the substantive rules was a possibility at all. An alternative explanation however is that the Commission did not just want to issue guidelines reiterating case law and repeating what had gone before. Arguably, the Commission wanted to evolve its policy, but was restricted by case law. Trying to make new law goes beyond the Commission's responsibility for orientating of competition policy.[38]

The *Discussion Paper* tried to push the Commission's policy beyond the framework set by the Community Courts by stating that the objective of Article 82 is consumer welfare. This is problematic. Chapter 4 concluded that consumer welfare is not the only objective of Article 82, but one objective amongst others. Thus, issuing guidelines stating that the main objective of Article 82 is consumer welfare requires judicial support, as the Commission cannot derogate from older case law by means of soft law.[39] There is a difference between (i) adopting priority guidelines stating that the Commission will focus its limited resources on cases where it believes consumers are harmed, and (ii) issuing substantive guidelines stating that the objective of Article 82 is consumer welfare if this is not supported in case law. The former is creating clarity as to where the Commission will focus its resources, whereas the latter is an interpretation of the law, which is not fully supported by Article 82 case law. Had the *Discussion Paper* turned into substantive Commission guidelines, it would have been in conflict with the case law pursuing objectives other than consumer welfare. A reminder that the Commission is bound by the framework set by the Community Courts came from Advocate General Kokott a couple of months after the release of the *Discussion Paper*. In her Opinion in *British Airways* she said: 'even if … [the Commission's] administrative practice were to change, the Commission would still have to act within the framework prescribed for it by Article 82 EC as interpreted by the Court of

37 The presentations and video link to the hearing are available at: http://ec.europa.eu/competition/antitrust/art82/hearing.html.

38 Case C-234/89 *Stergios Delimitis v. Henninger Bräu AG* [1991] ECR I-935.

39 F. Snyder, 'Soft Law and Institutional Practice in the European Community' in S. Martin (ed.), *The Construction of Europe: Essays in Honour of Emil Noel* (Dordrecht: Kluwer Academic Publishers, 1994) 199–201.

Justice'.[40] The Community Courts have made clear in several judgments that guidelines and notices cannot depart from case law.[41] Some argue that guidelines are only valid if they do not conflict with the courts' interpretation of the treaty provisions.[42]

If the Commission is extrapolating case law by means of soft law, it is going beyond its remit. Because the European Parliament is not involved in the enactment of guidelines, it is of immense importance that the Commission acts within the limits of the law, otherwise the guidelines are not legitimate. The European Parliament report,[43] referred to above, notes that use of soft law, such as guidelines, may be liable to circumvent the properly competent legislative bodies, contravene the principles of democracy and the rule of law, for example by avoiding the involvement of the Parliament and legal review by the ECJ, and may result in the Commission acting *ultra vires*. It states that 'soft law all too often constitutes an ambiguous and ineffective instrument which is liable to have a detrimental effect on Community legislation and institutional balance and should be used with caution, even where it is provided for in the Treaty'.[44] The Parliament report in particular warns against the use of soft law where 'it extrapolates the case-law of the European Court of Justice into uncharted territory'.[45] The procedures for adopting soft law generally tend to circumvent the more costly but more legitimate decision-making ways. That said, where the Commission does not act outside its remit, adopting guidelines seems sensible. This is particularly so within the area of Article 82, as limited tools are available to the Commission in modernising the provision.[46] Markets develop with high speed and the legislative process is slow and time-consuming. The political differences would also make it hard to adopt new legislation because it would require consensus from the different Member States.[47]

40 Advocate General Kokott's Opinion in Case C-95/04P *British Airways plc v. Commission* [2007] ECR I-2331, delivered on 23 February 2006, para. 28.

41 *Dansk Rørindustri*, supra note 5, para. 261; Case T-213/00 *CMA CGM and others v. Commission* [2003] ECR II-913, para. 262; Case T-65/99 *Strintzis Lines Shipping v. Commission* [2003] ECR II-5433, para. 168; Case T-9/99 *HFB Holding and others v. Commission* [2002] ECR II-1487, para. 446.

42 Senden, supra note 24, 373.

43 European Parliament Report, supra note 8, 6 point X.

44 Ibid., point Za(1). 45 Ibid., 7 point Za(5). 46 See chapter 1.

47 Consensus may be difficult to achieve as proven by F. Engelsing, P. Marsden and D. Möller, 'A Bundeskartellamt/Competition Law Forum Debate on Reform of Article 82: A "Dialectic" on Competing Approaches' 2 (special supplement) *European Competition Journal* (2006) 211.

The *Guidance Paper* makes clear that 'it is intended to provide greater clarity and predictability on the general framework of analysis which the Commission employs in determining whether it should pursue cases concerning various forms of exclusionary conduct and to help undertakings better assess whether a certain behaviour is likely to result in intervention by the Commission under Article 82'.[48] By producing the *Guidance Paper*, the Commission wants to bring an element of certainty as to how it prioritises its cases under Article 82 so that undertakings in the market are aware of the ways in which the Commission will apply its powers. In the absence of soft law, there would only be previous Commission decisions and the Community case law to rely on. The *Guidance Paper* emphasises in paragraph 3 that it 'is not intended to constitute a statement of the law and is without prejudice to the interpretation of Article 82 by the European Court of Justice or the Court of First Instance'. Commission guidelines usually adopt the general proposition that they are without prejudice to what the Community Courts say.[49] However, the unusual caveat that the *Guidance Paper* is not a statement of law becomes necessary because the *Guidance Paper* is *in effect* substantive guidelines which offer an interpretation of the law. That the *Guidance Paper* is comprised of substantive guidelines in disguise is not in itself a problem, but becomes a problem because the Commission's interpretation of substantive law ignores case law in several aspects.

A similar 'caveat' was given in the Commission's Notice on *The Application of Article 10a of Council Regulation (EEC) No. 3030/93 Concerning a Textiles Specific Safeguard Clause.* The Commission said:[50]

> These guidelines are for the information of interested parties and do not constitute a legal instrument. They reflect the policy intention of the Commission to follow certain procedures and criteria ... and therefore should not lead to any legally legitimate expectations regarding the individual decisions that the Commission will adopt.[51]

[48] *Guidance Paper*, supra note 1, para. 2.

[49] For example, OJ [2008] C265/6 *Guidelines on the Assessment of Non-horizontal Mergers under the Council Regulation on the Control of Concentrations between Undertakings*, para. 9; OJ [2004] C31/5 *Guidelines on the Assessment of Horizontal Mergers under the Council Regulation on the Control of Concentrations between Undertakings*, para. 7.

[50] OJ [2005] C101/02 Commission Notice, *The Application of Article 10a of Council Regulation (EEC) No. 3030/93 Concerning a Textiles Specific Safeguard Clause*. Available at: www.trade.ec.europa.eu/doclib/docs/2005/may/tradoc_123149.pdf.

[51] The guidelines followed the EU–China Textile Agreement. The massive influx of Chinese textile products onto the European market led the EC to regulate, by the signing of a bilateral agreement, the EU–China Textile Agreement of 10 June 2005 (MEMO 05/201, 12 June 2005).

Despite this, some argue that 'the Guidelines will have a de facto binding character, as they demonstrate how the external relations between Commission and economic operators will be configured'.[52] Similarly, the *Guidance Paper* may have binding character. Noting that the *Guidance Paper* is not a statement of law, the Commission is trying to avoid creating any legitimate expectations as to how it interprets the law when examining whether a dominant undertaking is abusing its position, as opposed to simply creating an expectation as to how it will prioritise its cases. There is a difference between, on the one hand, issuing priority guidelines setting out enforcement priorities and making clear that the Commission will focus its limited resources on cases where it believes consumers are harmed the most, and, on the other hand, issuing substantive guidelines interpreting the law. Despite this difference, the *Guidance Paper* is a hybrid between the two as the Commission sets out its enforcement priorities at the same time as it is interpreting the law. However, to avoid acting outside its remit, the Commission labelled the *Guidance Paper* 'enforcement priorities', although this is a false dichotomy as the *Guidance Paper* also goes into the substance of the law.[53]

3.2 Consumer welfare as a priority as opposed to a rule of substance

Unlike the *Discussion Paper* where DG COMP said that the aim of Article 82 is consumer welfare, the *Guidance Paper* does not try to impose an overall aim on Article 82. However, it makes clear that it will prioritise cases where consumers are harmed.[54] Having consumer welfare as a *priority* instead of a rule of substance shifts the discussion from being a discussion about whether or not certain conduct is competitive or anticompetitive in the light of consumer welfare to a discussion about whether or not it is legitimate for the Commission to intervene in the specific market where consumers are believed to be harmed. Prioritising cases where it is believed consumers are harmed does not elucidate which kinds of conduct are acceptable and which are not from a consumer welfare perspective. Rather, it determines which kinds of conduct are to be

[52] A. Rogmann and B. Stadtler, 'Is Free Trade with China in Peril?' 2(2) *World Customs Journal* (2005) 29, 34.

[53] L. L. Gormsen, 'Why the European Commission's Enforcement Priorities on Article 82 EC Should Be Withdrawn' 31(2) *European Competition Law Review* (2010), 45, 46.

[54] *Guidance Paper*, supra note 1, paras. 5 and 19.

subject to intervention and which are not. The point of making consumer welfare a priority is to demonstrate when the Commission will legitimately intervene. In this way, consumer welfare becomes a priority instead of a rule of substance. This is particularly important in relation to Article 82 as the substance of the law does not entirely support consumer welfare. However, labelling the *Guidance Paper* 'enforcement priorities' where it is *in effect* subtantive guidelines creates legitimate expectations that the Commission interprets the law in the light of consumer welfare. This is not supported by case law as shown in chapter 3.

3.3 *The Commission's framework*

The *Guidance Paper* is not nearly as detailed and in-depth as the analysis in the *Discussion Paper*, although it is twenty-six pages long, which is quite long for administrative guidelines. Moreover, one would have expected a priority paper to show how the Commission is going to prioritise specific market sectors where significant market power is likely. Besides the length and different omissions in the *Guidance Paper*, it goes into the substance of the law, as it specifically notes how the Commission will interpret different things. For example, it specifies how the Commission will interpret market shares in the light of the relevant market conditions, such as the dynamics of the market and the extent to which products are differentiated.[55] Moreover, the *Guidance Paper* ignores (or deliberately omits) the *AKZO* presumption that very large market shares (50 per cent or more) are in themselves considered evidence of a dominant position.[56] Perhaps this is sensible if the aim is consumer welfare, as market shares are not informative as to whether consumers are harmed or not. However, as chapter 5 explained, the focus in the *AKZO* case was on the structure of competition, considering whether ECS's economic freedom was restricted by AKZO's behaviour. A market share of 50 per cent may be enough to harm the structure and freedom of competition in a specific market. As long as economic freedom is considered a valid objective by the Community Courts, the Commission cannot ignore such a presumption as that would be to ignore Article 82 case law.

The *Guidance Paper* establishes a number of factors upon which the Commission will rely when analysing whether the allegedly abusive

[55] Ibid., para. 13.
[56] Case 62/86 *AKZO Chemie BV v. Commission* [1991] ECR I-3359, para. 60.

conduct is likely to lead to anticompetitive foreclosure.[57] To determine whether conduct is anticompetitive, the Commission will examine whether the dominant undertaking's competitors' access to suppliers or customers is foreclosed.[58] It will build a theory of harm by relying on some general factors such as the position of the dominant undertaking, its competitors and customers or input suppliers; the conditions on the relevant market; the extent of the allegedly abusive conduct; possible evidence of actual foreclosure; and direct evidence of any exclusionary strategy.[59] The assessment will consider the current or likely future situation in the relevant market relative to an appropriate counterfactual.[60] Besides the fact that these factors support the objective of economic freedom, the point is that they form part of the Commission's legal framework on how the Commission will go about analysing foreclosure, which creates legitimate expectation. This means that the Commission cannot divert from this methodology in individual cases without having to give reasons.[61]

For example, the Commission establishes a methodology for imposing a fine in its *Guidelines on the Method of Setting Fines.*[62] Whilst the fining guidelines do not constitute the legal basis for imposing a fine (the legal basis is in Regulation 1/2003), they form part of the legal framework of the fining decision and create legitimate expectations as to how the Commission is going to go about calculating the fine. The Commission will have to respect and follow that methodology although it has huge discretion as to the proportionality of the fine. This is underlined in the *Archer Daniels Midland* (*ADM*) case.[63] The CFI found that the Commission had wrongly calculated the fine by taking account only of the worldwide and not the EEA turnover of ADM,[64] but found that the fine imposed in the case was proportionate. On appeal, the ECJ found that the CFI had erred in law by directly judging on the proportionality of the fine, after having already established that the Commission had infringed its own fining guidelines.[65] The ECJ held that the principles of equality and legal certainty required that the CFI should have first determined whether, in taking into account the EEA turnover, the fine remained within the framework established by the guidelines. Only if this assessment was

57 *Guidance Paper*, supra note 1, para. 20. 58 Ibid., para. 19.

59 Ibid., para. 20. 60 Ibid., para. 20.

61 *Dansk Rørindustri*, supra note 5, para. 209.

62 OJ [2006] C210/2 *Guidelines on the Method of Setting Fines Imposed Pursuant to Article 23(2)(a) of Regulation No. 1/2003.*

63 Case T-224/00 *Archer Daniels Midland v. Commission* [2003] ECR II-2597.

64 Ibid., paras. 197 and 198. 65 *Archer Daniels Midland*, supra note 19.

satisfied should the CFI have gone on to consider the proportionality of the fine.[66]

Since the *Guidance Paper* considers the substance of the law, the following section examines whether that substantive discussion clarifies the uncertainties surrounding the application of Article 82.

PART II

In this part, section 4 examines whether the *Guidance Paper* has clarified the uncertainties surrounding the application of Article 82. This is essential as to which – if any – suggestions ought to be advanced in this area of law. Section 5 outlines the consequences of any remaining ambiguities. Section 6 provides some recommendations for the Commission.

4. The uncertainties surrounding the application of Article 82

According to former Competition Commissioner Monti, who initiated the review of Article 82, the purpose of re-examining Article 82 was to evaluate existing policy and how to make it more effective, as well as to define the most appropriate means to make it more transparent.[67] This is echoed in the *Guidance Paper*, which states that its aim is to provide greater clarity and predictability to the Commission's general framework of analysis.[68] Clarity is of immense importance given the current uncertainties surrounding the application of Article 82. Making its policy more transparent in this context implies explaining what the aim of its policy is and how it is going to be achieved. The benefit of transparency is legal certainty for undertakings subject to investigation under Article 82, although legal certainty is not the only value that legal systems promote.[69]

Another reason for initiating the review was a greater appreciation of micro-economic theory on the part of the policy-makers and the Commission's perception that the rules under Article 82 must be

[66] Ibid., para. 93.

[67] M. Monti, 'EU Competition Policy after May 2004', 24 October 2003, the Thirteenth Annual Conference on International Antitrust Law and Policy, Fordham Corporate Law Institute.

[68] *Guidance Paper*, supra note 1, para. 2.

[69] T. Frazer, 'Competition Policy after 1992: The Next Step' 53(5) *Modern Law Review* (1990) 609, 622 and 623.

sufficiently responsive to sound economics.[70] This part of the chapter assesses (i) whether the *Guidance Paper* is more responsive to economic principles, thereby clarifying the uncertainty about the interpretation of abuse and dominant undertakings' ability to defend themselves, and (ii) whether it is more transparent, thereby explaining the underlying purpose of Article 82. With that in mind, this section looks at whether the *Guidance Paper* achieves these goals. Where relevant, it will be compared to the *Discussion Paper.*

4.1 *The story of uncertainty continues*

Now that the Commission has issued its *Guidance Paper*, the question is whether it clarifies the underlying purpose of Article 82. In paragraph 5, the Commission says:

> In applying Article 82 to exclusionary conduct by dominant undertakings, the Commission will focus on those types of conduct that are most harmful to consumers. Consumers benefit from competition through lower prices, better quality and a wider choice of new or improved goods and services. The Commission, therefore, will direct its enforcement to ensuring that markets function properly and that consumers benefit from the efficiency and productivity which result from effective competition between firms.

Besides cases where consumers are believed to be harmed, the *Guidance Paper* makes clear that the purpose of Article 82 is to ensure that rivals of dominant undertakings are not excluded by means other than competition on the merits, because 'what really matters is to protect an effective competitive process and not simply protecting competitors'.[71] This is not particularly helpful, as the concept of competition on the merits is not precisely defined. Protecting an efficient competitive process is taken to mean that Article 82 is not aimed at protecting all competitors in the market, but only those competitors that make the competitive process efficient. This however may not only mean competitors which are as efficient as the dominant undertaking, since the Commission says in the *Guidance Paper* paragraph 23 that 'in certain circumstances a less efficient competitor may also exert a constraint which should be taken into account when considering whether a particular price-based conduct leads to anticompetitive foreclosure'. This appears to contradict the 'as

[70] See chapter 1. [71] *Guidance Paper*, supra note 1, para. 6.

efficient competitor' test, the adoption of which the Commission is, later in the *Guidance Paper*, suggesting. Chapter 5 explained that there may be situations where the presence of an inefficient competitor raises consumer welfare in the long term, because they become efficient over time. However, this would require price regulation until the inefficient competitor becomes efficient otherwise the inefficient competitor will not be able to stay in the market. If the aim is to protect an efficient competitive process, in the name of consumer welfare, the Commission needs to adopt a methodology capable of measuring how less efficient competitors make the competitive process efficient over time or price regulate. The *Guidance Paper* does not do that. Instead, it endorses an 'as efficient competitor' test[72] to accommodate a more economic approach to Article 82. This test is linked to the objective of consumer welfare and can therefore only be used in cases where that is the aim.

The 'as efficient competitor' test was accepted in *Deutsche Telekom*,[73] a case concerning margin squeeze.[74] Unlike the foreclosure test in Article 81, where it is necessary to examine whether access to the market is foreclosed and, if so, whether it is the specific agreement which leads to foreclosure,[75] the Commission suggests examining whether the conduct in question is capable of foreclosing the market for an 'as efficient' competitor.

The idea behind the test is that conduct would not be considered an abuse if it would not exclude a firm as efficient as the dominant firm. On the face of it, the test seems to be able to distinguish between efficient and inefficient competitors. This is to be welcomed in cases where the objective of Article 82 is consumer welfare, as protecting *inefficient* competitors against elimination goes beyond protecting the competitive process to the benefit of consumers.[76] To avoid concluding that the dominant undertaking's conduct is harmful to consumers where the excluded or impaired competitors are *inefficient*, the Commission must examine whether the

72 Ibid., para. 24.

73 Case T-271/03 *Deutsche Telekom v. Commission* [2006] ECR II-1747, para. 186.

74 The idea of margin squeeze is that the vertically integrated dominant undertaking can manipulate the relationship of the input price to the output price in such a way that it is impossible for an 'as efficient' competitor to compete in the downstream market. The Commission's description of a margin squeeze (price squeeze) is to be found in OJ [1998] C265/2 Commission Notice, *The Application of the Competition Rules to Access Agreements in the Telecommunications Sector*, paras. 117–18.

75 *Delimitis v. Henninger Bräu*, supra note 38, paras. 19–27.

76 R. Joliet, *Monopolization and Abuse of Dominant Position* (University of Liège, 1970) 250–1.

excluded or impaired competitor is *efficient* in the marketplace.[77] Being efficient does not necessarily have anything to do with size. Some competitors are 'as efficient' as the dominant undertaking despite being small, but because of their smaller financial resources such competitors could be excluded from the market where, for example, the dominant undertaking engages in pricing above AVC but below ATC.[78]

That said, it is a difficult test to apply in practice. It requires the Commission to gather evidence of price and cost data from the dominant firm,[79] and compare it with the costs of a competitor which is 'as efficient', i.e. a hypothetical competitor having the same costs as the dominant company.[80] Such evidence may not be easy to obtain, let alone reliable, and appears to be costly and time consuming to gather.[81] The test, however, does not appear to be able to address the problems discussed above about the protection of *not yet efficient competitors* or *potentially efficient* or even *inefficient competitors*, which shows that the test cannot be used in cases where the objective is economic freedom. Moreover, the 'as efficient competitor' test does not make it any easier to obtain evidence either; on the contrary, it makes it more difficult. Also, what happens if the dominant undertaking and its rivals have different cost curves?[82] Even if they have similar cost curves, the test seems unable to measure whether a less efficient competitor will become more efficient over time and increase consumer welfare in the long term, as the test is based on the dominant undertaking's costs at the time of the investigation.

Despite aiming at protecting an efficient competitive process, the Commission indicates that Article 82 can be used to protect weaker firms from stronger ones where an economic dependency exists. It notes that it is particularly concerned where the dominant firm is an 'unavoidable trading partner' for part of the customer demand. In such cases, rivals may not be able to compete for an individual customer's entire demand, either because the dominant undertaking supplies a 'must-stock' brand or because the competitors do not have the capacity to meet total customer demand. Where 'the dominant undertaking is an unavoidable

77 *Deutsche Telekom*, supra note 73, para. 194.

78 *AKZO*, supra note 56, para. 72.

79 *Deutsche Telekom*, supra note 73, para. 194.

80 *Guidance Paper*, supra note 1, para. 24.

81 Other drawbacks of the 'as efficient' competitor test are outlined in A. Jones and B. Sufrin, *EC Competition Law* (Oxford University Press, 3rd edn, 2007) 329.

82 B. Sher, 'Leveraging Non-contestability: Exclusive Dealing and Rebates under the Commission's Article 82 Guidance' *Global Competition Policy* (2009) 1, 9.

trading partner for all or most customers, even an exclusive purchasing obligation of short duration can lead to anticompetitive foreclosure'.[83]

The *Guidance Paper* notes that Article 82 must prohibit behaviour which undermines the effort to achieve an integrated internal market.[84] Unlike the *Discussion Paper*, which stated that the objective of Article 82 is consumer welfare,[85] the *Guidance Paper* tries to accommodate different objectives such as avoiding harm to consumers, to the process of competition and to the integration of the internal market. This is for good reason, since Article 82 is not only about promoting consumer welfare.[86] This was confirmed in the press release that followed the publication of the *Guidance Paper*, which states that 'the focus of the Commission's enforcement policy should be on protecting consumers, on *protecting the process of competition* and not on protecting individual competitors'.[87] Depending on how the Commission anticipates protecting the process of competition, this may or may not promote consumer welfare. However, trying to encompass different objectives requires the Commission to clarify what it intends to do in case of a conflict between those objectives. As discussed in chapter 4, economic freedom and consumer welfare may conflict where the protection of economic freedom does not promote consumer welfare. As it stands, the Commission ignores the possibility of a conflict between those objectives. The Community Courts will have to decide which objective is the more important one in each case, holding it against the benchmark of undistorted competition.[88] The courts are clearly capable of doing this.[89] By avoiding any consideration of the conflict between the different objectives and how this might be resolved, the *Guidance Paper* is not providing undertakings with much certainty about the balancing of conflicting objectives.[90]

4.2 *Effects on the structure of competition or on consumers*

Besides the uncertainty about the underlying purpose of Article 82, another doubt has been whether it is necessary to demonstrate actual

[83] *Guidance Paper*, supra note 1, para. 35. [84] Ibid., paras. 6–7.

[85] *Discussion Paper*, supra note 35, paras. 4 and 54. [86] See chapter 3.

[87] IP/08/1877 of 3 December 2008, 'Antitrust: Consumer Welfare at Heart of Commission Fight Against Abuses by Dominant Undertakings'. Emphasis added.

[88] This will be elaborated in chapter 7.

[89] Joined Cases C-468/06 to C-478/06 *Sot. Lelos kai Sia EE and others v. GlaxoSmithKline AEVE* [2008] ECR I-7139.

[90] For an analysis of this in Article 81, see C. Townley, *Article 81 EC and Public Policy* (Oxford: Hart Publishing, 2009) chapter 8.

or likely anticompetitive effects in the marketplace and what effects are relevant. This was discussed in chapter 5. The *Guidance Paper* confirms that between actual and likely harm, evidence of *likely* anticompetitive foreclosure suffices.[91] The Commission does not need to establish that the dominant undertaking's conduct actually harmed competition, only that there is convincing evidence that harm is likely.[92] This is in line with some case law.[93]

Unlike the *Discussion Paper*, which focused on conduct that has a market-distorting foreclosure effect,[94] the *Guidance Paper* does not use the terminology of market-distorting foreclosure effect, but of anti-competitive foreclosure.[95] Despite the omission of the word 'effect', the Commission purports to adopt an effects-based approach: '[t]he guidance paper sets out an economic and effects-based approach to exclusionary conduct under EC antitrust law'.[96] An approach based on effects implies a rejection of the use of *per se* rules. However, the question is whether the Commission will continue automatically to assume harmful effects to consumers where there is harm to economic freedom, or whether it will allow dominant undertakings the opportunity of advancing efficiencies for their behaviour. According to the *Guidance Paper*, the Commission will consider whether there are any economic efficiencies as possible justification for the alleged harmful conduct.[97] It notes that a dominant undertaking may justify conduct leading to foreclosure if it is able to show that the efficiency benefits to consumers outweigh any allegedly competitive harm to consumers and that the conduct generating the efficiencies does not eliminate all or most existing sources of competition.[98] However, upon analysing how efficiencies should be treated in Article 82, it transpired that the test for efficiencies is not whether the conduct in question is efficient or inefficient to the advantage or disadvantage of consumers, but rather whether effective competition is eliminated. Whether or not there is effective competition in the market ought not to matter if the conduct in question is beneficial to consumers. The benchmark of effective competition can be decided by analysing the structure of competition. The fear is that consumer harm is assumed by looking at the structure of competition only.

[91] *Guidance Paper*, supra note 1, para. 19. [92] Press release, supra note 87.

[93] See chapter 5. [94] *Discussion Paper*, supra note 35, section 5.

[95] *Guidance Paper*, supra note 1, paras. 66–72.

[96] Press release, supra note 87. [97] *Guidance Paper*, supra note 1, para. 27.

[98] Ibid., para. 29. The *Guidance Paper* also discusses efficiencies in relation to specific abuses: see paras. 45, 61, 73 and 89.

Whilst the *Guidance Paper* describes the conditions for efficiencies as a potential justification,[99] it only outlines a few examples of accepted efficiencies, such as technical improvements in the quality of goods, or a reduction in the cost of production or distribution.[100] Some argue that the *Guidance Paper* omits a discussion of the large number of potentially beneficial effects that economic literature identifies, especially for tying/bundling, refusal to supply and exclusive dealing practices.[101] Moreover, they claim that this asymmetric way of treating potential efficiencies relative to potentially harmful effects has no justification in current economic thinking,[102] and the Commission's reading of economics literature appears to be rather one-sided.[103] This, in conjunction with little knowledge about what kinds of efficiencies objective justifications include, increases uncertainty.[104] This makes it extremely difficult for dominant undertakings to assess whether the Commission will categorise their conduct as harmful or legitimate.

The *Guidance Paper* does not offer a particular test which applies across all kinds of conduct for a good reason, which is that different objectives are being pursued in different cases. Instead, it formulates legal standards for individual abuses. It is presumably very difficult to advance a test that applies to both pricing practices and non-pricing practices, so requiring one overall test may be unrealistic. However, the formulation of the individual legal standards is very broad. For example, in examining whether consumers are harmed by a dominant undertaking's refusal to supply, the Commission will assess whether 'the likely negative consequences of the refusal to supply in the relevant market outweigh over time the negative consequences of imposing an obligation to supply'.[105] Nothing is wrong with this balancing test, which follows the Commission's decision in *Microsoft*.[106] However, only a limited number of examples of which practices are likely to constitute a refusal to supply are mentioned.[107]

The *Guidance Paper* does not explicitly say that it will always investigate anticompetitive foreclosure. For example, sacrifice is presumed where the

[99] *Guidance Paper*, supra note 1, para. 29. [100] Ibid., para. 29.

[101] Y. Katsoulacos, 'Some Critical Comments on the Commission's Guidance Paper on Art. 82 EC' *Global Competition Policy* (February 2009) 1, 8.

[102] Ibid., 6. [103] Ibid., 100, 8.

[104] Although some clarity is provided by E. Rousseva, 'The Concept of "Objective Justification" of an Abuse of a Dominant Position: Can it Help to Modernise the Analysis under Article 82 EC?' 2(2) *Competition Law Review* (2006) 27.

[105] *Guidance Paper*, supra note 1, para. 85. [106] COMP/C-3/37.792 *Microsoft*.

[107] *Guidance Paper*, supra note 1, para. 77.

dominant undertaking prices below average avoidable cost. Moreover, the 'as efficient competitor' test is only applicable if the Commission has sufficient cost data, which could indicate an assumption of foreclosure in the absence of such data. The Commission is still willing to rely on direct evidence of any exclusionary strategy, which implies that intent still plays a role in reaching a conclusion of anticompetitive foreclosure. Chapter 5 explained that intent is relevant where the objective is economic freedom. In examining tying and bundling the Commission limits its analysis to *risk* of foreclosure,[108] which again is about harm to the structure of competition instead of harm to consumers. Whilst the *Guidance Paper* gives dominant undertakings the opportunity to advance efficiencies, this is impossible as long as the aim is not consumer welfare. Without knowing whether the Commission will rely on assumptions of harm to the structure of competition or whether it will examine the effects on consumers, it is still uncertain whether dominant undertakings can defend themselves in the form of efficiencies. This does not create clarity and certainty. Thus, whilst in some places the *Guidance Paper* provides a useful summary, it provides little direction additional to what was already available in the case law. This can create uncertainty in the business community as to how the Commission will enforce potentially abusive conducts under Article 82. The Commission does not solve the conflict between economic freedom and consumer welfare and therefore does not illuminate how conflicting objectives are to be balanced.

5. The consequences of continuous uncertainty

As noted above, the national courts and competition authorities are bound to apply Articles 81 and 82 in their entirety and cannot take decisions running counter to Commission decisions or Community case law. Thus, it would be advisable for the Commission to clarify the issues discussed above if national authorities and courts are to achieve a similar outcome to Community practice in future cases as they will need to know what the Commission is trying to achieve. When national courts are called upon to apply Community competition law, they can seek guidance in the case law of the Community Courts or in Commission regulations, decisions, notices and guidelines applying the competition rules.[109] Where

108 Ibid., para. 52.

109 OJ [2004] C101/54 Commission Notice, *The Co-operation Between the Commission and the Courts of the EU Member States in the Application of Articles 81 and 82 EC*, recital 27.

these tools are limited or do not offer sufficient guidance, the national court may ask the Commission for its opinion on economic, factual and legal matters regarding the application of Community competition law.[110] Thus, where guidelines are unclear the number of requests may increase as more national courts ask the Commission for its opinion on questions concerning the application of EC competition law. The Member States' courts may also ask the Commission to 'transmit to them information in its possession or its opinion on questions concerning the application of the Community competition rules'.[111] This workload is likely to increase if the national courts are given insufficient information about how to assess exclusionary conduct by dominant undertakings. Besides asking the Commission for its opinion on economic, factual and legal matters, national courts may refer questions to the ECJ under the Article 234 procedure, provided the criteria for admissibility are fulfilled.[112]

6. The way forward

For competition policy to be effective it will need support from the business community, which will only happen when businesses understand the Commission's policy. Although the *Guidance Paper* creates legitimate expectations as to how the Commission will interpret the law, it does not directly and explicitly address the uncertainties surrounding Article 82.

The *Guidance Paper* does not clarify whether the Commission will always investigate the possibility of consumer harm. The implication is that the Commission may still rely on assumptions of harm to consumers where economic freedom is harmed. This is not about consumer welfare and leaves dominant undertakings without an opportunity to advance efficiencies. When applying Article 82, the Commission aims to safeguard the process of competition in the internal market, and prohibit conduct which undermines the effort to achieve an integrated

[110] *Delimitis v. Henninger Bräu*, supra note 38, para. 53; Joined Cases C-319/93, C-40/94 and C-224/94 *Hendrik Evert Dijkstra v. Friesland (Frico Domo) Coöperatie BA and Cornelis van Roessel and others v. De coöperatieve vereniging Zuivelcoöperatie Campina Melkunie VA and Willem de Bie and others v. De Coöperatieve Zuivelcoöperatie Campina Melkunie BA* [1995] ECR I-4471, para. 34.

[111] Council Regulation 1/2003, supra note 18, Article 15.

[112] For example Cases 28/62 to 30/62 *Da Costa en Schaake NV, Jacob Meijer NV and Hoechst-Holland NV v. Nederlandse Belastingadministratie* [1963] ECR 31; Cases C-415/93 *Union Royal Belge des Sociétés de Football Association v. Bosman* [1995] ECR I-4921; Case C-379/98 *PreussenElektra AG v. Schleswag AG* [2001] ECR I-2099.

market.[113] Chapter 3 showed that integration of the market does not necessarily make consumers better off, as the underlying purpose of market integration is also about achieving freedom of competition. Protecting undistorted competition in the internal market safeguards economic freedom by eradicating barriers to trade within the common market, but protecting economic freedom may not always lead to consumer welfare. These two objectives may sometimes conflict. Thus, the Commission needs to explain which objective is the more important one in case of conflict. The *Guidance Paper* does not do that.

The author is not suggesting that the Commission find an overall objective of Article 82 that replaces all the other objectives of Article 82, as the *Discussion Paper* tried to do. There is no support for that in the jurisprudence. Instead, this author suggests that the Commission acknowledge that a conflict may sometimes exist between economic freedom and consumer welfare, and that in cases where such conflict does arise, the Commission should explain which of the two objectives is the more important in that particular case. How the Commission should decide this will be discussed in the next chapter. This will allow those enforcing Article 82 to better determine what value to ascribe to economic freedom and to consumer welfare where the two conflict. Such an approach would help to create a unified body of decisions, thus providing greater predictability, legal certainty and transparency to undertakings and their advisers. By determining the value of the conflicting objectives, the Commission would reduce its discretion and its decisions would not be perceived as being arbitrary. The approach outlined above is not easy but this is exactly why it must be done. Otherwise there will be no certainty for undertakings, national courts and competition authorities and the consequences will be an increase in workload for the Commission and the ECJ, as described in the previous section. The Commission has had the opportunity to produce guidelines. It opted for a hybrid between priority and substantive guidelines. Another set of guidelines is unlikely to add much. Thus, it is suggested that the Commission publish its future decisions, not only prohibition decisions but also non-infringement decisions and decisions which are closed because of administrative priorities. In this way, it would be possible for the business community to see what was important to the Commission in its enforcement of Article 82. This author also suggests that the Commission be clear on its counterfactuals

[113] *Guidance Paper*, supra note 1, paras. 6–7.

and explain why it relies on those counterfactuals. Intervention does not always lead to a prohibition decision; the Commission may close its file because it is convinced by the specific efficiencies advanced by a dominant undertaking. Publishing such decisions would allow undertakings to see what efficiencies the Commission considers important. This is of course only possible in cases where the starting point is consumer welfare.

As noted above, the Commission does not solve the conflict between economic freedom and consumer welfare and therefore does not illuminate how conflicting objectives are to be balanced. Thus, the next and final chapter discusses how to balance these objectives against the overarching objective of undistorted competition and advances some policy recommendations.

7

The way forward

This book has considered the legitimacy of consumer welfare as an objective of Article 82. It demonstrated that consumer welfare is only one amongst other relevant objectives within that provision. It suggested that consumer welfare cannot be given primacy in the hierarchy of goals in terms of excluding other goals. There are several reasons for this. Chapter 3 showed that Article 82 is not an end in itself, but rather an implementation provision of the wider Treaty goals. Article 82 must therefore be read in the context of the Treaty as a whole and cannot be narrowed down simply to focusing on consumer welfare. One of the Treaty's goals is a system ensuring that competition in the internal market is not distorted. The Community Courts have interpreted Article 82 in the light of undistorted competition since *Continental Can*.[1] The *Discussion Paper*[2] created a lot of ambiguity by treating consumer welfare as the main objective of Article 82, in particular because it is hard to see a concern for consumer welfare in the vast majority of cases. While many Community lawyers would readily accept, and indeed welcome, the focus on the objective of consumer welfare,[3] this is not always supported by case law. While the Community Courts have been concerned with both direct and indirect harm to consumers, there is little discussion of the efficiencies certain conduct may bring to consumers. This is because economic freedom has been the main concern for some time. As chapter 2 explained, this is a very different objective from an objective focusing on efficiency. Although the *Guidance Paper*[4] adopts a neo-classical definition of market power

[1] Case 6/72 *Europemballage Corporation and Continental Can Co. Inc. v. Commission* [1973] ECR 215.

[2] DG COMP's *Discussion Paper on the Application of Article 82 of the Treaty to Exclusionary Abuses* (December 2005) (*Discussion Paper*).

[3] The majority of submissions to the *Discussion Paper* welcomed the objective of consumer welfare. These are available at: http://ec.europa.eu/competition/antitrust/art82/contributions.html.

[4] OJ [2009] C45/7 *Guidance on the Commission's Enforcement Priorities in Applying Article 82 EC Treaty to Abusive Exclusionary Conduct by Dominant Undertakings* (*Guidance Paper*).

and links it to neo-classical price theory, the Chicago School cannot be injected into Article 82 as efficiency cannot be balanced against social justice. More fundamentally, chapter 4 found that consumer welfare is conflicting with the objective of economic freedom/freedom of competition and that the Community Courts do not necessarily favour consumer welfare at the expense of freedom of competition. Chapter 6 concluded that the *Guidance Paper* does not identify this conflict and therefore does not resolve it. Thus, this chapter suggests balancing these objectives against the overarching objective of undistorted competition.

The book then established that three main uncertainties surround Article 82. These are (i) what Article 82's underlying purpose is; (ii) whether it is necessary to demonstrate actual or likely anticompetitive effects in the marketplace when applying Article 82; and (iii) how dominant undertakings can defend themselves against a finding of abuse. These uncertainties led the Commission to initiate its review of Article 82.[5] Opinions as to what the Commission ought to do when applying the provision have been numerous. Some argue that 'a great deal of improvement could be achieved if the Community Courts were able, in these cases, to refine some of the earlier jurisprudence in the light of the debate that has taken place as a result of the Commission's review over the last couple of years'.[6] This is not a request for a re-interpretation of the case law in the light of past disappointments, but an appeal for a refinement. The Commission echoes this:[7]

> [T]he Commission must always work to improve its decisions and its policies. The review [of Article 82] is about a better focus and a better argumentation in future cases. Furthermore, the fact that if the discussion paper leads to a more refined economic analysis, the Commission would in future argue a case in a different way than in the past, does not mean that the decision taken in a past case was wrong, only that the argumentation would today have been different.

A '*more* refined economic analysis' would imply that the Commission is already employing an economic analysis when applying Article 82. Depending on what is meant by an economic analysis, this may be confirmed or rejected. The EAGCP Report's definition of an economic approach to Article 82, being an approach that 'requires a careful

[5] Chapter 1.

[6] R. Whish, 'Review of O'Donoghue and Padilla, *The Law and Economics of Article 82 EC*' 2(2) *Competition Policy International* (2006) 188, 192.

[7] Commission Discussion Paper on Abuse of Dominance – Frequently Asked Questions, Memo of 19 December 2005, MEMO/05/486.

examination of how competition works in each particular market in order to evaluate how specific company strategies affect consumer welfare' focuses 'on the effects of company actions rather than on the form that these actions may take'.[8] This definition requires the Commission to measure consumer welfare by adopting an approach focusing on the effects on consumers. This is not only a question of objectives, but also one of methodology.

A change of objectives and/or methodology

Chapter 5 argued that it is important to distinguish objectives and methodology, as they are two separate things. Methodology and objectives are sometimes intertwined and changing the underlying purpose of a provision may sometimes require a change of methodology, but this is not always the case, and in any event it does not alter the fact that they are two different things.[9] It was also argued that aiming at promoting consumer welfare does not mean that the Commission has to apply an effects-based test. If economic theory shows that consumers are almost always harmed when a dominant undertaking engages in certain kinds of behaviour, then the Commission can advance consumer welfare by prohibiting that conduct *per se*. To take an example from Article 81, consumers would in most cases be likely to be harmed by horizontal price fixing. There may be exceptions where horizontal price fixing does not harm consumers, but these are few, and so on a balance between efficient enforcement and getting the right outcome in every case, the former takes priority over the latter. The problem in Article 82, however, is that very few kinds of conduct can be categorised as almost always harming competition. Yet, chapter 5 discovered that the Commission prefers to rely on assumptions – at times conclusive presumptions – instead of analysing a specific conduct's economic impact. There has been a tendency to presume that conduct is abusive where a dominant undertaking engages in, for example, predatory pricing, awards customers with rebates or refuses to supply downstream customers. It was considered whether these presumptions are acceptable or unacceptable. It was argued that this depends on what the Commission is trying to achieve when applying Article 82. Depending on the underlying

[8] EAGCP Report on *An Economic Approach to Article 82 EC* (July 2005) 2.

[9] L. Lovdahl Gormsen, 'Article 82 EC: Where Are We Coming From and Where Are We Going To?' 2(2) *Competition Law Review* (2005) 5.

objective, it may or may not be ideal to have *per se* rules or conclusive presumptions.

If the aim of Article 82 is freedom of competition, the Commission can adopt a conclusive presumption of abuse where, for example, a dominant undertaking grants its customers a loyalty rebate, as the rebate is likely to foreclose the dominant undertaking's competitors' access to the customer base. The foreclosure impairs competitors' freedom to compete on the merits. Thus, if the underlying objective of Article 82 is economic freedom in the market, a presumption of abuse where a dominant undertaking engages in conduct likely to foreclose access is acceptable. Many kinds of conduct are capable of reducing or limiting other market participants' economic freedom, but may not necessarily harm consumers. Therefore, if the aim of Article 82 is consumer welfare then such a presumption of abuse, where foreclosure is likely, is not acceptable as foreclosure may not necessarily harm consumers. Whether foreclosure harms consumers depends on how significant the foreclosure is. Thus, a conclusive presumption of abuse where a dominant undertaking awards its customer rebates is not acceptable, because it is not certain that consumers are harmed by that conduct. Even if the dominant undertaking is able to foreclose the majority of the market, it still cannot automatically be concluded that consumers are harmed, because the dominant undertaking may be able to offer efficiencies to consumers that outweigh the lack of choice. However, where experience or economic theory tells the Commission that dominant undertakings rarely advance efficiencies which outweigh the lack of choice, it may consider adopting a presumption of abuse where the conduct in question is capable of foreclosing the majority of the market. Depending on experience or economic theory, pursuing an objective of consumer welfare may or may not require the Commission to adopt a methodology of effects. Relying on conclusive presumptions may however be acceptable in some situations, even where the Commission is trying to promote consumer welfare: for example, if the dominant undertaking enters into long-term exclusive dealing contracts with *all* the main customers in the market. Assumptions are very useful and necessary to make enforcement administrable and efficient. However, the assumptions need to be built on sound theory, economic evidence and many years of experience. For example, predatory pricing is usually considered abusive if the prices are below average variable costs, as it does not make any business sense. If the theory behind the assumption no longer reflects reality, the theory and the assumption must be changed. This suggession is based on Karl Popper's critical rationalism that we can never justify any scientific theory, but we can falsify it. To examine whether the current presumptions are in need of a change, chapter 5 analysed some of them. It argued that whether the presumptions ought to be changed depends on which objective Article 82 is trying to achieve. The Commission cannot claim to pursue an objective of consumer welfare as long as it keeps assessing the effects of the *structure of competition* instead of the effects on *consumers*.

Presumptions of harm

If the ultimate objective is consumer welfare, the question is whether consumer welfare is promoted by relying on an assumption of consumer harm where evidence of intent to eliminate a competitor is found. This is only a good presumption if it is obvious that consumers are likely to be harmed where there is intent (by a dominant firm) to eliminate competition, but as shown this is not always the case. Likewise, if the ultimate objective is freedom of competition, the question is whether this objective is safeguarded by relying on an assumption of harm to economic freedom where evidence of intent to eliminate a competitor is found. Again, unless it is obvious that competition is likely to be harmed, where there is evidence of intent to eliminate a competitor, then that is not a good presumption. There is an argument that exclusion is more likely to happen where intent to exclude is found than where no such intent is found, but the question is what are we trying to safeguard by protecting against likely exclusion. Freedom of competition is protected, because the potentially excluded competitor is saved from being excluded, but is consumer welfare promoted? An affirmative answer relies on a presumption that consumers are likely to be harmed by excluding a competitor. This goes back to the fundamental question raised, which is whether consumer welfare is promoted by protecting freedom of competition or, in other words, whether economic freedom is a means to an end of consumer welfare. Chapter 4 answered that question negatively.

Although economic freedom is not a means to an end of consumer welfare, this does not mean that safeguarding economic freedom never promotes consumer welfare. Even protecting less efficient competitors could promote consumer welfare either because those competitors are likely to become efficient over time or because they impose some constraint on the dominant undertaking (compared to no constraint at all). However, since protecting economic freedom just means protecting market players' freedom to participate in the marketplace, it will rarely automatically lead to increasing consumer welfare. Also, protecting inefficient competitors would require regulation. In terms of economic freedom, it does not matter whether the protected competitors are *efficient* or *inefficient*, as it is the freedom of all market players to participate in the marketplace that must be protected against exclusion or impairment. On the other hand, promoting consumer welfare means protecting only those competitors that are *efficient*, as only these competitors are believed to be able to bring consumers efficiencies.

Currently, the way in which the Commission and the Community Courts protect the process of competition is by safeguarding rivalry in the long term *without* considering whether only *efficient* competitors are protected. Thus, if the Commission wants to apply Article 82 to promote consumer welfare, it is crucial that it explains *how* safeguarding such rivalry, which may protect less efficient competitors, is able to promote consumer welfare. The Commission claims the aim of Article 82 is to advance consumer welfare, but continues to safeguard rivalry without explaining *how* protecting rivalry in specific cases promotes consumer welfare. Because it is not clear whether the process of competition is being protected to safeguard freedom of competition in itself or to promote consumer welfare, the Commission is easily accused of using Article 82 as a tool to protect *inefficient* competitors.

There may be several reasons why the Commission and the Courts do not explain why they protect rivalry: (i) they acknowledge that there is a conflict between economic freedom and consumer welfare, but believe it occurs so rarely that there is no need to resolve it by balancing the objectives; or (ii) they do not believe there is a conflict because they believe economic freedom is always a means to an end of consumer welfare; or (iii) they acknowledge that there is a conflict, but resolve it in favour of freedom of competition at the expense of consumer welfare. In the first scenario, the Commission and the Courts acknowledge that there is a conflict between the two objectives, but do not balance the objectives, because they choose efficiency of administration over a potentially wrong outcome in very few cases. In the second scenario, they incorrectly believe that there is no conflict where there is one. This fallacy is likely to lead to wrong outcomes either by allowing conduct which is abusive, or by prohibiting conduct which is legitimate. In the third scenario, they acknowledge there is a conflict, but choose to resolve it in favour of economic freedom at the expense of consumer welfare, because they believe that between the two types of errors, it is better to make type I errors than type II errors.

Because the Commission and Community Courts rarely articulate which objective they are trying to achieve in individual cases, it is extremely difficult to say whether the current presumptions are in need of a change. With that in mind, some policy recommendations are advanced.

Policy recommendations

Given the uncertainties surrounding the underlying objective of Article 82, the fundamental question is whether it is enough to *refine* the analysis of Article 82 to resolve the uncertainties or whether there is a need for a more revolutionary overhaul such as a departure from old case law. This author is not tempted to suggest the Community Courts ought to change their past jurisprudence, although the ECJ has done so in other areas of law.[10] Instead, this author suggests making undistorted competition (a concept which changes its meaning over time) the overarching objective in every case. Against this benchmark, the Commission would then decide, in every case, whether to balance it against consumer welfare or economic freedom. Enunciating an overall objective in every case would enhance clarity for those interpreting Article 82, so they know what they are trying to achieve.

As has been discussed in previous chapters, the objectives of consumer welfare and economic freedom sometimes clash, so it is necessary that the Commission decides which one is the most deserving in each case to balance this against undistorted competition. This is even more important because the Treaty does not provide for such a balancing, nor does it create a hierarchy of objectives, or even mention all the objectives considered relevant under Article 82. The Community Courts do however perform such balancing of objectives,[11] so the Commission should also be able to do it.[12] Balancing is not in itself enough; the Commission needs to make clear which objective is the main objective in the balance as the Courts rarely make that clear. The balance between different values will have to take

[10] For example, in Case C-10/89 *CNL-Sucal v. Hag* (*Hag II*) [1990] ECRI-3711 the ECJ reversed its judgment in Case 192/73 *Van Zuylen v. Hag* (*Hag I*) [1974] ECR 731 as it found the doctrine of 'common origin' somewhat incompatible with developing EC law.

[11] See, for example, Case C-418/01 *IMS Health GmbH & Co. OHG v. NDC Health GmbH & Co. KG* [2002] ECR I-3401; Case T-76/89 *Independent Television Publications Ltd v. Commission* [1991] ECR II-575.

[12] It was capable of doing it in COMP/C-3/37.792 *Microsoft*, para. 970.

place within the economic and legal context of the specific market where the conduct is taking place. Hopefully, by providing an overall objective and balancing it against other objectives, clarity will prevail, which will increase transparency to undertakings and their advisers, stakeholders and other market players. This is even more important given that the *Guidance Paper* ignores the issue of the conflict between objectives of Article 82, so that ambiguity remains. The *Guidance Paper* acknowledges that Article 82 aims at achieving different objectives. However, chapter 6 showed that the *Guidance Paper* does not acknowledge that these may clash at times. Instead, the *Guidance Paper* states it will pursue cases where the Commission believes consumers are harmed.[13] This means that the Commission will only intervene where it thinks there is consumer loss. Although the Commission is entitled to decide not to open a case or to close a case based on administrative priorities,[14] it may run the risk of legal action for 'failure to act' being taken against it in the case of such a decision not to intervene, especially if the Commission ignores other objectives that it acknowledges in the *Guidance Paper* are important.

It is suggested that the overall objective, against which other values must be balanced, must be to ensure competition in the internal market is not distorted. Chapter 3 explained that ensuring undistorted competition is not about protecting competition in itself against *any* distortion, but about the achievement of the broader objectives of the Treaty. This requires a fine balance between conduct which distorts competition in such a way that the wider objectives are jeopardised and conduct which distorts competition only insignificantly and therefore does not prevent the broader objectives from being achieved. As said, the overall objective of undistorted competition must be applied in its legal and economic context. Depending on the individual case, this could mean favouring economic freedom more or less in one case or favouring consumer welfare more or less in another case. The Commission will have discretion to decide which objective is more deserving in each case, but will have to explain which one it is relying on. Chapter 4 gave a couple of examples of markets where it would be preferable to give priority to freedom of competition regardless of whether this may sacrifice consumer welfare and vice versa. For example, in newly liberalised markets where the incumbent is all powerful, new entrants may be discouraged from entering the market unless they are protected for some time despite not being able to

[13] *Guidance Paper*, supra note 4, paras. 5 and 19.

[14] Case T-24/90 *Automec v. Commission* [1992] ECR II-2223, para. 77.

enhance consumer welfare. Similarly, freedom of competition may be given priority in markets where the dominant undertaking has a near-monopoly *if* this is not the most efficient supply structure for consumers, but that will have to be examined. On the other hand, in markets characterised by a less concentrated supply structure, it may not be necessary to protect freedom of competition, and may instead be better to promote efficiency to the benefit of consumers. The Commission will have to examine the individual market to assess whether it is better to sacrifice some competitors' economic freedom to the potential benefit of consumer welfare, or whether it should sacrifice some potential efficiencies to safeguard freedom of competition. It is difficult *a priori* to say which objective is the best in a given situation as it depends on the individual markets.

In this area of law, where the Commission and the Community Courts have been accused of protecting competitors instead of competition, it is important to achieve the right outcome not only to avoid prohibiting legitimate conduct, but also to make clear that Article 82 is about protecting competition, not inefficient competitors. However, this author acknowledges there is a balance between the right outcome in every case and efficient administration of the law. Therefore, this book does not go as far as saying that the Commission always has to examine the effects on consumers, as other objectives are important as well. However, the hope is that the Commission will stop pretending it is promoting consumer welfare where it is not and stop assuming harm to consumers from harm to economic freedom. If the aim is consumer welfare in a given case, the Commission can still rely on a presumption of consumer harm if it is based on a sound theory or on experience of similar cases of how consumers are harmed. Where the Commission is no longer certain that the presumption reflects reality, it is advised to revise or even abandon it. There is a hint of this in the *Guidance Paper*, which omits to mention the *AKZO* presumption that very large market shares above 50 per cent can in themselves be evidence of a dominant position.[15] This must be taken to mean that the Commission no longer believes it is a good presumption.

The Commission is advised to adopt rebuttable presumptions instead of conclusive presumptions. The consequence of a rebuttable presumption is that the evidential burden of proof shifts between the dominant undertaking and the Commission. A rebuttable presumption as opposed

[15] Case 62/86 *AKZO Chemie BV v. Commission* [1991] ECR I-3359, para. 60.

to a conclusive presumption would allow dominant undertakings to defend themselves, which would otherwise require an appeal (although dominant undertakings usually appeal anyway). Chapter 2 established that despite the lack of an explicit exemption provision in Article 82, dominant undertakings are allowed to advance objective justifications. This however is not possible where the Commission relies on conclusive presumptions. Moreover, chapter 3 showed that the Community Courts are currently adopting a narrow interpretation of which efficiencies dominant undertakings can advance. This is because advancing efficiencies is not a possibility where the aim is economic freedom, as this objective is about 'the protection of individual economic freedom of action as a value in itself, or vice versa, the restraint of undue economic power'.[16] Efficiency is not the aim. There will be cases where the Commission opens an investigation against a dominant undertaking, but decides to close the case due to the restriction of competition being outweighed by efficiencies. Depending on how far the Commission is into the investigation, it may decide either to close the case based on administrative priorities or to reach a non-infringement decision. The latter will be published, but chapter 6 suggested that the Commission also publish its decision to close cases based on administrative priorities. This may place a heavy burden upon the Commission, but would avoid any arbitrariness in its decision-making, and would help stakeholders, undertakings, national competition authorities and courts understand which efficiencies the Commission considers relevant or whether the Commission is relying on an objective of consumer welfare.

Overall conclusion

The aim of this book was to challenge the legitimacy of focusing on consumer welfare as the only or main goal of Article 82. This was necessary not only to see whether it was legitimate but also to test the implications of the Commission's presumptions. The introduction cited Amato, who has pointed out that 'it requires a frank discussion [of the goals of competition], because it is doubtful that we all agree on the goals of competition. Generally, however, we refrain from discussing it openly, and ambiguities

[16] W. Möschel, 'The Proper Scope of Government Viewed from an Ordoliberal Perspective: The Example of Competition Policy' 157 *Journal of Institutional and Theoretical Economics* (2001) 3; W. Möschel, 'Competition Policy from an Ordo Point of View' in H. Willgerodt and A. Peacock (eds.), *German Neo-liberals and the Social Market Economy* (London: Macmillan, 1989) 146.

remain.'[17] Whilst correct, the review of Article 82 was never about objectives only, but also about methodology. In particular, it considered the necessity of demonstrating actual or likely anticompetitive effects in the market when applying Article 82. Would this be solved by adopting a consumer welfare objective? This book has answered this negatively. It argued that consumer welfare can be achieved even without going into an analysis of effects on consumers in every case. Presumptions are acceptable if they are supported by good theory or experience as to how consumers are harmed. The Commission is entitled to rely on presumptions. However, where these no longer reflect reality, they must be revised or abandoned.

Another issue was whether freedom of competition was considered a fundamental right, in which case a priority of a utilitarian goal of consumer welfare would undermine the Community legal order, as it would be a priority of a utilitarian approach over a fundamental rights-based approach. Despite finding that economic freedom is not a fundamental right, it was established that there is a potential conflict between economic freedom and consumer welfare. Because of the clash between the two objectives, the Commission must find an overall objective in each case, so it is possible to balance the positive and negative effects of the conduct against that objective. The Commission must make clear in every decision what it is trying to achieve so as not to undermine clarity. The *Guidance Paper* does not deal with the conflict or the balance, so there is still much work to be done in this area of law. A start would be to publish all decisions to close cases based on administrative priority. Given the framework for anticompetitive foreclosure set forth in the *Guidance Paper*, the Commission has created legitimate expectations as to what framework it will apply when intervening. Where the Commission departs from the framework, it will have to give reasons. By publishing decisions to close cases, it will hopefully become clear why the Commission did not think the foreclosure in a specific case was anticompetitive.

[17] Panel discussion on Competition Policy Objectives in C. D. Ehlermann and L. L. Laudati (eds.), *European Competition Law Annual 1997: The Objectives of Competition Policy* (Oxford: Hart Publishing, 1998) 3.

BIBLIOGRAPHY

Books

Amato, G. *Antitrust and the Bounds of Power* (Oxford: Hart Publishing, 1997)

Arnull, A. *The European Union and its Court of Justice* (Oxford University Press, 1999)

Bain, J. *Barriers to New Competition: Their Character and Consequences in Manufacturing Industries* (Harvard University Press, 1956)

Industrial Organization (New York: Wiley, 2nd edn, 1968)

Bannock, G. *et al. Dictionary of Economics* (New York: Bloomberg Press, 4th edn, 2003)

Bishop, S. and Walker, M. *The Economics of EC Competition Law: Concepts, Application and Measurement* (London: Sweet & Maxwell, 2nd edn, 2002)

Böhm, F. *Wirtschaftsordnung und Staatsverfassung* (Tübingen: Mohr, 1950)

Bork, R. *The Antitrust Paradox: A Policy at War with Itself* (New York: Free Press, 1993)

Bouckaert, B. and De Geest, G. *Encyclopedia of Law and Economics* (Cheltenham: Elgar, 2000) vol. III

Carlton, D.W. and Perloff, J.M. *Modern Industrial Organization* (Boston: Addison Wesley, 4th edn, 2005)

Craig, P. and De Búrca, G. *EU Law: Text, Cases and Materials* (Oxford University Press, 3rd edn, 2003)

Cruz, J.B. *Between Competition and Free Movement: The Economic Constitutional Law of the European Community* (Oxford: Hart Publishing, 2002)

Cseres, K.J. *Competition Law and Consumer Protection* (The Hague: Kluwer Law International, 2005)

Deringer, A. *The Competition Law of the European Economic Community: A Commentary on the EEC Rules of Competition (Articles 85 to 90) Including the Implementing Regulations and Directives* (New York: Commerce Clearing House, 1968)

Douglas-Scott, S. *Constitutional Law of the European Union* (Harlow: Pearson Education, 2002)

Ehlermann, C. D. and Atanasiu, I. (eds.) *European Competition Law Annual 2003: What is an Abuse of a Dominant Position?* (Oxford: Hart Publishing, 2006)

Ehlermann, C.D. and Laudati, L.L. (eds.) *European Competition Law Annual 1997: The Objectives of Competition Policy* (Oxford: Hart Publishing, 1998)

Eucken, W. *The Unsuccessful Age* (Edinburgh: William Hodge, 1951)

Grundsätze der Wirtschaftspolitik (Berne, 1952)

Faull, J. and Nikpay, A. *The EC Law of Competition* (Oxford University Press, 2nd edn, 2007)

Furse, M. *Competition Law of the EC and UK* (Oxford University Press, 5th edn, 2006)

Gerber, D. *Law and Competition in Twentieth Century Europe: Protecting Prometheus* (Oxford University Press, 1998)

Giersch, H., Paque, K. H. and Schmieding, H. *The Fading Miracle: Four Decades of Market Economy in Germany* (Cambridge University Press, 1992)

Glöckler, G., Junius, L., Scappucci, G., Usherwood, S. and Vassallo, J. *Guide to EU Policies* (London: Blackstone Press, 1998)

Goldschmid, H., Mann, H. and Weston, J. (eds.) *Industrial Concentration: The New Learning* (New York: Columbia University Press, 1974)

Gormley, L. W. (ed.) *Introduction to the Law of the European Communities after the Coming into Force of the Single European Act* (Deventer: Kluwer, 2nd edn, 1989)

Goyder, D. *EC Competition Law* (Oxford University Press, 3rd edn, 1998)

Hartley, T. C. *The Foundations of European Community Law* (Oxford University Press, 5th edn, 2003)

Hawk, B. E. (ed.) *Annual Proceedings of the Fordham Corporate Law Institute: International Antitrust Law and Policy* (New York: Juris, 2004)

Hayek, F. A. *New Studies in Philosophy, Politics, Economics and the History of Ideas* (University of Chicago Press, 1978)

Hildebrand, D. *The Role of Economic Analysis in the EC Competition Rules* (The Hague: Kluwer Law International, 2nd edn, 2002)

Joliet, R. *Monopolization and Abuse of Dominant Position* (University of Liège, 1970)

Jones, A. and Sufrin, B. *EC Competition Law* (Oxford University Press, 2nd edn, 2004; 3rd edn, 2007)

Leoni, B. *Freedom and the Law* (Indianapolis: Liberty Fund, 3rd edn, 1991)

Lipsey, R. *An Introduction to Positive Economics* (London: Weidenfeld and Nicolson, 7th edn, 1989)

Mason, E. *Economic Concentration and the Monopoly Problem* (Harvard University Press, 1957)

Mestmäcker, E. J. *Europäisches Wettbewerbsrecht* (Munich: Beck, 1974)

Mestmäcker, E. J. and Schweitzer, H. *Europäisches Wettbewerbsrecht* (Munich: Beck, 2nd edn, 2004)

Miksch, L. *Wettbewerb als Aufgabe Grundsätze einer Wettbewerbsordnung* (Stuttgart: Godesberg, 2nd edn, 1947)

Monti, G. *EC Competition Law* (Cambridge University Press, 2007)

Motta, M. *Competition Policy: Theory and Practice* (Cambridge University Press, 2004)

O'Donoghue, R. and Padilla, A. J. *The Law and Economics of Article 82 EC* (Oxford: Hart Publishing, 2006)

Odudu, O. *The Boundaries of EC Competition Law: The Scope of Article 81* (Oxford University Press, 2006)

Pepall, L., Richards, D. and Norman, G. *Industrial Organization: Contemporary Theory and Practice* (Cincinnati, OH: South Western, 1999)

Posner, R. *Antitrust Law* (University of Chicago Press, 2nd edn, 2001)

Price, C. M. *Welfare Economics in Theory and Practice* (London: Macmillan, 1977)

Rasmussen, H. *EU-Ret i Kontekst* (Copenhagen: GadJura, 3rd edn, 1998)

Röpke, W. *German Commercial Policy* (London: Longmans, 1934)

Die Gesellschaftskrisis der Gegenwart (Erlenbach-Zurich, 1942)

Civitas Humana. Grundfragen der Gesellschafts- und Wirtschaftsreform (Erlenbach-Zurich, 1944)

Social Crisis of Our Time (London: Thames and Hudson, 1958)

Sauter, W. *Competition Law and Industrial Policy in the EU* (Oxford: Clarendon Press, 2003)

Senden, L. *Soft Law in European Community Law* (Oxford: Hart Publishing, 2004)

Scherer, F. M. *Competition Policies for an Integrated Work Economy* (Washington, DC: Brookings Institution, 1944)

Siragusa, M. *The Application of Art. 86: Tying Agreements, Refusal to Deal, Discrimination and Other Cases of Abuse* (Bruges, 1974)

Stigler, G. *The Organization of Industry* (Homewood, IL: R. D. Irwin, 1968)

Thorelli, H. B. *The Federal Antitrust Policy* (Boltimore: Johns Hopkins Press, 1955)

Townley, C. *Article 81 EC and Public Policy* (Oxford: Hart Publishing, 2009)

Tridimas, T. *The General Principles of EC Law* (New York: Oxford University Press, 1999)

Van Bael, I. and Bellis, J. F. *Competition Law of the European Community* (The Hague: Kluwer Law International, 4th edn, 2005)

Van den Bergh, R. and Camesasca, P. D. *European Competition Law and Economics: A Comparative Perspective* (Antwerp: Intersentia, 2001)

Viscusi, W. K., Vernon, J. M. and Harrington, J. E. *Economics of Regulation and Antitrust* (MIT Press, Cambridge, MA, 2nd edn, 1995)

Walker, D. M. *The Oxford Companion to Law* (Oxford: Clarendon Press, 1980)

Weatherill, S. and Beaumont, P. *EU Law* (London: Penguin Books, 3rd edn, 1999)

Whish, R. *Competition Law* (Oxford University Press, 6th edn, 2009)

Wils, W. *Efficiency and Justice in European Antitrust Enforcement* (Oxford: Hart Publishing, 2008)

Articles and chapters

Abbot, K. and Sindal, D. 'Hard and Soft Law in International Governance' 54(3) *International Organization* (2000) 421

Adams, W. and Brock, J. W. 'Antitrust and Efficiency: A Comment' 62 *New York University Law Review* (1987) 1116

Ahlborn, C. 'Competition Policy in the New Economy: Is European Competition Law up to the Challenge?' 22(5) *European Competition Law Review* (2001) 156

Ahlborn, C. and Evans, D. 'The *Microsoft* Judgment and its Implications for Competition Policy Towards Dominant Firms in Europe', 25–6, available at: http://papers.ssrn.com/sol3/papers.cfm?abstract_id=1115867

Ahlborn, C. and Grave, C. 'Walter Eucken and Ordoliberalism: An Introduction from a Consumer Welfare Perspective' 2(2) *Competition Policy International* (2006) 196

Akman, P. '"Consumer Welfare" and Article 82 EC: Practice and Rhetoric' 32(1) *World Competition* (2009) 71

Allan, B. 'Article 82: A Commentary on DG Competition's Discussion Paper' 2(1) *Competition Policy International* (2006) 42

Areeda, P. and Turner, D. 'Predatory Pricing and Practices under Section 2 of the Sherman Act' 88 *Harvard Law Review* (1975) 697

Bain, J. 'Relation of Profit Rate to Industry Concentration: American Manufacturing, 1936–40' 65 *Quarterly Journal of Economics* (1951) 293

Baker, J. 'Recent Developments in Economics that Challenge the Chicago School Views' 58(3) *Antitrust Law Journal* (1989) 645

Beveridge, F. and Nott, S. 'A Hard Look at Soft Law' in P. Craig and C. Harlow (eds.), *Lawmaking in the European Union* (The Hague: Kluwer Law International, 1998) 285

Bishop, W. 'Price Discrimination under Article 86: Political Economy in the European Court' 44 *Modern Law Review* (1981) 282

Böhm, F. 'Democracy and Economic Power' in *Cartel and Monopoly in Modern Law* (Karlsruhe: C. F. Müller, 1961)

Bork, R. H. 'Legislative Intent and the Policy of the Sherman Act' 9 *Journal of Law and Economics* (1966) 7

'The Role of the Courts in Applying Economics' 54 *Antitrust Law Journal* (1985) 21

Bowman, W. 'Tying Arrangements and the Leverage Problem' 67 *Yale Law Journal* (1957) 19

Brodley, J. F. 'The Economic Goals of Antitrust: Efficiency, Consumer Welfare and Technological Progress' 62 *New York University Law Review* (1987) 1020

Budzinski, O. 'Monoculture versus Diversity in Competition Economics' 32(2) *Cambridge Journal of Economics* (2008) 295

Burstein, M. 'The Economics of Tie-in Sales' 42 *Review of Economics and Statistics* (1960) 68

'A Theory of Full-line Forcing' 55 *Northwestern University Law Review* (1960) 62

Coppel, J. and O'Neill, A. 'The European Court of Justice: Taking Rights Seriously?' 29 *Common Market Law Review* (1992) 669

Cosma, H. and Whish, R. 'Soft Law in the Field of EU Competition Policy' 14(1) *European Business Law Review* (2003) 25

Dabbah, M. M. 'Conduct, Dominance and Abuse in "Market Relationship": Analysis of Some Conceptual Issues under Article 82 EC' 21(1) *European Competition Law Review* (2000) 45

Easterbrook, F. H. '*The Limits of Antitrust*' 63 *Texas Law Review* (1984) 1

Edlin, A. S. 'Stopping Above-cost Predatory Pricing' 4 *Yale Law Journal* (2002) 941

Eilmansberger, T. 'How to Distinguish Good from Bad Competition under Article 82 EC: In Search of Clearer and More Coherent Standards for Anticompetitive Abuses' 42 *Common Market Law Review* (2005) 129

'Dominance – the Lost Child? How Effects-based Rules Could and Should Change Dominance Analysis' *European Competition Journal* (July 2006) 15

Elzinga, K. G. 'The Goals of Antitrust: Other than Competition and Efficiency, What Else Counts?' 125 *University of Pennsylvania Law Review* (1977) 1191

Engelsing, F., Marsden, P. and Möller, D. 'A Bundeskartellamt/Competition Law Forum Debate on Reform of Article 82: A "Dialectic" on Competing Approaches' 2 (special supplement) *European Competition Journal* (2006) 211

Eucken, W. 'Die Wettbewerbsordnung und ihre Verwirklichung' 2 *ORDO* (1949) 1

Eucken, W. and Grossman-Doerth, H. 'What Kind of Economic and Social System?' in H. Willgerodt and A. Peacock (eds.), *Germany's Social Market Economy: Origins and Evolution* (Basingstoke: Macmillan, 1989) 34

Evans, D. 'Roundtable Discussion about the US Supreme Court's Decision in *Verizon v. Trinko*' 7(2) *Global Competition Review* (2004) 26

Farrell, J. and Katz, M. L. 'The Economics of Welfare Standards in Antitrust' 2(2) *Competition Policy International* (2006) 1

Forrester, I. 'The Modernisation of EC Antitrust Policy: Compatibility, Efficiency, Legal Security' in C. D. Ehlermann and I. Atanasiu (eds.), *The Modernisation of EC Antitrust Policy* (Oxford: Hart Publishing, 2001) 75

Fox, E. 'Monopolization and Dominance in the United States and the European Community: Efficiency, Opportunity, and Fairness' 61 *Notre Dame Law Review* (1986) 981

'What is Harm to Competition? Exclusionary Practices and Anticompetitive Effect' 70 *Antitrust Law Journal* (2002) 371

Fox, E. and Sullivan, L. 'Antitrust – Retrospective and Prospective: Where Are We Coming From? And Where Are We Going?' 62 *New York University Law Review* (1987) 936

Frazer, T. 'Competition Policy after 1992: The Next Step' 53(5) *Modern Law Review* (1990) 609

Geradin, D. and Petit, N. 'Price Discrimination under EC Competition Law: Another Antitrust Doctrine in Search of Limiting Principles?' 2(3) *Journal of Competition Law and Economics* (2006) 479

Gerber, D. 'Constitutionalizing the Economy: German Neo-liberalism, Competition Law and the "New" Europe' 42 *American Journal of Comparative Law* (1994) 25

Gormsen, L. L. 'Article 82 EC: Where Are We Coming From and Where Are We Going To?' 2(2) *Competition Law Review* (2005) 5

'The Conflict between Economic Freedom and Consumer Welfare in the Modernisation of Article 82 EC' 3(2) *European Competition Journal* (2007) 329

'The Parallels between the Harvard Structural School and Article 82 EC and the Divergences between the Chicago and Post-Chicago Schools and Article 82 EC' 4(1) *European Competition Journal* (2008) 221

'The European Commission's Priority Guidelines on Article 82 EC' 14(3) *Communication Law* (2009) 83

'Why the European Commission's Enforcement Priorities on Article 82 EC Should Be Withdrawn' 31(2) *European Competition Law Review* (2010) 45

Gyselen, L. 'Rebates: Competition on the Merits or Exclusionary Practice?' in C. D. Ehlermann and I. Atanasiu (eds.), *European Competition Law Annual 2003: What is an Abuse of a Dominant Position?* (Oxford: Hart Publishing, 2006) 287

Haracoglou, I. 'Competition Policy Law, Consumer Policy and the Retail Sector: The Systems' Relation and the Effects of a Strengthened Consumer Protection Policy on Competition Law' 3(2) *Competition Law Review* (2007) 175

Haubert II, W. M. H. '*Continental Can*: New Strength for Common Market Anti-trust' 11 *San Diego Law Review* (1973–4) 227

Hawk, B. E. 'The American (Anti-trust) Revolution: Lessons for the EEC' 9(1) *European Competition Law Review* (1988) 53

'Article 82 and Section 2' in OECD Paper on Competition on the Merits, DFA/COMP (2005) 27, 253

Hepple, B. 'Social Values and European Law' 48 *Current Legal Problems* (1995) 39

Hondius, F. W. 'The New Architecture of Europe and *Ius Commune Europaeum*' in B. de Witte and C. Forder (eds.), *The Common Law of Europe and the Future of Legal Education* (Deventer: Kluwer Law International, 1992) 215

Hovenkamp, H. 'Antitrust Policy after Chicago' 84 *Michigan Law Review* (1985) 213

Hur, J. Seon 'The Evolution of Competition Policy and its Impact on Economic Development in Korea' in UNCTAD Report on Competition, Competitiveness, and Development: Lessons from Developing Countries (2004) 227

Jacobs, F. G. 'Human Rights in the European Union: The Role of the Court of Justice' 26(4) *European Competition Law Review* (2001) 331

Jacobs, M. 'An Essay on the Normative Foundations of Antitrust Economics' 74 *North Carolina Law Review* (1995) 219

Jebsen, P. and Stevens, R. 'Assumptions, Goals and Dominant Undertakings: The Regulation of Competition under Article 86 of the European Union' 64 *Antitrust Law Journal* (1996) 443

Kallaugher, J. and Sher, B. 'Rebates Revisited: Anticompetitive Effects and Exclusionary Abuse under Article 82' 5 *European Competition Law Review* (2004) 263

Karsten, S. 'Eucken's "Social Market Economy" and its Test in Post-war West Germany. The Economist as Social Philosopher Developed Ideas that Paralleled Progressive Thought in America' 44(2) *American Journal of Economics and Sociology* (1985) 169

Katsoulacos, Y. 'Some Critical Comments on the Commission's Guidance Paper on Art. 82 EC' *Global Competition Policy* (February 2009) 1

Kenny, A. 'Intention and Purpose' 63 *Journal of Philosophy* (1966) 642

Korah, V. '*Istituto Chemioterapico Italiano SpA and Commercial Solvents Corporation v. Commission of the European Communities*' 11 *Common Market Law Review* (1974) 248

'The Interface between Intellectual Property Rights and Antitrust: The European Experience' 69(3) *Antitrust Law Journal* (2001) 801

Kovacic, W. 'The Intellectual DNA of Modern US Competition Law for Dominant Firm Conduct: The Chicago/Harvard Double Helix' *Columbia Business Law Review* (2007) 1

Lande, R.H. 'Wealth Transfers as the Original and Primary Concern of Antitrust: The Efficiency Interpretation Challenged' 34 *Hastings Law Journal* (1982) 65

'The Rise and (Coming) Fall of Efficiency as the Rule of Antitrust' 33 *Antitrust Bulletin* (1988) 429

Maduro, M. P. 'Reforming the Market or the State? Article 30 and the European Constitution: Economic Freedom and Political Rights' 3(1) *European Law Journal* (1997) 55

Manow, P. 'Ordoliberalismus als Ökomische Ordnungstheologie' 29 *Leviathan* (2001) 179

Marburg, T. 'Government and Businesses in Germany: Public Policy towards Cartels' 38(1) *Business History Review* (1964) 78

Marenco, G. 'Competition between National Economies and Competition between Businesses: A Response to Judge Pescatore' 10 *Fordham International Law Journal* (1987) 420

Marsden, P. and Bishop, S. 'Intellectual Leaders Still Need Ground to Stand On' editorial 3(2) *European Competition Journal* (2007) 315

Marsden, P. and Waller, S. W. 'Antitrust Marathon II' 4(1) *European Competition Journal* (2008) 213

Marsden, P. and Whelan, P. '"Consumer Detriment" and its Application in EC and UK Competition Law' 27(10) *European Competition Law Review* (2006) 569

May, J. 'Antitrust in the Formative Era: Political and Economic Theory in Constitutional and Antitrust Analysis, 1880–1918' 50 *Ohio State Law Journal* (1989) 257

McDonnell, B. and Farber, D. A. 'Are Efficient Antitrust Rules Always Optimal?' 48(3) *Antitrust Bulletin* (2003) 807

McNulty, P. 'Economic Theory and the Meaning of Competition' 82(4) *Quarterly Journal of Economics* (1968) 639

Mertikopoulou, V. 'DG Competition's Discussion Paper on the Application of Article 82 of the EC Treaty to Exclusionary Abuses: The Proposed Economic Reform from a Legal Point of View' 28(4) *European Competition Law Review* (2007) 241

Messina, M. 'Article 82 and the New Economy: Need for Modernisation?' 2(2) *Competition Law Review* (2005) 73

Mestmäcker, E. J. 'Die Beurteilung von Unternehmenszusammenschlüssen nach Artikel 86 des EWG-Vertrags' in *Festschrift für Walter Hallstein zu seinem 60: Probleme des Europäischen Rechts* (Frankfurt am Main: Klostermann, 1966)

'Competition Policy and Antitrust: Some Comparative Observations' 136 *Zeitschrift für die Gesamte Staatswissenschaft* (1980) 387

'Sur Anwendung der Wettbewerbsregeln auf die Mitgliedstaaten und auf die Europaischen Gemeinschaft' in J. F. Baur, P.-C. Müller-Graff and M. Zuleeg (eds.), *Europarecht, Energierecht, Wirtschaftsrecht: Festschrift für Bodo Borner sum 70. Geburtstag* (Cologne: Carl Heymanns Verlag, 1992)

'On the Legitimacy of European Law' 58 *Rabels Zeitschrift für Ausländisches und Internationales Privatrecht* (1994) 615

'The EC Commission's Modernization of Competition Policy: A Challenge to the Community's Constitutional Order' 1 *European Business Organization Law Review* (2000) 401

'Bausteine zu einer Wirtschaftsverfassung: Franz Böhm in Jena', reprinted in Mestmäcker, *Wirtschaft und Verfassung in der Europäischen Union* (Baden-Baden: Nomos Verlagsgesellschaft, 2nd edn, 2006)

Miksch, L. 'Walter Eucken' 4 *Kyklos* (1950) 279

Monti, G. 'Article 81 EC and Public Policy' 39 *Common Market Law Review* (2002) 1057

Monti, M. 'European Competition Policy for the 21st Century' in *International Antitrust Law and Policy* (Fordham Corporate Law Institute, 2000)

Möschel, W. 'Competition Policy from an Ordo Point of View' in H. Willgerodt and A. Peacock (eds.), *German Neo-liberals and the Social Market Economy* (London: Macmillan, 1989) 146

'The Proper Scope of Government Viewed from an Ordoliberal Perspective: The Example of Competition Policy' 157 *Journal of Institutional and Theoretical Economics* (2001) 3

Nazzini, R. 'The Wood Began to Move: An Essay on Consumer Welfare, Evidence and Burden of Proof in Article 82 Cases' 31(4) *European Law Review* (2006) 518

Neven, D. J. 'Competition Economics and Antitrust in Europe' 21(48) *Economic Policy* (2006) 741

Pathak, A. S. 'Articles 85 and 86 and Anticompetitive Exclusion in EEC Competition Law: Part 1' 10(1) *European Competition Law Review* (1989) 74

Pejovich, S. 'From Socialism to the Market Economy: Postwar West Germany versus Post-1989 East Bloc' 1 *Independent Review* (2001) 27

Peltzman, S. 'Aaron Director's Influence on Antitrust Policy' 43 *Journal of Law and Economics* (2005) 313

Peritz, R. J. 'A Counter-History of Antitrust Law' 40(2) *Duke Law Journal* (1990) 263

Pitofsky, R. 'The Political Content of Antitrust' 127 *University of Pennsylvania Law Review* (1979) 1051

Posner, R. 'The Chicago School of Antitrust Analysis' 127 *University of Pennsylvania Law Review* (1979) 925

Rasmussen, H. 'Between Self-Restraint and Activism: A Judicial Policy for the European Court' 13 *European Law Review* (1988) 28

Rawlinson, F. 'The Role of Policy Frameworks, Codes and Guidelines in the Control of State Aid' in I. Harden (ed.), *State Aid: Community Law and Policy* (Cologne: Bundesanzeiger, 1993) 52

Rogmann, A. and Stadtler, B. 'Is Free Trade with China in Peril?' 2(2) *World Customs Journal* (2005) 29

Rousseva, E. 'Modernizing by Eradicating: How the Commission's New Approach to Article 81 EC Dispenses with the Need to Apply Article 82 EC to Vertical Restraints' 42 *Common Market Law Review* (2005) 587

'The Concept of "Objective Justification" of an Abuse of a Dominant Position: Can it Help to Modernise the Analysis under Article 82 EC?' 2(2) *Competition Law Review* (2006) 27

Sauter, W. 'The Economic Constitution of the European Union' 4 *Columbia Journal of European Law* (1998) 27

Scherer, F. M. 'Antitrust, Efficiency, and Progress' 63 *New York University Law Review* (1987) 998

Schmidtchen, D. 'German Ordnungspolitik as Institutional Choice' 140 *Zeitschrift für die Gesamte Staatswissenschaft* (1984) 60

Senden, L. 'Soft Law, Self-regulation and Co-regulation in European Law: Where Do They Meet?' 9(1) *Electronic Journal of Comparative Law* (2005) 1

Sher, B. 'Price Discounts and *Michelin 2*: What Goes Around, Comes Around' 23(10) *European Competition Law Review* (2002) 482

'The Last of the Steam-Powered Trains: Modernising Article 82' 25(5) *European Competition Law Review* (2004) 243

'Leveraging Non-contestability: Exclusive Dealing and Rebates under the Commission's Article 82 Guidance' *Global Competition Policy* (2009) 1

Snyder, F. 'Soft Law and Institutional Practice in the European Community' in S. Martin (ed.), *The Construction of Europe: Essays in Honour of Emil Noel* (Dordrecht: Kluwer Academic Publishers, 1994)

Spector, D. 'Loyalty Rebates: An Assessment of Competition Concerns and a Proposed Structured Rule of Reason' 1(2) *Competition Policy International* (2005) 88

Ştefan, O. A. 'European Competition Soft Law in the European Courts: A Matter of Hard Principles?' 14(6) *European Law Journal* (2008) 753

Stigler, G. 'The Dominant Firm and the Inverted Price Umbrella' 8 *Journal of Law and Economics* (1965) 167

Swaine, E. T. 'Subsidiarity and Self-interest: Federalism at the European Court of Justice' 41 *Harvard International Law Journal* (2000) 1

Telser, L. 'Why Should Manufacturers Want Fair Trade?' 3 *Journal of Law and Economics* (1960) 86

Temple Lang, J. 'Legal Certainty and Legitimate Expectations as General Principles of Law' in U. Bernitz and J. Nergelius (eds.), *General Principles of European Community Law* (The Hague: Kluwer Law International, 2000) 163

'The Requirements for a Commission Notice on the Concept of Abuse under Article 82 EC' CEPS Special Report (2008) 1

Townley, C. 'Is Anything More Important than Consumer Welfare (in Article 81 EC)? Reflections of a Community Lawyer' in *Cambridge Yearbook* (Cambridge University Press, 2007) 9

Trubek, D., Cottrell, P. and Nance, M. '"Soft Law", "Hard Law", and the EU Integration' in G. de Búrca and J. Scott (eds.), *Law and New Governance in the EU and the US* (Oxford: Hart Publishing, 2006) 65

Van Den Bergh, R. 'Modern Industrial Organisation versus Old-fashioned European Competition Law' 17(2) *European Competition Law Review* (1996) 75

Vickers, J. 'Abuse of Market Power' 115 *Economic Journal* (2005) F244

Völcker, S. 'Developments in EC Competition Law in 2003: An Overview' 41 *Common Market Law Review* (2004) 1027

Waelbroeck, D. '*Michelin II*: A *Per Se* Rule against Rebates by Dominant Companies?' 1(1) *Journal of Competition Law and Economics* (2005) 149

Waelbroeck, M. 'Competition, Integration and Economic Efficiency in the EEC from the Point of View of the Private Firm' in *Festschrift zu Ehren von Eric Stein* (Baden-Baden: Nomos Verlagsgesellschaft, 1987)

'Price Discrimination and Rebate Policies under EU Competition Law' in B. Hawk (ed.), *International Antitrust Law and Policy: Fordham Corporate Law 1995* (New York: Juris Publishing, 1996) 160

Waldron, J. 'Rights' in R. E. Goodin and P. Pettit (eds.), *A Companion to Contemporary Political Philosophy* (Oxford: Blackwell Publishing, 1995) 581

Watrin, C. 'Germany's Social Market Economy' in A. Kilmarnock (ed.), *The Social Market and the State* (London: Social Market Foundation, 1999) 91

Weiler, J. 'The Transformation of Europe' 100 *Yale Law Journal* (1991) 2403

Wellens, K. and Borchardt, G. 'Soft Law in European Community Law' 14(5) *European Law Review* (1989) 267

Whish, R. 'Review of O'Donoghue and Padilla, *The Law and Economics of Article 82 EC*' 2(2) *Competition Policy International* (2006) 188

White, E. 'Some Important Aspects of the *Hoffmann-La Roche* Judgment' 77 *Law Society's Gazette* (1980) 246

Williamson, O. E. 'Economies as an Antitrust Defense: The Welfare Tradeoffs' 58(1) *American Economic Review* (1968) 18

'Economies as an Antitrust Defense Revisited' 125 *University of Pennsylvania Law Review* (1977) 699

Wood, D. P. 'The Role of Economics and Economists in Competition Cases' 1(1) *OECD Journal of Competition Law and Policy* (1999) 82

Zanon, L. 'Price Discrimination under Article 86 of the EEC Treaty: *The United Brands Case' 31 International and Comparative Law Quarterly* (1982) 36

Working and conference papers

Barrell, R. and Dury, K. 'Choosing the Regime: Macroeconomic Effects of UK Entry into EMU' NIESR Discussion Paper No. 168 (2000)

Geradin, D. and Petit, N. 'Price Discrimination under EC Competition Law: The Need for a Case-by-Case Approach' GCLC Working Paper (July 2005)

Goldsmith, N. and Berndt, A. 'Leonhard Miksch (1901–1950): A Forgotten Member of the Freiburg School', Walter-Eucken-Institute, Freiburg Discussion Papers on Constitutional Economics No. 3 (2002)

Joerges, C. 'The Law in the Process of Constitutionalising Europe' EUI Working Paper Law No. 4 (2002)

'What is Left of the European Economic Constitution?' EUI Working Paper Law No. 13 (2004)

Themaat, V. Van 'Zusammenschlüsse über die Grenze im Rahmen des EWG-Bereichs' presented at the Fourth International Conference on European Law (Rome, 1968)

White, L. 'The Growing Influence of Economics and Economists on Antitrust: An Extended Discussion' Working Article 08–05 (2008) 6

Speeches

Kroes, N. 'Preliminary Thoughts on Policy Review of Article 82', 23 September 2005, Fordham Corporate Law Institute, New York (speech/05/537)

'The Commission's Review of Exclusionary Abuses of Dominant Position', 26/27 June 2006 at the Korean Competition Forum

'European Competition Policy in a Changing World and Globalised Economy: Fundamentals, New Objectives and Challenges Ahead', 5 June 2007, GCLC/College of Europe Conference on '50 years of EC Competition Law', Brussels (speech/07/364)

'Exclusionary Abuses of Dominance: The European Commission's Enforcement Priorities', 25 September 2008 at the Fordham Corporate Law Institute, New York (speech/08/457)

Lowe, P. 'The Thirteenth Annual Conference on International Antitrust and Policy', 23 October 2003, Fordham Antitrust Conference in Washington

'New Challenges in Europe', 24 June 2005, King's College London

'Remarks on Unilateral Conduct', 11 September 2006, Washington, DC

'Consumer Welfare and Efficiency: New Guiding Principles of Competition Policy?', 27 March 2007, Thirteenth International Conference on Competition and Fourteenth European Competition Day

'The European Commission Formulates its Enforcement Priorities as Regards Exclusionary Conduct by Dominant Undertakings', Global Competition Policy (February 2009) 1

Monti, M. 'EU Competition Policy after May 2004', 24 October 2003, the Thirteenth Annual Conference on International Antitrust Law and Policy, Fordham Corporate Law Institute

'Comments to the Speech given by Hew Pate, Assistant Attorney General, US Department of Justice, at the Conference "Antitrust in a Transatlantic Context"', 7 June 2004, Brussels

Paulis, E. 'The Burden of Proof in Article 82 Cases', 13 September 2006, Fordham Corporate Law Institute, New York

Rule, C. F. 'Consumer Welfare, Efficiencies, and Mergers', 17 November 2005, the hearing of the Antitrust Modernization Commission

Salop, S. C. 'Efficiencies in Dynamic Merger Analysis', Statement before the US Federal Trade Commission (FTC) Hearings on Global and Innovation-Based Competition (2 November 1995)

Van Miert, K. 'Competition Policy in the 1990s', 11 May 1993, Royal Institute of International Affairs

'The Future of European Competition Policy', 17 September 1998, Ludwig Erhard Foundation in Bonn (speech/98/1351)

INDEX